Death, Dying, and the Biological Revolution

Death, Dying, and the Biological Revolution

Our Last Quest for Responsibility

Robert M. Veatch

Yale University Press   New Haven and London

1976

for Laurie

Library of Congress catalog card number: 75-43337
International standard book number: 0-300-01949-1

Designed by John O. C. McCrillis and set in Baskerville type.
Printed in the United States of America by The Vail-Ballou Press, Inc.,
Binghamton, N.Y.

Published in Great Britain, Europe, Africa, and Asia (except Japan) by Yale
University Press, Ltd., London. Distributed in Latin America by Kaiman & Polon,
Inc., New York City; in Australia and New Zealand by Book & Film Services,
Artarmon, N.S.W., Australia; in Japan by John Weatherhill, Inc., Tokyo.

Contents

WITHDRAWN

Preface

In the last days of the final editing of this book the Supreme Court of the State of New Jersey overturned a lower court decision and, in effect, granted Karen Quinlan's father the right and responsibility, once it has been confirmed that there is no reasonable possibility of Karen's ever emerging from her present comatose condition, to decide whether life-supporting interventions must continue. Karen Quinlan's fate, of course, could be that of any one of us. The ethical, legal, and social dilemmas confronting us in her tragic case are the subject of this volume.

My objective has not been to write a philosophical analysis of the ethics of death and dying—or at least not that alone. Rather, it has been much broader. At the Institute of Society, Ethics and the Life Sciences, where for most of the past six years I have had the privilege of being the Director of its Research Group on Death and Dying, we are convinced that the best hope for gaining insight into the complex dilemmas posed by the technological and biological revolutions is an eclectic spirit combining contributions from many disciplines. This volume is written in that spirit. It begins with more theoretical reflection—sometimes philosophical, sometimes more theological—and moves through a maze of technical medical and legal facts toward examination of alternative public and personal policy. The biological revolution has challenged us in our dying and our death, much as it has challenged us in our living.

In a simpler day we often knew, or thought we knew, what our objectives were for medicine. Someone dying of pneumonia, who had heard that some drug would restore his health, needed to know what the drug was or at least how to get it. No obvious moral problem arose. It was clear what would produce the best consequences and, for the most part, what was the right thing to do. Now, however, with miraculous but only partially successful interventions, such as those given to Karen Quinlan, it is not at all clear what alternative actions will produce the best consequences. It is even less clear what is morally right. The biological revolution poses for us new problems: what a good life is, what our rights are, and what our responsibilities are in the process of our dying.

These questions of rights and responsibilities in our final days are critical—literally matters of life and death. Yet it would be unfair to say that those difficult questions alone are the subject matter of this book. Many years ago I originally became interested in the social and ethical problems of death and dying not only because they were themselves fundamental questions but also because dealing with those questions provided a context for struggling with even more basic questions. To ask the meaning of death is, in an indirect way, to ask the meaning of life. To ask what are the rights of the dying is to ask what are the rights of human beings. To decide the nature of questions in the care of the dying—who is an expert and who shall control the decision making—is to decide even more fundamental questions about expertise and decision making—or at least to give us a context for grappling with those questions. If individuals and societies are to retain their freedom and dignity, their responsibility, in the living of their lives then they must do so in their last quest for responsibility.

My debt to the Research Group on Death and Dying and the institute staff and fellows in the writing of this volume is greater than can be expressed. Virtually every idea here was tested in that group or at least in late evening, heated debate with members of it. Many of the ideas originally took their shape in the context of the research group and the institute more generally. I am particularly grateful to Daniel Callahan, director of the institute, for the freedom and encouragement to pursue this writing and to Willard Gaylin, institute president, with both of whom I have debated these issues over the years. Among the members of the research group, Paul Ramsey, Henry Beecher, Leon Kass, and Eric Cassell have read and more or less formally criticized specific chapters, but all have an impact they will recognize. Of course, the views presented here are mine and not necessarily theirs or the institute's. The help of Sharmon Sollitto, Nancy Taylor, Leslie English, and Patricia Pierce is gratefully acknowledged, as is the support and patience of Laurelyn, Paul, and Carl, a family who have tolerated a great deal.

I do not yet know what Karen Quinlan's fate will be. For her and her family, of course, that is crucial. But her legacy to the rest of us is also crucial. In her dying she has helped us begin the process of clarifying our rights and responsibilities in the face of the biological revolution. It is my hope that this volume continues that process.

May 1976   R.V.

Is Death Moral? An Introduction

Late one evening a thirty-three-year-old man was deposited at the door of the emergency room of a metropolitan hospital by three anonymous friends who made a swift departure. He showed no sign of life. A nurse initiated mouth-to-mouth resuscitation until the respirator team could attach the appropriate mechanical devices. Laboratory analysis confirmed the visual diagnosis of the resident on duty: heroin overdose. Lack of oxygen to the brain left the patient in a deep coma, but by morning the heart was functioning normally while respiration was being maintained by machinery.

After an extensive examination, the neurologist announced that the patient showed no signs of brain activity; he met the criteria of irreversible coma proposed by the Harvard Medical School Ad Hoc Committee to Examine the Definition of Brain Death. The tests were repeated after the heroin had clearly been metabolized and again twenty-four hours later as called for by the Harvard committee.

At this point there was complete agreement among the medical staff about the patient's medical condition. All the evidence indicated that the patient would never recover consciousness, although the respirator, combined with intravenous feeding and careful monitoring, might keep his cells and organs functioning for an indefinite period, perhaps years. The neurologist claimed that the patient was dead; the Harvard criteria were met. He suggested that they go ahead and remove the kidneys, which were urgently needed by a young girl on the nephrology service. The sooner they operated the better if she were to get the organs in good condition.

At this point dispute broke out among the medical staff, and three camps emerged. The first, representing about 40 percent of the staff, agreed with the neurologist that the patient could be considered dead. A second group, perhaps another 40 percent, argued that the patient's heart was still beating. "How," one of them asked, "can you possibly call the patient dead when he has a functioning heart?" This group conceded that he was in irreversible coma. In fact, he had reached a point where he should be allowed to die with dignity, but he was still living. The third and smaller group took one of the traditional positions of physician ethics that the medical professional's duty is to preserve life when it can be preserved. They agreed with the second group that a patient with a beating heart is still alive, but they differed in saying that treatment, by whatever means, should be continued.

This debate took place even though all of the medical staff involved were agreed about the medical facts of the patient's condition. It took place because the issues dividing the groups are ethical issues. Recent advances in the biomedical revolution have made possible intervention into the once irreversible and simple process of dying, permitting ever greater prolongation of dying or, if not dying, of the functioning of body organs and tissues. This has raised ethical and social issues so fundamental and controversial that the debate can no longer be contained within hospital walls. The public as well as professionals—physicians and philosophers and lawyers— must confront these issues raised by our partially successful biological revolution.

Is Death Moral in a Technological Age?

Death has always been inevitable—a "fact of life." But where humans were once helpless onlookers in the presence of death, we are now increasingly able to intervene in the process, using technological resources to direct or delay the inevitable.

A surgeon has removed the heart from a living human being and maintained him for sixty-five hours by mechanical devices while waiting for a suitable heart for transplantation. A human being's cells can be kept alive virtually indefinitely through the use of artificial respirators, artificial cardiac pacemakers, and intravenous feeding with artificial food—giving rise to what many would call an artificial human being. A man's body has been frozen immediately after death to await discovery of a cure for his particular disease with a faith in technology that someday we shall be able to thaw him out and cure his disease.

Efforts like these make it appear that we are engaged in a struggle against death itself. Death, as never before, is looked upon as an evil, and we are mobilizing technology in an all-out war against it. If not death itself, at least certain types of deaths are beginning to be seen as conquerable. We are being forced to ask the question, "Is death moral in a technological age?"

Last year, the world saw about fifty million people die. Because of the partial success of our new techniques of biomedical intervention, more and more of these people underwent a prolonged dying process. In the United States alone, perhaps a million people are now in the process of dying. The exact number depends upon what we mean by *dying*. If in this confusing time, we cannot agree on a definition of death, we have hardly begun to ask what it means to be dying.[1]

A casual look at American records of causes of death reveals a predominance of lingering deaths, that is, deaths anticipated over months or years. Communicable diseases of childhood and rapid infectious diseases do not cause enough deaths to warrant tabulation in most lists. Among the causes of rapid death only accidents, suicides, and homicides, together with some cardiovascular diseases, ever claim a place on the lists, and even they are sometimes the result of some of the most horrible biomedical interventions. All other deaths in the list are chronic. Until recently they were often masked by early death from now vanquished organisms. Now we confront chronic death in ever increasing proportions.

We can anticipate not only that the cause of our death will be different from what it would have been in previous eras, but that the place will be different as well. The scene of the family gathered in the bedroom of the dying is now little more than a poignant memory. Seventy-three percent of adult

---

1. In one sense, of course, we are all dying from the moment we are conceived, but that is not what interests us in any practical sense. *Dying* is used here to refer to anyone with a specific, progressive, normally irreversible ailment which will eventually end in death and which has become so debilitating that it has seriously disrupted normal life patterns.

Americans dying in 1965 had hospital or other institutional care during the last year of their lives.[2] If you are average, in your dying you will spend eighty days during your last year in a hospital or institution.[3] The chances are thirty-eight in a hundred that your medical bills will be over $1,000; over 50 percent if death is from cancer. In Michigan recently a family lost everything it had in meeting over $160,000 in medical bills for the care of a relative who was kept alive although there was "no chance of rehabilitation." [4]

The cost of dying and the chances of dying in an institution have both increased dramatically. In 1958 (the latest figures available) 61 percent of all deaths in the United States occurred in hospitals or other institutions. In 1949 the figure was 49.5 percent; in 1937, 37 percent.[5] Later figures for New York City indicate that this trend has continued: deaths in hospitals and other institutions rose from 66 percent in 1955 to 73 percent in 1967.[6]

Average life expectancy at birth has risen from 47.3 years in 1900 to over 71 years now, largely because of the precipitous decline in deaths of children and young adults. Today 60 percent of Americans die after 65 years of age.[7] About one in ten of these live alone at the time of their death or onset of the illness that sends them into an institution. In short, people have radically changed their style of dying. Scientific advance has meant that more die in institutions, die older, take longer to die, and spend more money doing it. Somehow in the

2. U. S. Department of Health, Education, and Welfare, Public Health Service, *Expenses for Hospital and Institutional Care During the Last Year of Life for Adults Who Died in 1964 or 1965 United States.* Vital and Health Statistics, series 22, no. 11 (Washington, D.C.; U. S. Government Printing Office, 1971), p. 14.

3. Ibid., p. 36.

4. "Euthanasia Questions Stir New Debate," *Medical World News* (September 14, 1973), p. 78.

5. U.S. Department of Health, Education, and Welfare, Public Health Service, *Episodes and Duration of Hospitalization in the Last Year of Life United States-1961.* Vital and Health Statistics, series 22, no. 2 (Washington, D.C.: U.S. Government Printing Office, 1966), p. 3.

6. Monroe Lerner, "When, Why and Where People Die," in *The Dying Patient,* ed. Orville G. Brim, Jr. *et al.* (New York: Russell Sage Foundation, 1970), pp. 21–122.

7. U. S. Department of Health, Education, and Welfare, Public Health Service, *Socioeconomic Characteristics of Deceased Persons.* Vital and Health Statistics, series 22, no. 9 (Washington, D.C.: U. S. Government Printing Office, 1965), pp. 1–2.

emergence of our technologized, expertized society, we even seem to have developed the bizarre notion that we need "permission to die." [8] Medical professionals are asking on hospital floors and in medical magazines whether they should let the dying go ahead and die. Citizens who are winning a prolonged struggle for individual freedoms from oppressive governments may at the same time be losing that freedom to a technocratic elite. They now have to ask if there is a "right to die." What was once inevitable now must be defended as one's moral right.

This new potential for controlling life means there is a new potential for controlling death. This technological power makes many deaths either tragic accidents or, where social injustice permits inadequate health care services, intolerable outrages. Responsibility must now be borne for deaths that could have been prevented, had adequate health care services been available. As humans close in first on infectious diseases, then social diseases, and now chronic illnesses; they seem to close in on death itself, leading some to treat it as an immoral power to be driven from the community like the Salem witch.

Is Death Moral or Technical?

In one sense, then, the impact of modern biomedical technology has made mortality itself in the eyes of some an immorality. In another sense the question, "Is Death Moral?" still remains to be answered. Was the debate about whether the heroin overdose victim was alive or dead a dispute over technical medical facts or was it a debate about morality? While technology has given men greater power to control death, paradoxically it has also generated confusion over the once simple concepts of life and death. As one scholar observed, "If whether a man is alive or dead cannot be determined by medical experts, then just what can be?" But an increasing number of cases have come up in which medical experts, along with the rest of us, are in total confusion over whether individuals are alive or dead.

8. Eric Cassell, "Permission to Die," *BioScience* 23 (1973), pp. 475–78.

On May 7, 1968, the heart of Clarence Nicks was removed and transplanted into the chest of John Stuckwish, a sixty-two-year-old man suffering from a severe heart condition. Nicks had been beaten by a group of assailants in a brawl. His breathing had stopped and his brain waves were flat, according to reports of the case. He would not regain brain function again. He was pronounced dead by one physician. Another disagreed, claiming Nicks was not yet dead since his heart was still beating—although its continuation required the introduction of artificial respiration. It is not difficult to imagine what the assailants' legal counsel chose as a defense against the charge of murder: according to them, the victim was not dead until the heart was removed. If anyone was responsible for the immediate cause of death, it was the physician who removed the heart.

The physicians in both this case and in the case of the heroin overdose victim were surprised at the disagreement among their colleagues. They were for the first time forced to ask what the real meaning of death is. In both cases there was little disagreement over the technical facts yet substantial disagreement over what ought to be done. We are forced to ask in what sense death is a "fact" at all: in what sense death is a technical question to be decided by experts with appropriate scientific training and in what sense it is a moral or philosophical or theological question to be decided by criteria of a radically different kind. That death can be a matter of moral judgment rather than of biological fact seems strange. That possibility will be explored in chapter 1 of this book.

It is not enough, however, to speculate about the philosophical meaning of death. The heroin overdose victim is in the intensive care unit. The medical staff is waiting to prepare two patients for kidney transplants. In chapter 2 we shall ask the practical policy questions. Exactly when should public policy permit or require death to be pronounced? Who should determine when death should be pronounced, and by what concept, locus, and criteria? Kansas and Maryland have recently adopted new laws permitting the use of so-called "brain definitions of death." We shall explore some of the pitfalls of such legislation. More fundamentally we shall ask exactly who has the right to select a concept of death for a particular patient?

IS A PARTICULAR DEATH MORAL?

What about the debate between the second and third groups of physicians attending the overdose victim? These two groups agreed that the patient was "alive" in spite of the fact that his brain was irreversibly destroyed. He was, according to them, still a human being possessing fundamental rights, including, for example, the right not to have kidneys removed even to save other human beings.

The second and third groups of the medical staff were also in fundamental disagreement, though. One group considered themselves morally obligated to preserve life as long as possible. The other group made a different moral assessment. According to them it was immoral to maintain a patient, still alive but irreversibly dying, by useless and inappropriate intervention.

Even if we conclude that it is still morally acceptable to die in a technological age, and even if we conclude that the definition of death is a moral rather than a technical or biological problem, still we must ask whether a particular death—a particular way of dying—is moral. If there are a million people dying at this moment in the United States (and who knows how many in the rest of the world), a tragically large percentage of them will do their dying in what many would consider outrageously immoral ways. Some will die through starvation, war, drugs, and the blight of poverty; others because they cannot obtain needed medical care. Still others will do their dying in an atmosphere of mystery where they know their own condition only vaguely or are given medical treatment that they or their agents are desperately trying to refuse.

Certain philosophical distinctions must be made in attempting to resolve issues of medical morality. They arise most commonly in what some call the euthanasia debate. *Euthanasia,* however, is a very confusing term. To some it means literally "a good death." To others it means a morally outrageous death. When one term has such contradictory meanings it is

probably better that it disappear from the language. I shall
generally avoid it. The questions in that debate, however, cannot be avoided. Is there, for instance, a moral difference between actively killing dying patients and allowing them to die,
or between stopping treatment and deciding not to start? Is it
morally acceptable to relieve pain or induce sleep with drugs
whose side effects may hasten death? Is this the same as actively killing the patient? Is stopping a treatment morally more
like actively killing or like not starting the treatment in the
first place? Is there a difference between "ordinary" and "extraordinary" treatments, and if there is, has it any practical
significance? What is the distinction between a medical treatment that saves life and one that merely forestalls death?
These questions will be dealt with in chapter 3.

The Patient's Right to Refuse Treatment

It is an unfortunate aspect of modern medical ethics that
these questions are frequently asked in a way that assumes the
decisions will be made by someone acting on the patient's behalf. Our technocracy even assigns experts to decide the life
and death fate of the terminal patient. A fundamental thesis
of this book is that, especially in issues as basic as these, the patient must be the one who decides. The question should never
be, "When should we stop treating this patient?" as if the patient were an object to be repaired or discarded. Rather the
moral question must be, "When, if ever, should it be morally
and/or legally possible for the patient to decide to refuse medical treatment even if that may mean that dying will no longer
be prolonged?" Chapter 4 examines cases where patients and
their agents have tried to refuse medical treatment, often to
the point of legal battles.

We shall see that despite the seeming inconsistency in court
opinions, a few basic principles appear to account for every
decision. The problem is that some of these principles seem
intolerable, and some new kinds of cases lack clear legal prece-
dents. Certain changes in public policy are being proposed to
ensure humane and dignified treatment of the dying. Chapter

4 closes with some guidelines for deciding when patients should be legally free to refuse treatment.

It is not enough, however, to explore the legal side of refusing treatment—it is not even enough to propose some guidelines for changes in our case law. Only the force of an informed and concerned public will insure that our public policy regarding death and dying is examined and modified. Cases such as that of Karen Anne Quinlan, the twenty-one-year-old who spent months in a coma before her parents went to court seeking authorization to have her respirator turned off,[9] have generated enormous amounts of press coverage and public debate. We are now asking if we can continue our current practice of permitting individual physicians standing at the bedside to decide whether a patient shall live or die. Committees are being proposed—sometimes called God Squads—to take the burden off the individual physician. Model letters patterned after the Living Will are being drafted for people to use to instruct family, friends, physician, lawyer, or clergyman about their wishes for their own terminal care. At least fourteen state legislatures have considered some form of a bill to permit "euthanasia" or the refusal of treatment. Chapter 5 offers an analysis of these policy alternatives, leading to two constructive proposals that I feel would best protect the autonomy of patients in their last quest for dignity and moral responsibility.

Telling the Dying Patient

For some patients their particular deaths are morally questionable, not because of their medical treatment or lack of treatment, but because critical information is withheld from them. They may suspect a fatal diagnosis or be informed through other channels, but too often they are not given a clear picture of their condition. Of the roughly one million individuals dying in the United States at this moment, as many

9. In the Matter of Karen Quinlan, An Alleged Incompetent (Superior Court of New Jersey, Chancery Division, Morris County, Docket No. C-201-75, 1975).

as 880,000 may not even know it. In one study of physicians, 88 percent claimed that they would tend not to tell cancer patients their diagnosis even though it was "certain" and "treatment may be possible (but) the prognosis is grave." [10] Yet 82–98 percent of medical laypeople apparently want to be told if they have cancer.[11] This issue may signal an approaching crisis in medicine, a polarization of health care professionals and laypeople. The physicians' accustomed position of respect and authority is being challenged. Different ethical norms may be partly responsible for this dilemma, as well as differences in beliefs about important facts. What then is to be done? Again, it is a question of policy. In chapter 6 we shall explore the types of cases where withholding of diagnosis or outright deception are often considered, asking when, if ever, it is acceptable to withhold the truth from the dying patient.

Transplants and Other Uses of Spare Parts

When the heroin overdose victim was deposited at the hospital, the dispute over his mortal status arose, at least in part, because there was a more than passing interest in his kidneys. The debate between the first and second groups of medical staff was occasioned by the fact that the dying (or already dead) individual possessed some now possibly spare parts which had life and death significance for others. Joseph Fletcher has called it a "shameful waste of human tissue" simply to let patients pass from hospital bed to coffin without tapping vital resources remaining in their bodies.[12] But should the need for body parts for transplantation be relevant to the issue of who is to die and who is to call them dead?

Although transplantation gets most of the publicity sur-

10. Donald Oken, "What to Tell Cancer Patients: A Study of Medical Attitudes," *Journal of the American Medical Association* 175 (1961), pp. 1120–28. A thorough discussion of these data will be undertaken in chapter 6.

11. See W. D. Kelly and S. R. Friesen, "Do Cancer Patients Want to Be Told?" *Surgery* 27 (1950) pp. 822–26; and C. H. Branch, "Psychiatric Aspects of Malignant Disease," *CA: Bulletin of Cancer Progress* 6 (1956), pp. 102–04.

12. Joseph Fletcher, "Our Shameful Waste of Human Tissue: An Ethical Problem for the Living and the Dead," in *Updating Life and Death,* ed. Donald R. Cutler (Boston: Beacon Press, 1969), pp. 1–30.

rounding the responsible care and use of the new corpse, other uses are envisioned. The Uniform Anatomical Gift Act, now passed in all fifty states, specifies that a body donated under its provisions may be used for "medical or dental education, research, advancement of medical or dental science, therapy or transplantation. . . ." Some proposed uses of newly dead bodies, however, are controversial, and it must be asked whether certain ingenious techniques being developed are morally tolerable or practically necessary.

The human body has traditionally been considered a "temple of God" and treated with sacred awe by even the most secular. The defensive humor of first-year medical students entering the anatomy laboratory only betrays their uneasiness at treating this temple so irreverently.[13] Once again, the question of policy must be resolved: Who should authorize the use of human flesh and blood and under what circumstances? These issues are examined in chapter 7.

In all our discussions, certain moral principles are central. These themes underlie the arguments of this book:

(1) patients' control of decisions affecting their death and dying;

(2) preservation of patients' freedom and dignity in the last of it;

(3) rejection of the assumption that moral policy expertise is the exclusive prerogative of technical experts;

(4) substitution of the patient's agent, normally the next of kin, when the individual is unable to act; and

(5) modification of public policy to allow individual autonomy and dignity to the greatest extent tolerable to the moral sense of society.

It is strange that we have to ask whether the dying continue to have rights of their own. It is sad that at the same time the individual is winning political and legal victories for freedom and justice, he must surrender his moral autonomy to a technocratic elite. By confronting the moral and policy crisis pre-

13. Harold I. Lief and Renée C. Fox, "Training for Detached Concern in Medical Students," in *The Psychological Basis of Medical Practice*, ed. Harold I. Lief *et al.* (New York: Harper & Row, 1963), pp. 12–35.

cipitated by the biological revolution in human death and
dying, we hope to advance human freedom and justice and
once again make at least some people's dying a moral experience.

A Historical Perspective

The business of death and dying, with life in the last of it,
has not always commanded the same attention from the philosopher, theologian, and political theorist that it does in the
day of the biological revolution. Most so-called primitive societies, from what we know of them, had a very limited perspective of death. Their myths and symbols were intimately related
to the realities of the actual world, of the immediate surround-
ings.[14] Death was not considered a necessary attribute of the
human condition.[15] Consciousness of death requires a separation of individual identity from that of the tribe. A concept of
death must be the product of a long-developing cultural system, of a set of myths, rituals, and symbols giving perspective
on an event modern man takes for granted to be inevitable.
To the extent that death was conceived of at all by early man,
it was seen as the result of evil powers inflicted by human or
spiritual enemies.

When more highly structured cultures emerged with more
complex cosmologies and otherworldly perspectives, death
began to play a major part in the constructive symbolism of
the society, and humans began the philosophical struggle to
come to terms with their own deaths. From this point on, the
debate dominates Eastern and Western philosophy in myriad
forms—the Eastern doctrines of transmigration and ultimate
release from the world,[16] for example, or the notions of the

14. Robert N. Bellah, "Religious Evolution," *American Sociological Review* 29 (1964),
pp. 358–74.

15. See Jacques Choron, *Death and Western Thought* (New York: Macmillan, 1963),
p. 14.

16. For summaries of death in Eastern thought see Frederick Holck, ed., *Death and
Eastern Thought* (Nashville: Abingdon, 1974); and Frank E. Reynolds and Earle H.
Waugh, eds., *Religious Encounters with Death: Essays in the History and Anthropology of
Religion* (University Park, Pa.: Pennsylvania State University Press, forthcoming
1976). For a classic document see *The Tibetan Book of the Dead*, trans. W. Y. Evans-
Wentz (New York: Causeway Books, 1973).

immortality of the soul found in Egyptian *Book of the Dead* [17] and in Greek thought.[18]

The older Hebraic strand of the Judeo-Christian tradition showed remarkably little interest in the question of death. The inevitability of death in a world created by an all-powerful and benevolent suzerain was considered perplexing, true, but virtually no attention was given to the problem of men's fate after their worldly death. Only in the later accounts, in Ezekiel's vision of the Valley of the Dry Bones coming to life and the explicit reference to the resurrection of the dead in Daniel, were there intimations of the struggle that was to play so dominant a role in Greek and Christian thought.

In Western philosophical thought, death became a major theme, capturing the imagination of the great thinkers of the day. But in the philosophical debates of fifth and fourth century Greece (which really continue into modern times), the main concern was the period after death, not death itself or the period of dying. The great argument was whether some form of life existed after death (the view of archaic societies such as the Babylonians, and also of Homer, Pythagoras, Plato, Seneca, and the later strands of the Judeo-Christian tradition) or whether life ended in annihilation (the view suggested in Heraclitus and found more clearly in Aristotle, Lucretius, Marcus Aurelius, Averroes, Montaigne, and the eighteenth-century rationalists). Those who believed in life after death disagreed about the nature of that existence: the Eastern and Pythagorean transmigration of the soul competed with the Platonic immortality of the soul, and the Judeo-Christian resurrection of the body.[19]

17. *Book of the Dead,* translation and introduction by E. A. Wallis Budge (New Hyde Park, New York: University Books, 1960).

18. For summaries of death in Western thought, see Philippe Ariès, *Western Attitudes toward Death: From the Middle Ages to the Present* (Baltimore: Johns Hopkins University Press, 1974); T. S. R. Boase, *Death in the Middle Ages: Mortality, Judgment and Remembrance* (New York: McGraw-Hill, 1972); Krister Stendahl, *Immortality and Resurrection* (New York: Macmillan, 1965); and Milton McC. Gatch, *Death: Meaning and Mortality in Christian Thought and Contemporary Culture* (New York: Seabury Press, 1969); as well as Choron, *Death and Western Thought.*

19. Choron, *Death and Western Thought;* Oscar Cullmann, "Immortality of the Soul or Resurrection of the Dead," in *Immortality and Resurrection,* ed. Krister Stendahl (New York: Macmillan, 1965), pp. 9–53.

The premodern philosophical mind found death fasci-
nating because of its cosmological significance for man's
relation to the transcendent, but also devoted thought to the
social and ethical problems of death and dying.[20] Questions on
the meaning of death and the appropriate care of the dying
often arose in the context of rather mundane matters of governmental and social relations. Aristotle discussed the killing
of deformed infants while instructing the legislator how to
govern well.[21] He saw suicide as an act related not fundamentally to oneself but to the state.[22]

In the *Phaedo*, Socrates ponders the absolute prohibition on
suicide, concluding that although the philosopher is one who
is ready and willing to die, he must await God's call. The
otherworldly *Republic* began by pondering the fate of man
after death and questioned the expansion of "strange and
new-fangled" names and treatment for disease. Plato saw
Herodicus as the corrupter of the tradition of Asclepius:

> But Herodicus, being a trainer, and himself of a sickly
> constitution, by a combination of training and doctoring
> found out a way of torturing first and chiefly himself, and
> secondly the rest of the world . . . by the invention of
> lingering death; for he had a mortal disease which he per-
> petually tended, and as recovery was out of the question,
> he passed his entire life as a valetudinarian; he could do
> nothing but attend upon himself, and he was in constant
> torment whenever he departed in anything from his usual
> regimen, and so dying hard, by the help of science he
> struggled on to old age.[23]

In contrast, Plato had Socrates say of Asclepius:

> . . . bodies which disease had penetrated through and
> through he would not have attempted to cure by gradual
> processes of evacuation and infusion: he did not want to

20. See Thomas W. Furlow Jr., "A Matter of Life and Death," *The Pharos* (July
1973), pp. 84–90.
21. "As to the exposure and rearing of children, let there be a law that no deformed child shall live. . . ." Aristotle, *Politics* 7, chap. 16.
22. Aristotle, *Nicomachean Ethics* 5, chap. 11.
23. Plato, *The Republic* 3, 406 A-B.

lengthen out good-for-nothing lives, or to have weak fathers begetting weaker sons;—if a man was not able to live in the ordinary way he had no business to cure him.[24]

What is striking is the oblique treatment of the subject in classical literature. Epicureans and Stoics, who find so little to agree on, seem quite compatible on the subject of suicide, although they approve it for quite different reasons. Especially Marcus Aurelius and Seneca make suicide a major theme, a release from the burdens of the world. "For mere living is not good, but living well. Accordingly, the wise man will live as long as he ought, not as long as he can." [25] Although for the Stoic, suicide may offer solace to a body tormented with disease, there is yet no specific development of the ethics of the treatment of the dying, such as will be seen in, say, the Roman Catholic moral theology of the sixteenth century and later.

In the Middle Ages a series of handbooks on the ars moriendi, the art of dying, began to signal a shift in attention to the moral and social problems of the dying. The books were part of a movement that also gave rise to a series of hospices for the care of the dying at religious centers throughout Europe. (These are the historical precursors of the present day hospices such as St. Christopher's in England and the planned center in New Haven, Connecticut, where the goal is to provide humane care for the dying without resort to endless technological interventions.) There remained, however, a distinct focus on preparing properly for the transition to the world beyond, to the life of real and everlasting significance. It was the psychology of dying rather than the social and ethical aspects of death and dying on this side of the death event that were important.

THE CONTEMPORARY INTEREST IN DEATH

The modern spirit in the West, characterized so clearly by Max Weber and more recently by Talcott Parsons as in-

24. Ibid., 3, 407 D-E.

25. Seneca, *Ad Lucilium Espistulae Morales* 2, trans. R. M. Gummere (London: William Heinemann, 1920), epis. 70, cited in Furlow, "A Matter of Life and Death," p. 87.

traworldly, instrumental, and activist, has a new attitude toward death.[26] Modern man (and Americans particularly) tend
to focus on the active and rational control of day-to-day
events. This orientation is basic to both technological society
and the biomedical attack on death.

It cannot exactly be said of modern man that the total annihilation view of death has won out. There are still spokes-
men for existence after death (Spinoza, Leibnitz, Kant, Fichte,
Schelling, Bergson, and, in the twentieth century, Whitehead,
Kierkegaard, or Marcel, as well as most interpreters of orthodox Christianity). Still, concern for what follows this earthly
life has become less pressing to secular man. Rather, we seem
to be fascinated by the rational solution of worldly problems,
including the problem of death. The biological revolution
which resulted from our activist approach to nature has made
possible the attack on death. But this alone cannot account for
the suddenly renewed interest in death and its problems.
There are at least two additional reasons for the current interest in public policy for dealing with death.

First, as with ecology, civil rights, overpopulation, or any
other infatuation, many deep-seated and unmet needs must
be involved when a topic attracts wide public concern. People
are seeking ultimate answers about the nature of man and the
meaning of life in the face of the social crisis and chaos of the
last decade.

As we come closer and closer to controlling our biological
processes through new biomedical technological breakthroughs, death stands as an ultimate abyss, a final unknown.
Medical research has conquered a few infectious diseases
—smallpox, salmonella, syphilis, polio, pellagra, and even the
plague—but not one piece of medical research has ever told us

26. Max Weber, *Sociology of Religion* (Boston: Beacon Press, 1963); Talcott Parsons
and Winston White, "The Link Between Character and Society," in Talcott Parsons,
Social Structure and Personality (New York: Free Press, 1964), pp. 183–235; and Talcott
Parsons, *The System of Modern Societies* (Englewood Cliffs, N.J.: Prentice Hall, 1971).
For a specific application of this analysis to the American response to death, see Tal-
cott Parsons and Victor Lidz, "Death in American Society," in *Essays in Self-Destruction,*
ed. Edwin S. Schneidman (New York: Science House, 1967), pp. 133–70; and Talcott
Parsons, Renée C. Fox, and Victor Lidz, "The 'Gift of Life' and Its Reciprocation,"
Social Research 39 (1972), pp. 367–415.

a thing about the meaning of death. It stands before us as something completely outside the scientific point of view, probably more awe-inspiring than ever before.

Thus death is both an enemy to be conquered by our activist faith in man's ability to solve his own problems and an unknown of infinite proportions. There is in our culture a simultaneous obsession with the phenomenon of death and a compulsion to conceal it. To use the religious term, death is taboo. This concurrent preoccupation with and avoidance of the subject of death reveals that even the most secularized of us still treats death as a sacred event. It is elevated to ultimate significance and at the same time viewed with ultimate dread. To lift the shroud and bring the subject into the open will permit profound questions to be raised giving perspective on our situation and dealing with the fundamental problems facing our society.

Second, we are in the midst of not only a biological revolution but also a social revolution, one that began with the rise of individualism. This movement appeared in embryo in the fourteenth century, grew among the radical religious sectarians and spiritualists of the sixteenth century, and was full grown among the liberal political philosophies of the eighteenth century. The banners of personal freedom and the right of individuals to hold and act on their own values in accordance with their own life styles were advanced by the political revolutions of eighteenth-century France and America. These began an egalitarian social revolution that sought freedom and justice for all. The instrumental activism that spawned our technological society has also produced the social egalitarianism that now resists vesting authority over life and death in the medical specialist. We must find ways to reap the dramatic benefits of controlling or partially controlling the dying process without rendering the patient powerless before the paraphernalia of a new priesthood.

This book should be seen then, in relation to these twin revolutions, the biological and the social. Death is of interest in part because it offers man—the ordinary man—his last chance to express his human potential to determine his own destiny.

It is not a belated contribution to the philosophical debate about the possibility and nature of a life after death. Neither is it another exploration of the psychology of the dying. Understanding the dying process through social science techniques is part of modern man's intense drive to grasp and rationalize his experience in this world; it may well contribute to the humane care of the dying, although this is an art that cannot entirely be reduced to a science. To the extent that it can be learned, however, there are others who have addressed the psychological issues.[27]

Nor will this book be a theology of death. Death as a sacred event will always be subject to theological analysis. Although this volume may be seen by some as a medical book my intention is to deal with ethics, philosophy, sociology, law, and public policy—and with people first and foremost. My concern is our struggle for freedom and justice in a world increasingly moved by a technological priesthood who can lead us simultaneously to salvation and damnation. I want to probe the new social and ethical problems of death and dying that have been generated by those revolutions.

The questions at stake are, as I have said, fundamentally philosophical or ethical. That they arise in a medical context should not lead anyone to conclude that they are the exclusive purview of the scientific expert. They are in but not of the realm of science. I shall attempt to clarify the issues on a theoretical level, then proceed with matters of practical policy. This approach goes against the scholarly tradition of the scientific era, in which moral neutrality is an attractive refuge. It once was fashionable to say that scientific and other scholarly pursuits were morally neutral, tools in the hands of man to be put to good or evil purpose. There is a certain naive simplicity about this view that is attractive to scientific minds who would just as soon skirt the complex ethical issues. It is true that the same atomic theory produces the bomb and potential medical

27. For a discussion of the psychological ramifications of dying, refer to: Elisabeth Kübler-Ross, *Death and Dying* (New York: Macmillan, 1969); Robert Kastenbaum and Ruth Aisenberg, *The Psychology of Death* (New York: Springer, 1972); Robert E. Neale, *The Art of Dying* (New York: Harper & Row, 1973); Leonard Pearson, ed., *Death and Dying* (Cleveland: Press of Case Western Reserve University, 1969); Bernard Schoenberg *et al.*, eds., *Loss and Grief: Psychological Management in Medical Practice* (New York: Columbia University Press, 1970).

cures. The same genetic theory may soon permit selective change in a fetus's genetic code to avoid a potentially fatal genetic disease or to produce a monstrosity. The same technology lets us save a drowning child whose breathing has stopped and prolong the dying of an semicomatose octogenarian whose time has long since come.

It is undeniable that the products of research can be used either for good or evil. Yet the claim of the "pure scientist" (including the philosophers and policy researchers) that scientific facts can be isolated from the moral judgments necessary to make use of the facts is no longer tenable.[28] In the first place, ethical and other values are essential inputs into what is normally considered the purely investigatory stage, the mere gathering of data and testing of hypotheses. Values are involved willy-nilly at every step: in selecting a significant problem for study, forming meaningful hypotheses, choosing methods, selecting analytical tests (levels of significance for instance), and, most important, deciding what is worth reporting.

All scientific investigators must also decide at the research stage whether their proposed research is morally tolerable, whatever the morality of the use made of the results. The research process itself is not morally neutral, no more than are the technological applications of that research.

There are at least two additional ways in which technology is not morally neutral. First, new technologies seem to set up feedback loops with the basic value orientations of the culture. In the Judeo-Christian tradition, man is duty-bound to "have dominion over the earth and subdue it." The resulting control mentality has generated the technological revolution and in turn is spurred on by technological progress. Technology feeds and feeds on the control mentality. People are no longer able to return to the simple solutions of the past. They are no longer able to participate in a simple religious healing ceremony supported by their communities or to let nature do its own healing without their domination. Cannon's *Wisdom*

---

28. See my *Value-Freedom in Science and Technology: A Study of the Religious, Ethical and Other Socio-Cultural Factors in Selected Medical Decisions Regarding Birth Control*, (Missoula, Montana: Scholars Press, forthcoming, 1976).

of the Body has been superseded by the wisdom of the technocracy.

Second, technology shifts the bulk of decision making to
those who have technological expertise. Not long ago anyone
could decide to conceive a child or brew an herbal tea or walk
off into the wilderness. We are now at the point when most
couples would not think of going through a pre- and post-na-
tal period without following doctor's orders. We have lost almost entirely the art of self-medication, ceding these operations to the medical priests. Now countless hopelessly ill and
suffering patients literally cannot avoid death-prolonging intervention. This may occur, ironically, while others who desperately need medical interventions lack the social and economic keys to unlock the chambers where technology's priests
practice their life-saving craft. If technology does nothing
more, it radically shifts the locus of decision-making.

If it is the case that the biological sciences as well as the analysis of philosophy, theology and the social sciences cannot really be value-free, but only "value-disguising," then we not
only can, but must carry our discussion on to the crucial policy
questions and make at least a first effort to form some answers. Whether or not the reader agrees with those answers,
he at least knows the value framework which went into the
analysis of the more theoretical questions. Those questions are
of interest not only because of the literally life and death
issues which are at stake, but also because hidden among them
are the even more fundamental issues society must face: the
nature of man, the nature of authority, and man's last quest
for freedom in a technological society.

1

Defining Death Anew:
Technical and Ethical Problems

It seems strange to ask what death means. Throughout history men have had a good enough idea to transact the business of society—to cover the corpse, bury the dead, transmit authority. But now that technology permits us to treat the body organ by organ, cell by cell, we are forced to develop a more precise understanding of what it means to call a person dead. There is a complex interaction between the technical aspects of deciding a person is dead—all the business involving stethoscopes, electroencephalograms, and intricately determined medical diagnoses and prognoses—and the more fundamental philosophical considerations which underlie the judgment that a person in a particular condition should be called dead.

On May 24, 1968, a black laborer named Bruce Tucker fell and suffered a massive head injury. He was rushed by ambulance to the emergency room of the Medical College of Virginia Hospital where he was found to have a skull fracture, a subdural hematoma, and a brain stem contusion. At eleven o'clock that evening an operation was performed (described as "a right temporoparietal craniotomy and right parietal bur hole" in a later court record of the case), opening the skull to relieve the strain on the brain. A tracheostomy was also done to help his labored breathing. By the next morning Tucker was being fed intravenously, had been given medication, and was attached to a respirator. According to the court record, he was "mechanically alive"; the treating physician noted, his "prognosis for recovery is nil and death imminent."

In cases like Tucker's, the patient has frequently stopped breathing by the time he arrives at the hospital, and his heart may have gone into fibrillation. However, the rapid application of an electrical shock can cajole the heart back into a normal rhythm, while a respirator forces the breath of life from the tube of the machine into the tube of the patient's trachea. Thus technology can arrest the process of dying.

The Medical College of Virginia, where Tucker was taken, is the hospital of David M. Hume who, until his own recent accidental death, headed one of the eminent heart transplant teams of the world. At the time Tucker was brought in, there was a patient on the ward named Joseph Klett who was an ideal recipient. Bruce Tucker, with irreversible loss of brain function from a period of oxygen starvation in the brain and an otherwise healthy body, was an ideal heart donor.

Early in the afternoon a neurologist obtained an electroencephalogram (EEG) to determine the state of Tucker's brain activity. He saw that the electrical tracing was a flat line "with occasional artifact." Assuming the artifacts were the kind normally found from extraneous causes, this meant there was no evidence of cortical activity at that time. If the flat line on the EEG is not caused by drug overdose or low body temperature and is found again in repeated tests over several hours, most neurologists would take it to mean that consciousness would never return. Nevertheless, the respirator continued pumping oxygen into Tucker's lungs and, according to the judge's later summary, "his body temperature, pulse, and blood pressure were all normal for a patient in his condition."

In August of the same year a prestigious committee from the Harvard Medical School published more rigorous criteria for irreversible coma. Drafts of the report were circulating among professionals early in the year, but there is no evidence that the physicians in Virginia had access to it. Their use of their own judgment about criteria for diagnosing irreversible coma is still the subject of controversy.

At 2:45 that afternoon Tucker was taken back into the operating room to be prepared for the removal of his heart and both kidneys. Oxygen was given to preserve the viability of these organs. According to the court record, "he maintained, for the most part, normal body temperature, normal blood pressure and normal rate of respiration," but, in spite of the presence of these vital signs, at 3:30 the respirator was cut off. Five minutes later the patient was pronounced dead and the mechanical support was resumed to preserve the organs, and his heart was removed and transplanted to Joseph Klett. According to the record, Tucker's vital signs continued to be normal until 4:30, soon before the heart was removed.

The heart was removed although it had continued functioning while the respirator continued to pump. It was removed without any attempt to get the permission of relatives although Tucker's wallet contained his brother's business card with a phone number and an address only fifteen blocks away. The brother was in his place of business that day and a close friend had made unsuccessful inquiries at three information desks in the hospital. The heart was removed although Virginia law, according to the interpretation of the judge in the subsequent trial, defines death as total cessation of all body functions.

William Tucker, the "donor's" brother, brought suit against the surgical team for wrongfully ending Bruce Tucker's life. During the trial, physicians testified that Tucker was "neurologically dead" several hours before the transplant and that his heart and respiratory system were being kept viable by mechanical means. To this William Tucker responded, "There's nothing they can say to make me believe they didn't kill him." [1] Commenting on the decision in favor of the surgeons, Dr. Hume said, "This simply brings the law in line with medical opinion."

The *New York Times* headline read, "Virginia Jury Rules That Death Occurs When Brain Dies." Victor Cohn's *Washington Post* story announced, " 'Brain Death' Upheld in Heart Transplant." The medical news services were equally quick to treat this unquestioningly as a brain death case. The *Internal Medicine News* claimed, " 'Brain Death' Held Proof of Demise in Va. Jury Decision." Even a law review article considered the judgment to affirm that cesession of brain activity can be used in determining the time of death.[2] There has been some out-

1. "Clear MD's in 'Living' Donor Case," *New York Post*, May 26, 1972, p. 2.
2. Richmond Stanfield Frederick, "Medical Jurisprudence—Determining the Time of Death of the Heart Transplant Donor," *North Carolina Law Review* 51 (1972), pp. 172–84. For another review of the case see Ronald Converse, "But *When* Did He Die?: *Tucker v. Lower* and the Brain-Death Concept," *San Diego Law Review* 12 (1975), pp. 424–35.

cry, especially in the black community, over the hasty removal
of a man's heart without permission from the next of kin, but
the general public seemed undisturbed by the decision. The
medical community felt that one of their outstanding members had been exonerated.

Although the press, public, and some legal opinion treat this
case as crucial in establishing the legitimacy of the use of brain
criteria for death (thus bringing the law in line with "medical
opinion"), more issues than that are at stake. The case raises
basic questions about the definition of death.

The debate has become increasingly heated in the past decade, because fundamental moral and religious issues are at
stake. The very meaning of the word *definition* is ambiguous.
Some of the issues are indeed matters of neurobiological fact
and as such are appropriate for interpretation by medical
opinion. But judgments about facts made by scientists with expertise in a particular and relevant field can be called *definitions* only in an operational sense. The debate over the definition of death also takes place at philosophical, religious, and
ethical levels, probing into the meaning of life and its ending.
The more practical, empirical problems are an important part
of the debate, but they must be separated from the philosophical issues. The philosophical question is, What is lost at
the point of death that is essential to human nature? We can
avoid the serious philosophical errors committed in the
Virginia trial only by carefully separating the levels of the
debate.

Four separate levels in the definition of death debate must
be distinguished. First, there is the purely formal analysis of
the term *death,* an analysis that gives the structure and specifies the framework that must be filled in with content. Second,
the *concept* of death is considered, attempting to fill the content of the formal definition. At this level the question is,
What is is so essentially significant about life that its loss is
termed *death?* Third, there is the question of the locus of
death: where in the organism ought one to look to determine
whether death has occurred? Fourth, one must ask the question of the criteria of death: what technical tests must be applied at the locus to determine if an individual is living or
dead?

Serious mistakes have been made in slipping from one level of the debate to another and in presuming that expertise on one level necessarily implies expertise on another. For instance, the Report of the Ad Hoc Committee of the Harvard Medical School to Examine the Definition of Brain Death is titled "A Definition of Irreversible Coma." [3] The report makes clear that the committee members are simply reporting empirical measures which are criteria for predicting an irreversible coma. (I shall explore later the possibility that they made an important mistake even at this level.) Yet the name of the committee seems to point more to the question of locus, where to look for measurement of death. The committee was established to examine the death of the brain. The implication is that the empirical indications of irreversible coma are also indications of "brain death." But by the first sentence of the report the committee claims that "Our primary purpose is to define irreversible coma as a new criterion for death." They have now shifted so that they are interested in "death." They must be presuming a philosophical concept of death—that a person in irreversible coma should be considered dead—but they nowhere argue this or even state it as a presumption.

Even the composition of the Harvard committee membership signals some uncertainty of purpose. If empirical criteria were their concern, the inclusion of nonscientists on the panel was strange. If the philosophical concept of death was their concern, medically trained people were overrepresented. As it happened, the committee did not deal at all with conceptual matters. The committee and its interpreters have confused the questions at different levels. The remainder of this chapter will discuss the meaning of death at these four levels.

THE FORMAL DEFINITION OF DEATH

A strictly formal definition of death might be the following:

> Death means a complete change in the status of an living entity characterized by the irreversible loss of those characteristics that are essentially significant to it.

3. Ad Hoc Committee of the Harvard Medical School to Examine the Definition of Brain Death, "A Definition of Irreversible Coma," *Journal of the American Medical Association* 205 (1968), pp. 337–40.

Such a definition would apply equally well to a human being, a nonhuman animal, a plant, an organ, a cell, or even metaphorically to a social phenomenon like a society or to any temporally limited entity like a research project, a sports event, or a language. To define the death of a human being, we must recognize the characteristics that are essential to humanness. It is quite inadequate to limit the discussion to the death of the heart or the brain.

Henry Beecher, the distinguished physician who chaired the Harvard committee that proposed a "definition of irreversible coma," has said that "at whatever level we *choose* . . . , it is an arbitrary decision" [italics added].[4] But he goes on, "It is *best* to choose a level where although the brain is dead, usefulness of other organs is still present" [italics added]. Now, clearly he is not making an "arbitrary decision" any longer. He recognizes that there are policy payoffs. He, like the rest of us, realizes that death already has a well-established meaning. It is the task of the current debate to clarify that meaning for a few rare and difficult cases. We use the term *death* to mean the loss of what is essentially significant to an entity—in the case of man, the loss of humanness. The direct link of a word *death* to what is "essentially significant" means that the task of defining it in this sense is first and foremost a philosophical, theological, ethical task.

Furthermore, we behave socially in a very different way when we determine that a living individual has become a corpse. This new, now appropriate behavior might be called *death behavior*. We may pronounce death, go into mourning, begin a funeral or other ritual, conduct an autopsy under certain conditions, read the will, perhaps remove organs which could not have been removed previously. Death changes the roles of others as well. Lyndon Johnson has told of the awful feeling of being elevated to the presidency upon hearing of the death of President Kennedy. We are saying that the dead person has so changed in essence that entirely different behavior is not only permitted but required. Thus important

4. Henry K. Beecher, "The New Definition of Death, Some Opposing Views," unpublished paper presented at the meeting of the American Association for the Advancement of Science, December 1970, p. 2.

policy payoffs ride on the definition of death debate, no matter how tenuous some of the fine distinctions may seem in critical borderline cases.

It is important to realize that stopping medical treatment is not directly linked to the judgment that a person is dead. Some kinds of treatment might well be stopped long before anyone would want to call the patient dead. Even conservative thinkers, traditional Roman Catholic medical ethicists for instance, consider it appropriate to stop certain procedures being used with the dying—especially those labeled heroic, extraordinary, or simply useless. This certainly is not the same as saying the patient is dead. Others hold that treatment should continue until the patient is indeed considered dead. The question of stopping treatment on a dying but not yet dead individual is quite separate from deciding when a person is dead; this question we shall take up later in the book.

The actions of the physicians in the Tucker case are ambiguous. The physicians turned off the respirator after deciding that their patient was in an irreversible coma. They argued that their patient was "neurologically dead" for several hours before the transplant, and that his heart and respiratory system were kept functioning by artificial means merely to keep his heart and kidneys viable for transplant purposes. Yet they felt it necessary to shut off the respirator before pronouncing death—and Tucker's attorney charged that the patient's death was hastened by shutting off the mechanical support systems.

This reported sequence of events is morally as well as factually confusing. If the physicians really believed that Tucker was dead when he was in a confirmed irreversible coma, why did they feel compelled to turn off the mechanical oxygenating devices? On the other hand if their purpose was to preserve the organs of the corpse for transplantation, there were physiological reasons at least for not turning off the equipment. It might be not only morally acceptable but also required to continue oxygenation of a new corpse for purposes of preserving transplantable organs. If this were the interpretation of the case it would be appropriate for the debate to center on the use of neurological criteria for death. To this one would have to add a moral argument about the practice of continued oxygenation of known corpses.

What the physicians did, however, was to turn off the mechanical respirator, wait five minutes, pronounce Tucker dead, and then start the respiration again in order to preserve the organs. Did they do this to satisfy themselves and others that the patient had died "all the way?" This sequence of events implies that the patient might be considered still living at least "part of the way." The physician who finally pronounced death had only said that death was "imminent" after the EEG had shown a flat line.

Given this sequence of events, their use of a "new definition of death" as a legal defense makes no sense, since in reality the physicians were using the same old definition—the time when the heart and lungs stop functioning. It would seem that they had available a much more substantial defense—they were continuing a practice long accepted in the tradition of law and medical ethics of allowing an inevitably dying (but not yet dead) patient to die by discontinuing the use of an extraordinary, clearly useless medical procedure.

It is clear at least that death is a dramatic change in the status of the entity. For this reason we have spoken of death as a "complete change," a change in status so radical that totally different behavior is called for. But can we define the time period over which this change takes place? Robert S. Morison, a physician who is the former director of the Division of Biological Sciences at Cornell University, argues that death must be viewed as a process. "The life of a complex vertebrate like man," he has written, "is not a clearly defined entity with sharp discontinuities at both ends." [5]

Most people would agree that there are gradual changes in man's status at both ends of living, yet there are dissenters. Leon Kass, the former executive secretary of the Committee on the Life Sciences and Social Policy of the National Research Council / National Academy of Sciences, and currently professor of bioethics at the Kennedy Center for Bioethics at Georgetown University, argues in a reply to Morison that, while dying is often a continuous process, death itself is not:

5. Robert S. Morison, "Death: Process or Event?" *Science* 173 (1971), pp. 694–98.

What dies is the organism as a whole. It is this death, the death of the individual human being, that is important for physicians and for the community, not the "death" of organs or cells, which are mere parts.[6]

This argument does not depend on whether an individual organ, tissue, or cell can die independently of the organism as a whole. Obviously they can, but from the perspective of policy—of doing anything about the individual—this is usually irrelevant. The philosophical ramifications of focusing on the death of the organism as a whole have been explored by Dallas M. High, the chairman of the Philosophy Department of the University of Kentucky. He argues that life, especially human life, cannot be reduced to its physiological, biological, and physio-chemical components.[7] In the case of the human being, the whole is more than the sum of its parts.

This does not necessarily mean that certain organs, cells, or functions are not more central to what is important in life. What Kass and High recognize is that the debate about the definition of death is a search for what is *important,* to use Kass's term.

The change in the status of the whole organism may still be considered a process, but the fact that cells, tissues, and organs die at different times in itself does not establish this. Most types of death behavior (religious ritual, will reading, succession to the presidency) either happen or they do not. A point must be established at which the individual is no longer treated as living. When short-hand terms like *brain death* or *heart death* are used, it must be clear whether the reference is simply to the death of the organ or to the event which signifies the change in status of the organism as a whole.

The Concept of Death

To ask what is essentially significant to a human being is a philosophical question—a question of ethical and other values.

6. Leon R. Kass, "Death as an Event: A Commentary on Robert Morison," *Science* 173 (1971), pp. 698–702.
7. Dallas M. High, "Death: Its Conceptual Elusiveness," *Soundings* 55 (Winter 1972), p. 447.

Many elements make human beings unique—their opposing thumbs, their possession of rational souls, their ability to form cultures and manipulate symbol systems, their upright postures, their being created in the image of God, and so on. Any concept of death will depend directly upon how one evaluates these qualities. Four choices seem to me to cover the most plausible approaches.

Irreversible Loss of Flow of Vital Fluids

At first it would appear that the irreversible cessation of heart and lung activity would represent a simple and straightforward statement of the traditional understanding of the concept of death in Western culture. Yet upon reflection this proves otherwise. If patients simply lose control of their lungs and have to be permanently supported by a mechanical respirator, they are still living persons as long as they continue to get oxygen. If modern technology produces an efficient, compact heart-lung machine capable of being carried on the back or in a pocket, people using such devices would not be considered dead, even though both heart and lungs were permanently nonfunctioning. Some might consider such a technological man an affront to human dignity; some might argue that such a device should never be connected to a human; but even they would, in all likelihood, agree that such people are alive.

What the traditional concept of death centered on was not the heart and lungs as such, but the flow of vital fluids, that is, the breath and the blood. It is not without reason that these fluids are commonly referred to as "vital." The nature of man is seen as related to this vitality—or vital activity of fluid flow—which man shares with other animals. This fluidity, the movement of liquids and gases at the cellular and organismic level, is a remarkable biological fact. High school biology students are taught that the distinguishing characteristics of "living" things include respiration, circulation of fluids, movement of fluids out of the organism, and the like. According to this view the human organism, like other living organisms, dies when there is an irreversible cessation of the flow of these fluids.

Irreversible Loss of the Soul from the Body

There is a longstanding tradition, sometimes called vitalism, that holds the essence of man to be independent of the chemical reactions and electrical forces that account for the flow of the bodily fluids. Aristotle and the Greeks spoke of the soul as the animating principle of life. The human being, according to Aristotle, differs from other living creatures in possessing a rational soul as well as vegetative and animal souls. This idea later became especially pronounced in the dualistic philosophy of gnosticism, where salvation was seen as the escape of the enslaved soul from the body. Christianity in its Pauline and later Western forms shares the view that the soul is an essential element in the living man. While Paul and some later theologian-scholars including Erasmus and Luther sometimes held a tripartite anthropology that included spirit as well as body and soul, a central element in all their thought seems to be animation of the body by a noncorporeal force. In Christianity, however, contrasting to the gnostic tradition, the body is a crucial element—not a prison from which the soul escapes, but a significant part of the person. This will become important later in this discussion. The soul remains a central element in the concept of man in most folk religion today.

The departure of the soul might be seen by believers as occurring at about the time that the fluids stop flowing. But it would be a mistake to equate these two concepts of death, as according to the first fluid stops from natural, if unexplained, causes, and death means nothing more than that stopping of the flow which is essential to life. According to the second view, the fluid stops flowing at the time the soul departs, and it stops because the soul is no longer present. Here the essential thing is the loss of the soul, not the loss of the fluid flow.

The Irreversible Loss of the Capacity for Bodily Integration

In the debate between those who held a traditional religious notion of the animating force of the soul and those who had the more naturalistic concept of the irreversible loss of the

flow of bodily fluids, the trend to secularism and empiricism
made the loss of fluid flow more and more the operative concept of death in society. But man's intervention in the dying
process through cardiac pacemakers, respirators, intravenous
medication and feeding, and extravenous purification of the
blood has forced a sharper examination of the naturalistic
concept of death. It is now possible to manipulate the dying
process so that some parts of the body cease to function while
other parts are maintained indefinitely. This has given rise to
disagreements within the naturalistic camp itself. In its report,
published in 1968, the interdisciplinary Harvard Ad Hoc
Committee to Examine the Definition of Brain Death gave two
reasons for their undertaking. First, they argued that im-
provements in resuscitative and supportive measures had
sometimes had only partial success, putting a great burden on
"patients who suffer permanent loss of intellect, on their families, on the hospitals, and on those in need of hospital beds already occupied by these comatose patients." Second, they
argued that "obsolete criteria for the definition of death can
lead to controversy in obtaining organs for transplantation."

These points have proved more controversial than they may
have seemed at the time. In the first place, the only consideration of the patient among the reasons given for changing the
definition of death was the suggestion that a comatose patient
can feel a "great burden." If the committee is right, however,
in holding that the person is in fact dead despite continued
respiration and circulation, then all the benefits of the change
in definition will come to other individuals or to society at
large. For those who hold that the primary ethical consideration in the care of the patient should be the patient's own interest, this is cause for concern.

In the second place, the introduction of transplant concerns
into the discussion has attracted particular criticism. Paul
Ramsey, among others, has argued against making the issue of
transplant a reason for updating the definition of death:

If no person's death should *for this purpose* be hastened,
then the definition of death should not *for this purpose* be
updated, or the procedures for stating that a man has

died be revised as a means of affording easier access to organs.[8]

Clearly, the need for organs cannot in itself be a legitimate cause for adopting a new concept of death. The need of someone else for organs is simply not an adequate reason for changing our view about what it is in an individual that is so significant that when it has been lost the person is no longer considered alive. This does not mean that the search for a new concept of death must be abandoned or even that the need for organs is not a relevant factor. Even if the need for organs is not a legitimate reason for adopting a new concept of death, it may very well be one legitimate reason among others for taking up the tasks of searching for a new and more carefully stated concept. Henry Beecher argues:

> There is indeed a life-saving potential in the new definition, for, when accepted, it will lead to greater availability than formerly of essential organs in viable condition, for transplantation, and thus countless lives now inevitably lost will be saved.[9]

When he says this is one of the reasons for accepting a new definition (granted that it is only one of the reasons) he has made an ambiguous statement. If he means that it is a reason for adopting the new concept, he is making an unacceptable compromise with the value of the individual human being. If, however, he means that this is a reason for undertaking the task of philosophical examination of the meaning of death, that is something quite different. It would indeed be morally outrageous if "countless lives" were lost simply because society was too lazy to undertake the philosophical task of reexamining and clarifying its precise understanding of death.

Nevertheless, this reason for undertaking the reexamination of the concept of death must still be subordinated to the primary one. It is morally wrong to treat a dead man as if he were alive, but it is certainly morally relevant that others may

8. Paul Ramsey, "On Updating Procedures for Stating That a Man Has Died," in *The Patient as Person* (New Haven: Yale University Press, 1970), p. 103.

9. Beecher, "The New Definition of Death," p. 1.

benefit from a clarity of definition. This is true even without consideration of transplantation and is a legitimate reason for undertaking the reexamination. I would argue, however, that even if no one were to benefit—even if no family members would suffer psychologically and economically from the needless preservation of a corpse as if it were alive, even if no one needed the hospital bed, and even if no one needed the organs of the corpse mistakenly thought to be alive—it would still be a moral affront to the dignity of man to treat a corpse as if it were a living person.

We now must consider whether concepts of death that focus on the flow of fluids or the departure of the soul are philosophically appropriate. The reason that the question arises as a practical matter is fear of a "false positive" determination that human life is present. There are several ways of handling doubtful cases. Many would argue that when there is moral or philosophical doubt about whether someone is dead, it would be (morally) safer to act as if the person were alive. At the most rigorous extreme of this course, those advocating a position called tutiorism say that if there is any question at all that an action may be morally wrong, it should be avoided. In this case, the presence of any doubt about whether a person is dead would lead us to err on the safe side and consider the person to be living. An intermediate position, called probabiliorism, is that when there is moral doubt, we may follow a course of action whose morality is in doubt if (and only if) the probability that it is moral is more likely than that it is not. Another position, called probabilism, offers the most leeway, holding that a "probable opinion" may be followed even though the contrary opinion is also probable or even more probable. In the case under consideration, the probabilist could consider the individual dead even though moral doubt, even perhaps serious doubt, remained; while holders of the more rigorous positions would argue that we should take the morally safer course and consider the person alive even though the heart and lungs had permanently stopped functioning and fluid flow could never be restored.

Even the probabilist, however, traditionally has placed restrictions on legitimizing actions supported by a probable opinion—for instance, when a life may be saved by taking one of the probable courses of action. This is clearly the sort of case involved in trying to decide whether to treat an individual as dead.

Thus, when modifying our traditional concept of death to pronounce dead some individuals who would under older concepts be considered alive (that is, those with heart and lung but no brain function), the problem of moral doubt must be resolved. Three basic approaches can be used. First, one may argue that there is really no doubt to deal with, since the older concepts of death which depend on fluid flow or soul departure are now so implausible that they are not even viable candidates. This seems a very difficult argument to sustain in view of the apparent continued acceptance of precisely these concepts by large portions of the public. Even the physicians in the Tucker case apparently harbored some lingering doubts about the newer concept, because they did not pronounce death when the brain had irreversibly ceased functioning, but only after they had turned off the respirator.

Second, one might reject the exception to the probabilist rule in cases where a life may be saved. Since many would argue that the newer concepts of death are morally probable, even more probable than the older concepts, simply rejecting the exception in life-saving cases would justify the use of the newer concepts. This seems morally risky, however. We should continue to err in the direction of protecting the lives of individual patients, particularly those who are helpless, in need of protection, or from ethnic and income groups traditionally ill-treated by the health care system.

The real problem with treating the concept of death debate as a problem of moral doubt is that it assumes that only one moral norm—preserve life wherever possible—should be applied. Thus it is hard to avoid the conclusion that we should err on the side of assuming the doubtfully living patient is alive. There are also sound moral reasons for treating the patients as if they were dead. While benefit to others is one such factor, the crucial point is that, as we have said above, it is an affront to the dignity of individual persons to treat them as alive if they are dead.

This leads to a third solution, the one which is most plausible: to treat the real situation as one of perplexed conscience. There are two relevant and important moral principles at stake—preservation of an individual life and preservation of the dignity of an individual by being able to distinguish a dead person from a living one. The introduction of a moral obligation to treat the dead as dead leaves one perplexed. It creates moral pressures in each direction. The defenders of the older concepts, which may lead to false pronouncements of living, must defend their action as well. It seems to me that only when such positive moral pressure is introduced on both sides of the argument can we plausibly overcome the claim that we must take the morally safer course. We must consider that it may be not only right to call persons dead, but also wrong to call them alive. This will still mean minimizing the life-saving exception, but at least at this point there will be a positive moral argument for doing so. It can be seen that it is quite difficult to justify any divergence from the older, more traditional concepts of death. Nevertheless, the case is being made for a neurologically centered concept.

At first it would appear that the irreversible loss of brain activity is the concept of death held by those no longer satisfied with the vitalistic concept of the departure of the soul or the animalistic concept of the irreversible cessation of fluid flow. This is why the name *brain death* is frequently given to the new proposals, but the term is unfortunate for two reasons.

First, as we have seen, it is not the heart and lungs as such that are essentially significant but rather the vital functions— the flow of fluids—which we believe according to the best empirical human physiology to be associated with these organs. An "artificial brain" is not a present-day possibility but a walking, talking, thinking individual who had one would certainly be considered living. It is not the collection of physical tissues called the brain, but rather their functions—consciousness; motor control; sensory feeling; ability to reason; control over bodily functions including respiration and circulation; major integrating reflexes controlling blood pressure, ion levels, and pupil size; and so forth—which are given essential significance by those who advocate adoption of a new concept of death or clarification of the old one. In short they see the body's capacity for integrating its functions as the essentially significant indication of life.

Second, as suggested earlier, we are not interested in the death of particular cells, organs, or organ systems, but in the death of the person as a whole—the point at which the person as a whole undergoes a quantum change through the loss of characteristics held to be essentially significant, the point at which "death behavior" becomes appropriate. Terms such as *brain death* or *heart death* should be avoided because they tend to obscure the fact that we are searching for the meaning of the death of the person as a whole. At the public policy level, this has very practical consequences. A statute adopted in Kansas specifically refers to "'alternative definitions of death" and says that they are "to be used for all purposes in this state. . . ." According to this language, which has resulted from talking of brain and heart death, a person in Kansas may be simultaneously dead according to one definition and alive according to another. When a distinction must be made, it should be made directly on the basis of the philosophical significance of the functions mentioned above rather than on the importance of the tissue collection called the brain. For purposes of simplicity we shall use the phrase *the capacity for bodily integration* to refer to the total list of integrating mechanisms possessed by the body. The case for these mechanisms being the ones that are essential to humanness can indeed be made. Man is more than the flowing of fluids. He is a complex, integrated organism with capacities for internal regulation. With and only with these integrating mechanisms is homo sapiens really a human person.

There appear to be two general aspects to this concept of what is essentially significant: first, a capacity for integrating one's internal bodily environment (which is done for the most part unconsciously through highly complex homeostatic, feedback mechanisms) and, secondly, a capacity for integrating one's self, including one's body, with the social environment through consciousness which permits interaction with other persons. Clearly these taken together offer a more profound understanding of the nature of man than does the simple flow of bodily fluids. Whether or not it is more a profound concept of man than that which focuses simply on the presence or absence of the soul, it is clearly a very different one. The ultimate test between the two is that of meaningfulness and plausibility. For many in the modern secular society, the concept of loss of capacity for bodily integration seems much more meaningful and plausible, that is, we see it as a much more accurate description of the essential significance of man and of what is lost at the time of death. According to this view, when individuals lose all of these "truly vital" capacities we should call them dead and behave accordingly.

At this point the debate may just about have been won by the defenders of the neurologically oriented concept. For the most part the public sees the main dispute as being between partisans of the heart and the brain. Even court cases like the Tucker suit and the major articles in the scientific and philosophical journals have for the most part confined themselves to contrasting these two rather crudely defined positions. If these were the only alternatives, the discussion probably would be nearing an end. There are, however, some critical questions that are just beginning to be asked. This new round of discussion was provoked by the recognition that it may be possible in rare cases for a person to have the higher brain centers destroyed but still retain lower brain functions including spontaneous respiration.[10] This has led to the question of just what brain functions are essentially significant to man's nature. A fourth major concept of death thus emerges.

The Irreversible Loss of the Capacity for Social Interaction

The fourth major alternative for a concept of death draws on the characteristics of the third concept and has often been confused with it. Henry Beecher offers a summary of what he considers to be essential to man's nature:

10. J. B. Brierley, J. A. H. Adams, D. I. Graham, and J. A. Simpson, "Neocortical Death after Cardiac Arrest," *Lancet*, September 11, 1971, pp. 560–65.

the individual's personality, his conscious life, his uniqueness, his capacity for remembering, judging, reasoning,
acting, enjoying, worrying, and so on. . . .[11]

Beecher goes on immediately to ask the anatomical question
of locus. He concludes that these functions reside in the brain
and that when the brain no longer functions, the individual is
dead. We shall take up the locus question later in this chapter.
What is remarkable is that Beecher's list, with the possible exception of "uniqueness," is composed entirely of functions explicitly related to consciousness and the capacity to relate to
one's social environment through interaction with others. All
the functions which give the capacity to integrate one's internal bodily environment through unconscious, complex, homeostatic reflex mechanisms—respiration, circulation, and
major integrating reflexes—are omitted. In fact, when asked
what was essentially significant to man's living, Beecher replied simply, "Consciousness."

Thus a fourth concept of death is the irreversible loss of the
capacity for consciousness or social integration. This view of
the nature of man places even more emphasis on social character. Even, given a hypothetical human being with the full capacity for integration of bodily function, if he had irreversibly
lost the capacity for consciousness and social interaction, he
would have lost the essential character of humanness and, according to this definition, the person would be dead.

Even if one moves to the so-called higher functions and
away from the mere capacity to integrate bodily functions
through reflex mechanisms, it is still not clear precisely what is
ultimately valued. We must have a more careful specification
of "consciousness or the capacity for social integration." Are
these two capacities synonymous and, if not, what is the relationship between them? Before taking up that question, we
must first make clear what is meant by capacity.

Holders of this concept of death and related concepts of the
essence of man specifically do not say that individuals must be
valued by others in order to be human. This would place life
at the mercy of other human beings who may well be cruel or

11. Beecher, "The New Definition of Death," p. 4.

insensitive. Nor does this concept imply that the essence of man is the fact of social interaction with others, as this would also place a person at the mercy of others. The infant raised in complete isolation from other human contact would still be human, provided that the child retained the mere capacity for some form of social interaction. This view of what is essentially significant to the nature of man makes no quantitative or qualitative judgments. It need not, and for me could not, lead to the view that those who have more capacity for social integration are more human. The concepts of life and death are essentially bipolar, threshhold concepts. Either one has life or one does not. Either a particular type of death behavior is called for or it is not. One does not pronounce death half-way or read a will half-way or become elevated from the vice presidency to the presidency half-way.

One of the real dangers of shifting from the third concept of death to the fourth is that the fourth, in focusing exclusively on the capacity for consciousness or social interaction, lends itself much more readily to quantitative and qualitative considerations. When the focus is on the complete capacity for bodily integration, including the ability of the body to carry out spontaneous respiratory activity and major reflexes, it is quite easy to maintain that if any such integrating function is present the person is alive. But when the question begins to be, "What kinds of integrating capacity are really significant?" one finds oneself on the slippery slope of evaluating kinds of consciousness or social interaction. If consciousness is what counts, it might be asked if a long-term, catatonic schizophrenic or a patient with extreme senile dementia really has the capacity for consciousness. To position oneself for such a slide down the slope of evaluating the degree of capacity for social interaction is extremely dangerous. It seems to me morally obligatory to stay off the slopes.

Precisely what are the functions considered to be ultimately significant to human life according to this concept: There are several possibilities.

The capacity for rationality is one candidate. Homo sapiens is a rational animal, as suggested by the name. The human capacity for reasoning is so unique and so important that some would suggest that it is the critical element in man's nature. But certainly infants lack any such capacity and they are considered living human beings. Nor is possession of the potential for reasoning what is important. Including potential might resolve the problem of infants, but does not explain why those who have no potential for rationality (such as the apparently permanent back ward psychotic or the senile individual) are considered to be humanly living in a real if not full sense and to be entitled to the protection of civil and moral law.

Consciousness is a second candidate that dominates much of the medical and biological literature. If the rationalist tradition is reflected in the previous notion, then the empiricalist philosophical tradition seems to be represented in the emphasis on consciousness. What may be of central significance is the capacity for experience. This would include the infant and the individual who lacks the capacity for rationality, and focuses attention on the ability for sensory activity summarized as consciousness. Yet, this is a very individualistic understanding of man's nature. It describes what is essentially significant to the human life without any reference to other human beings.

Social interaction is a third candidate. At least in the Western tradition, man is seen as an essentially social animal. Perhaps it is man's capacity or potential for social interaction that has such ultimate significance that its loss is considered death. Is this in any sense different from the capacity for experience? Certainly it is conceptually different and places a very different emphasis on man's essential role. Yet it may well be that the two functions, experience and social interaction, are completely conterminous. It is difficult to conceive a case where the two could be separated, at least if social interaction is understood in its most elementary form. While it may be important for a philosophical understanding of man's nature to distinguish between these two functions, it may not be necessary for deciding when a person has died. Thus, for our purposes we can say that the fourth concept of death is one in which the essential element that is lost is the capacity for consciousness or social interaction or both.

The concept presents one further problem. The Western tradition which emphasizes social interaction also emphasizes, as we have seen, the importance of the body. Consider the admittedly remote possibility that the electrical impulses of the brain could be transferred by recording devices onto magnetic computer tape. Would that tape together with some kind of minimum sensory device be a living human being and would erasure of the tape be considered murder? If the body is really essential to man, then we might well decide that such a creature would not be a living human being.

Where does this leave us? The alternatives are summarized in the table at the end of the chapter. The earlier concepts of death—the irreversible loss of the soul and the irreversible stopping of the flow of vital body fluids—strike me as quite implausible. The soul as an independent nonphysical entity that is necessary and sufficient for a person to be considered alive is a relic from the era of dichotomized anthropologies. Animalistic fluid flow is simply too base a function to be the human essence. The capacity for bodily integration is more plausible, but I suspect it is attractive primarily because it includes those higher functions that we normally take to be central—consciousness, the ability to think and feel and relate to others. When the reflex networks that regulate such things as blood pressure and respiration are separated from the higher functions, I am led to conclude that it is the higher functions which are so essential that their loss ought to be taken as the death of the person. While consciousness is certainly important, man's social nature and embodiment seem to me to be the truly essential characteristics. I therefore believe that death is most appropriately thought of as the irreversible loss of the embodied capacity for social interaction.

THE LOCUS OF DEATH

Thus far I have completely avoided dealing with anatomy. Whenever the temptation arose to formulate a concept of death by referring to organs or tissues such as· the heart, lungs, brain, or cerebral cortex, I have carefully resisted. Now finally I must ask, "Where does one look if one wants to know whether a person is dead or alive?" This question at last leads into the field of anatomy and physiology. Each concept of death formulated in the previous section (by asking what is of essential significance to the nature of man) raises a corresponding question of where to look to see if death has occurred. This level of the definitional problem may be called the locus of death.

The term *locus* must be used carefully. I have stressed that we are concerned about the death of the individual as a whole, not a specific part. Nevertheless, differing concepts of death will lead us to look at different body functions and structures in order to diagnose the death of the person as a whole. This task can be undertaken only after the conceptual question is resolved, if what we really want to know is where to look to determine if a person is dead rather than where to look to determine simply if the person has irreversibly lost the capacity for vital fluid flow or bodily integration or social interaction. What then are the different loci corresponding to the different concepts?

The *loci* corresponding to the irreversible loss of vital fluid flow are clearly the heart and blood vessels, the lungs and respiratory tract. At least according to our contemporary empirical knowledge of physiology and anatomy, in which we have good reason to have confidence, these are the vital organs and organ systems to which the tests should have applied to determine if a person has died. Should a new Harvey reveal evidence to the contrary, those who hold to the concept of the irreversible loss of vital fluid flow would probably be willing to change the site of their observations in diagnosing death.

The locus, or the "seat," of the soul has not been dealt with definitively since the day of Descartes. In his essay, "The Passions of the Soul," Descartes pursues the question of the soul's dwelling place in the body. He argues that the soul is united to all the portions of the body conjointly, but, nevertheless, he concludes:

> There is yet . . . a certain part in which it exercises its functions more particularly than in all the others; and it is usually believed that this part is the brain, or possibly the heart: the brain, because it is with it that the organs of sense are connected, and the heart because it is ap-

parently in it that we experience the passions. But in examining the matter with care, it seems as though I had clearly ascertained that the part of the body in which the soul exercises its functions immediately is in no wise the heart, not the whole of the brain, but merely the most inward of all its parts, to wit, a certain very small gland which is situated in the middle of its substance. . . .[12]

Descartes is clearly asking the questions of locus. His anatomical knowledge is apparently sound, but his conclusion that the soul resides primarily and directly in the pineal body raises physiological and theological problems which most of us are unable to comprehend today. What is significant is that he seemed to hold that the irreversible loss of the soul is the critical factor in determining death, and he was asking the right kind of question about where to look to determine whether a man is dead.

The fact that the Greek term *pneuma* has the dual meaning of both breath and soul or spirit could be interpreted to imply that the presence of this animating force is closely related to (perhaps synonymous with) breath. This gives us another clue about where holders of the irreversible loss of the soul concept of death might look to determine the presence or absence of life.

The locus for loss of capacity for bodily integration is a more familiar concept today. The anatomist and physiologist would be sure that the locus of the integrating capacity is the central nervous system, as Sherrington has ingrained into the biomedical tradition. Neurophysiologists asked to find this locus might reasonably request a more specific concept, however. They are aware that the automatic nervous system and spinal cord play a role in the integrating capacity, both as transmitters of nervous impulses and as the central analyzers for certain simple acts of integration (for example, a withdrawal reflex mediated through the spinal cord); they would have to know whether one was interested in such simple reflexes.

12. René Descartes, "The Passions of the Soul," in *The Philosophical Works of Descartes*, vol. 1 (Cambridge: Cambridge University Press, 1911), p. 345.

Beecher gives us the answer quite specifically for his personal concept of death: he says spinal reflexes are to be omitted.[13] This leaves the brain as essentially the place to look to determine whether a man is dead according to the third concept of death. The brain's highly complex circuitry provides the minimal essentials for the body's real integrating capacity. This third concept quite specifically includes unconscious homeostatic and higher reflex mechanisms such as spontaneous respiration and pupil reflexes. Thus, anatomically, according to our reading of neurophysiology, we are dealing with the whole brain, including the cerebellum, medulla, and brain stem. This is the basis for calling the third concept of death *brain death,* and we already discussed objections to this term.

Where to seek the locus for irreversible loss of the capacity for social interaction, the fourth conception of death, is quite another matter. We have eliminated unconscious reflex mechanisms. The answer is clearly not the whole brain—it is much too massive. Determining the locus of consciousness and social interaction certainly requires greater scientific understanding, but evidence points strongly to the neocortex or outer surface of the brain as the site.[14] Indeed, if this is the locus of consciousness, the presence or absence of activity in the rest of the brain will be immaterial to the holder of this view.

THE CRITERIA OF DEATH

Having determined a concept of death, which is rooted in a philosophical analysis of the nature of man, and a locus of death, which links this philosophical understanding to the anatomy and physiology of the human body, we are finally ready to ask the operational question, What tests or measurements should be applied to determine if an individual is living or dead? At this point we have moved into a more technical realm in which the answer will depend primarily on the data gathered from the biomedical sciences.

Beginning with the first concept of death, irreversible loss of

13. Beecher, "The New Definition of Death," p. 2.
14. Brierley *et al.,* "Neocortical Death."

vital fluid flow, what criteria can be used to measure the activity of the heart and lungs, the blood vessels and respiratory track? The methods are simple: visual observation of respiration, perhaps by the use of the classic mirror held at the nostrils; feeling the pulse; and listening for the heartbeat. More technical measures are also now available to the trained clinician: the electrocardiogram and direct measures of oxygen and carbon dioxide levels in the blood.

If Descartes' conclusion is correct that the locus of the soul is in the pineal body, the logical question would be "How does one know when the pineal body has irreversibly ceased to function?" or more precisely "How does one know when the soul has irreversibly departed from the gland?" This matter remains baffling for the modern neurophysiologist. If, however, holders of the soul-departing concept of death associate the soul with the breath, as suggested by the word *pneuma,* this might give us another clue. If respiration and specifically breath are the locus of the soul, then the techniques discussed above as applying to respiration might also be the appropriate criteria for determining the loss of the soul.

We have identified the (whole) brain as the locus associated with the third concept of death, the irreversible loss of the capacity for bodily integration. The empirical task of identifying criteria in this case is to develop accurate predictions of the complete and irreversible loss of brain activity. This search for criteria was the real task carried out by the Ad Hoc Committee to Examine the Definition of Brain Death of Harvard Medical School; the simple criteria they proposed have become the most widely recognized in the United States:

1. Unreceptivity and unresponsitivity
2. No movements or breathing
3. No reflexes
4. Flat electroencephalogram

The report states that the fourth criterion is "of great confirmatory value." It also calls for the repetition of these tests twenty-four hours later. Two types of cases are specifically excluded: hypothemia (body temperature below 90° F) and the presence of central nervous system depressants such as barbiturates.[15]

Other criteria have been proposed to diagnose the condition of irreversible loss of brain function. James Toole, a neurologist at the Bowman Gray School of Medicine, has suggested that metabolic criteria such as oxygen consumption of the brain or the measure of metabolic products in the blood or cerebral spinal fluid could possibly be developed as well.[16]

European observers seem to place more emphasis on demonstrating the absence of circulation in the brain. This is measured by angiography, radioisotopes, or sonic techniques.[17] In Europe sets of criteria analogous to the Harvard criteria have been proposed. G. P. J. Alexandre, a surgeon who heads a Belgian renal transplant department, reports that in addition to absence of reflexes as criteria of irreversible destruction of the brain, he uses lack of spontaneous respiration, a flat EEG, complete bilateral mydriasis, and falling blood pressure necessitating increasing amounts of vasopressive drugs.[18] J. P. Revillard, a Frenchman, reportedly uses these plus angiography and absence of reaction to atropine.[19] Even among those who agree on the types of measures, there may still be disagreement on the levels of measurement. This is especially true for the electroencephalogram, which can be recorded at varying sensitivities and for different time periods. The Harvard-proposed twenty-four-hour period is now being questioned as too conservative.

15. Ad Hoc Committee of the Harvard Medical School, "A Definition of Irreversible Coma," pp. 337–38. See also F. Mellerio, "Clinical and EEG Study of a Case of Acute Poisoning with Cerebral Electrical Silence, Followed by Recovery," *Electroencephalography Clinical Neurophysiology* 30 (1971), pp. 270–71.

16. James F. Toole, "The Neurologist and the Concept of Brain Death," *Perspectives in Biology and Medicine* (Summer 1971), p. 602.

17. See, for example, A. A. Hadjidimos, M. Brock, P. Baum, and K. Schurmann, "Cessation of Cerebral Blood Flow in Total Irreversible Loss of Brain Function," in *Cerebral Blood Flow*, ed. M. Brock, C. Fieschi, D. H. Ingvar, N. A. Lassen, and K. Schurmann (Berlin: Springer-Verlag, 1969), pp. 209–12; A. Beis *et al.*, "Hemodynamic and Metabolic Studies in 'Coma Depasses,' " ibid., pp. 213–15.

18. G. E. W. Wolstenholme and Maeve O'Connor, eds., *Ethics in Medical Progress: With Special Reference to Transplantation* (Boston: Little, Brown, 1966), p. 69.

19. Ibid., p. 71.

While these alternate sets of criteria are normally described as applicable to measuring loss of brain function (or "brain death" as in the name of the Harvard committee), it appears that many of these authors, especially the earlier ones, have not necessarily meant to distinguish them from criteria for measuring the narrower loss of cerebral function.

The criteria for irreversible loss of the capacity for social interaction are far more selective. It should be clear from the above criteria that they measure loss of all brain activity, including spontaneous respiration and higher reflexes and not simply loss of consciousness. This raises a serious problem about whether the Harvard criteria really measure "irreversible coma" as the report title indicates. Exactly what is measured is an entirely empirical matter. In any case, convincing evidence has been cited by the committee and more recently by a committee of the Institute of Society, Ethics and the Life Sciences that no one will falsely be pronounced in irreversible coma. In 128 patients who underwent autopsy, the brain was found to be "obviously destroyed" in each case.[20] Of 2,650 patients with isoelectric EEGs of twenty-four hours' duration, not one patient recovered ("excepting three who had received anesthetic doses of CNS depressants, and who were, therefore, outside the class of patients covered by the report.") [21]

What then is the relationship between the more inclusive Harvard criteria and the simple use of electrocerebral silence as measured by an isoelectric or flat electroencephalogram? The former might be appropriate for those who associate death with the disappearance of any neurological function of the brain. For those who hold the narrower concept based simply on consciousness or capacity for social interaction, however, the Harvard criteria may suffer from exactly the same problem as the old heart- and lung-oriented criteria. With those criteria, every patient whose circulatory and respiratory

20. Task Force on Death and Dying of the Institute of Society, Ethics, and the Life Sciences, "Refinements in Criteria for the Determination of Death: An Appraisal," *Journal of the American Medical Association* 221 (1972), pp. 50–51.
21. Daniel Silverman, Richard L. Masland, Michael G. Saunders, and Robert S. Schwab, "Irreversible Coma Associated with Electrocerebral Silence," *Neurology* 20 (1970), pp. 525–33.

function had ceased was indeed dead, but the criteria might be too conservative, in that some patients dead according to the "loss of bodily integrating capacity" concept of death (for which the brain is the corresponding locus) would be found alive according to heart- and lung-oriented criteria. It might also happen that some patients who should be declared dead according to the irreversible loss of consciousness and social interaction concept would be found to be alive according to the Harvard criteria.[22] All discussions of the neurological criteria fail to consider that the criteria might be too inclusive, too conservative. The criteria might, therefore, give rise to classifying patients as dead according to the consciousness or social interaction conception, but as alive according to the full Harvard criteria.

A report in *Lancet* by the British physician J. B. Brierley and his colleagues, implies this may indeed be the case.[23] In two cases in which patients had undergone cardiac arrest resulting in brain damage, they report, "the electroencephalogram (strictly defined) was isoelectric throughout. Spontaneous respiration was resumed almost at once in case 2, but not until day 21 in case 1." [24] They report that the first patient did not "die" until five months later. For the second patient they report, "The Patient died on day 153." Presumably in both cases they were using the traditional heart and lung locus and correlated criteria for death as they pronounced it. They report that subsequent detailed neuropathological analysis confirmed that the "neocortex was dead while certain brainstem and spinal centers remained intact." These intact centers specifically involved the functions of spontaneous breathing and reflexes: eye-opening, yawning, and "certain reflex activities at brainstem and spinal cord levels." As evidence that lower brain ac-

22. The inclusion of absence of breathing and reflexes in the criteria suggests this, but does not necessarily lead to this. It might be that, empirically, it is necessary for lower brain reflexes and breathing to be absent for twenty-four hours in order to be sure that the patient not only will never regain these functions but will never regain consciousness.

23. Brierley et al., "Neocortical Death." See also Ricardo Ceballos and Samuel C. Little, "Progressive Electroencephalographic Changes in Laminar Necrosis of the Brain," *Southern Medical Journal* 64 (1971), pp. 1370–76.

24. Ibid., p. 560.

tivity remained, they report that an electroretinogram (measuring electrical activity of the eye) in patient 1 was normal on day 13. After day 49 there still remained reactivity of the pupils to light in addition to spontaneous respiration.

If this evidence is sound, it strongly suggests that it is empirically as well as theoretically possible to have irreversible loss of cortical function (and therefore loss of consciousness) while lower brain functions remain intact.

This leaves us with the empirical question of the proper criteria for the irreversible loss of consciousness which is thought to have its locus in the neocortex of the cerebrum. Brierley and his colleagues suggest that the EEG alone (excluding the other three criteria of the Harvard report) measures the activity of the neocortex.[25] Presumably this test must also meet the carefully specified conditions of amplifier gain, repeat of the test after a given time period, and exclusion of the exceptional cases, if it is to be used as the criterion for death according to our fourth concept, irreversible loss of capacity for social interaction. The empirical evidence is not all in, but it would seem that the 2,650 cases of flat EEG without recovery which are cited to support the Harvard criteria would also be persuasive preliminary empirical evidence for the use of the EEG alone as empirical evidence for the irreversible loss of consciousness and social interaction which (presumably) have their locus in the neocortex. What these 2,650 cases would have to include for the data to be definitive would be a significant number of Brierley-type patients where the EEG criteria were met without the other Harvard criteria being met. This is a question for the neurophysiologists to resolve.

There is another problem with the use of electroencephalogram, angiography, or other techniques for measuring cerebral function as a criterion for the irreversible loss of consciousness. Once again we must face the problem of a false positive diagnosis of life. The old heart and lung criteria may provide a false positive diagnosis for a holder of the bodily integrating capacity concept, and the Harvard criteria may give false positive indications for a holder of the consciousness or

25. Brierley *et al.,* "Neocortical Death."

social interaction concept. Could a person have electroencephalographic activity but still have no capacity for consciousness or social interaction? Whether this is possible empirically is difficult to say, but at least theoretically there are certainly portions of the neocortex which could be functioning and presumably be recorded on an electroencephalogram without the individual having any capacity for consciousness. For instance, what if through an accident or vascular occlusion the motor cortex remained viable but the sensory cortex did not? Even the most narrow criterion of the electroencephalogram alone may still give false positive diagnoses of living for holders of the social interaction concept.

COMPLEXITIES IN MATCHING CONCEPTS WITH LOCI AND CRITERIA

It has been our method throughout this chapter to identify four major concepts of death and then to determine, primarily by examining the empirical evidence, what the corresponding loci and criteria might be. But there are good reasons why the holders of a particular concept of death might not want to adopt the corresponding criteria as the means of determining the status of a given patient. These considerations are primarily pragmatic and empirical. In the first place, as a matter of policy we would not want to have to apply the Harvard criteria before pronouncing death while standing before every clearly dead body. It is not usually necessary to use such technical measures as an EEG, whether one holds the fluid-flow concept, the loss of bodily integration concept, or the loss of social interaction concept.

Reliance on the old circulatory and respiratory criteria in cases where the individual is obviously dead may be justified in either of two ways. First, there is the option implied in the new Kansas statute (to be discussed in the next chapter) of maintaining two operating concepts of death, either of which will be satisfactory. This appears, however, to be philosophically unsound, since it means that a patient could be simultaneously dead and alive. If the philosophical arguments for either of the neurological concepts are convincing, and I think they are, we should not have to fall back on the fluid-flow concept for pronouncing death in the ordinary case.

A second way to account for the use of the heart- and lung-oriented criteria is that they do indeed correlate empirically with the neurological concepts. When there is no circulatory or respiratory activity for a sufficient time, there is invariably a loss of capacity for bodily integration or capacity for consciousness or social interaction. Using circulatory and respiratory activity as tests is crude and in some cases the presence of such activity will lead to a false positive diagnosis of life; but the prolonged absence of circulation and respiration is a definitive diagnosis of death even according to the neurologically-oriented concepts. Their use is thus an initial shortcut; if these criteria are met, one need not go on to the other criteria for the purpose of pronouncing death. This would appear to be a sound rationale for continuing the use of the old criteria of respiratory and circulatory activity.

A second practical difficulty is inherent in correlating concept and criteria. Let us examine this by asking why one might not wish at this time to adopt the EEG alone as a definitive criterion for pronouncing death. There are two possible reasons. First, quite obviously, there will be those who do not accept the correlated concept of death. They reject the irreversible loss of the capacity for consciousness or social interaction in favor of the irreversible loss of capacity for bodily integration or for fluid flow. Second, there are those who accept the concept of irreversible loss of consciousness or social interaction, but still are not convinced that the EEG unfailingly predicts this. If and when they can be convinced that the EEG alone accurately predicts irreversible loss of consciousness or social interaction without any false diagnosis of death, they will adopt it as the criterion. In the meantime they would logically continue to advocate the concept while adhering to the more conservative Harvard criteria, which appear to measure the loss of whole brain function. Since the distinction is a new one and the empirical evidence may not yet be convincing, it is to be expected that many holders of this concept will, for the time being and as a matter of policy, prefer the Harvard committee's older and more conservative criteria for determining

TABLE 1 Levels of the Definition of Death

Formal Definition: Death means a complete change in the status of a living entity characterized by the irreversible loss of those characteristics that are essentially significant to it.

Concept of death: philosophical or theological judgment of the essentially significant change at death.	Locus of death: place to look to determine if a person has died.	Criteria of death: measurements physicians or other officials use to determine whether a person is dead—to be determined by scientific empirical study.
1. The irreversible stopping of the flow of "vital" body fluids, i.e., the blood and breath	Heart and lungs	1. Visual observation of respiration, perhaps with the use of a mirror 2. Feeling of the pulse, possibly supported by electrocardiogram
2. The irreversible loss of the soul from the body	The pineal body? (according to Descartes) The respiratory track?	Observation of breath?
3. The irreversible loss of the capacity for bodily integration and social interaction	The brain	1. Unreceptivity and unresponsivity 2. No movements or breathing 3. No reflexes (except spinal reflexes) 4. Flat electroencephalogram (to be used as confirmatory evidence) —All tests to be repeated 24 hours later (excluded conditions: hypothermia and central nervous system drug depression)
4. Irreversible loss of consciousness or the capacity for social interaction	Probably the neocortex	Electroencephalogram

Note: The possible concepts, loci, and criteria of death are much more complex than the ones given here. These are meant to be simplified models of types of positions being taken in the current debate. It is obvious that those who believe that death means the irreversible loss of con- sciousness (4) have no reservations about pronouncing death when the heart and lungs have ceased to function. This is because they are willing to use loss of heart and lung activity as shortcut criteria for death, believing that once heart and lungs have stopped, the brain or neocortex will necessarily stop as well.

death. The entire analysis of the four levels of definition presented thus far is summarized in table 1.

Having examined the theoretical distinctions associated with different concepts of death, as well as their related loci and the empirical criteria for determining when death has occurred according to any one of the concepts, we now may turn our attention to the critical policy question. Which concept, locus, and criteria should be used as a matter of public policy to pronounce a human being dead? This is the subject of the next chapter.

2

Defining Death Anew: Policy Options

While we philosophize about the meaning of death in the age of the biological revolution, people are being pronounced dead (or alive) by physicians who choose one definition or another. The philosophical discussion becomes literally a matter of life and death. You may be pronounced dead by a randomly available physician even if you and your family believe (or have belived) you are still alive and even if you would be considered alive at another hospital down the block. Or you may be considered living by a physician who has chosen to reject the newer notions of death centered on the brain or some part of it, even if you have thought about the issue and decided in favor of a brain-oriented concept.

Doctors in the forty states that have not adopted specific legislation are taking it upon themselves to use a brain-oriented concept of death although the laws in these states do not authorize them to. Other doctors are reluctant to use newer concepts of death, fearing they may offend the patient's family or some district attorney. The fact is, "there is currently no way to be certain that a doctor would not be liable, criminally or civilly, if he ceased treatment of a person found to be dead according to the Harvard Committee's criteria, but not according to the 'complete cessation of all vital functions' test presently employed by the courts." [1]

Some order must be brought out of this confusion. A public policy must be developed that will enable us to know who should be treated as alive and who should be treated as dead.

If it is true that there are several levels in the definition of death debate, it may be that different public actions will be required at the different levels. It would be foolish to use a

1. Alexander Morgan Capron and Leon R. Kass, "A Statutory Definition of the Standards for Determining Human Death: An Appraisal and a Proposal," *University of Pennsylvania Law Review* 121 (1972), p. 97.

Gallup poll or a group of legislators to determine how many minutes of flat electroencephalogram readings are necessary before we can predict confidently that a patient will not regain consciousness. The question whether to treat a person who will never regain consciousness as dead is really one of what concept of death ought to be used by society. It is, as I have argued in chapter 1, a philosophical question which can be answered independent of medical training or healing skills.

Our options are more numerous than they once were. Once, our *de facto* public policy was that the physician should (even must) pronounce death when the patient dies. Everyone knew when that was: when the individual was no longer able to circulate his vital bodily fluids, determined by looking at heart and lung functioning. We now must move beyond this traditional policy; the new pluralism denies us the luxury of drifting along with unexamined assumptions any longer. In this chapter we shall look at four of the policy proposals that are now receiving serious consideration.

First, many have argued forcefully that medical professionals should be free to use the definition of death they deem appropriate. Others, including state legislators in Kansas and Maryland, take a second position, that physicians should be required by law to pronounce death when the individual's brain is completely destroyed. This proposal seems very attractive today. A third proposal beginning to receive some consideration reflects a different concept of death; holders of this view would pronounce death when there is irreversible loss of the capacity for consciousness or social interaction, that is, when there is no longer any cerebral cortical activity in the brain. The debate among these approaches leads me to offer a fourth proposal which, although it has not yet received consideration in the public debate, may be the most reasonable and workable solution in the terribly confusing state in which we find ourselves. In a pluralistic world, different philosophical interpretaions may well have to operate simultaneously. We may wish to give patients and their agents some choice in deciding the meaning of death in their individual cases. If we are dealing at the conceptual level with philosphical choices about what is essential to human living, we may have to tolerate philosophical pluralism.

Of course there is a fifth alternative: the traditional concept, locus, and criteria of death focusing on the functioning of the heart and lungs could be reaffirmed. If we are to continue to use this older concept, however, we now must choose consciously to establish it as a public policy. As yet no such choice has been made. The remainder of this chapter discusses the four new policy alternatives that offer some hope of resolving this chaotic situation.

THE MEDICAL PROFESSIONAL CHOICE

At first it seems obvious and reasonable to let the choice of a definition of death rest in the hands of the physicians. The medical journals are filled with articles claiming that the physician is the only one with adequate experience and knowledge to make such a determination.[2] The World Medical Association, meeting in Sydney, Australia, in 1968 was eager to retain this role for the physicians:

> The determination of the time of death in most countries is the legal responsibility of the physician and should remain so . . . This determination will be based on clinical judgment supplemented if necessary by a number of diagnostic aids, of which the electroencephalogram is currently the most helpful. However, no single technological criterion is entirely satisfactory in the present state of medicine, nor can any one technological procedure be substituted for the overall judgment of the physician.[3]

"With scientific advances and new methods of resuscitation always coming up," said the group's president, Sir Leonard

2. "What and When Is Death?" *Journal of the American Medical Association* 204 (1968), pp. 539–40; "A Definition of Irreversible Coma: Report of the Ad Hoc Committee of the Harvard Medical School to Examine the Definition of Brain Death," *Journal of the American Medical Association* 204 (1968), pp. 337–40; A. Sadler *et al.*, "The Uniform Anatomical Gift Act: A Model for Reform," *Journal of the American Medical Association* 204 (1968), pp. 2501–06; J. Dukeminier and D. Sanders, "Organ Transplantation: A Proposal for Routine Salvaging Cadaver Organs," *New England Journal of Medicine* 279 (1968), pp. 403–19; "Report of the Special Committee on Organ Transplantation," *British Medical Journal* 1 (1970), pp. 750–51; British Medical Association, "The Problem of Euthanasia," (London: B.M.A., 1971), p. 3.

3. World Medical Association, Declaration of Sydney, 1968, cited in David Hendin, *Death as a Fact of Life* (New York: Norton, 1973), p. 36.

Mallen, "it would be silly of us to give a definition which could be outmoded within half an hour."

This bestowing of the decison-making authority on the physician is implied in the oft-cited Black's Law Dictionary definition of death: "The cessation of life; the ceasing to exist; *defined by physicians* as a total stoppage of the circulation of the blood, and a cessation of the animal and vital functions consequent thereupon, such as respiration, pulse, etc." (italics added). The question now raised by advocates of newer notions of death is, what if physicians decide to define death otherwise? If the physicians' old view of death was accorded legal standing, why should not any new medical consensus have legal significance? A *Health Law Bulletin*, for instance, argues: "Thus, courts are actually free to accept new definitions by physicians and to recognize other manifesting signs of death besides respiration and pulsation." [4]

Other authorities are also willing to give special weight to physicians' opinions about what counts as significant for life. Pope Pius XII, at a 1957 meeting of the International Congress of Anesthesiologists, recognized that what was at stake was determining when a body no longer has its "vital functions." This the Pope distinguished from "the simple life of the organs." But then he said, "The task of determining the exact instant of death is that of the physician." It is not clear whether he was ceding to the medical community the role of determining what bodily functions are really vital or simply the more limited technical task of making empirical observations about various body functions.

A lawyer, Walter C. Ward, is more explicit in his willingness to leave to the physician the critical policy choices:

> There is no need for a specific legislative definition of death. Such an effort would be futile in that the use of a flexible definition is required for differing circumstances. There is also the likelihood that currently accepted medical definitions will change or expand in the future or that medical science will discover new methods of death deter-

4. David G. Warren, "Developing a New Definition of Death," *Health Law Bulletin*, no. 35 (July 1972), p. 3.

mination. What is needed is legislative recognition that, if done without negligence, physicians may apply criteria other than cessation of respiration and circulation in death determination without fear of adverse consequences.[5]

According to this view all that is needed is legal protection for physicians so that they can use "criteria other than cessation of respiration and circulation," that is, so they can choose other concepts of death according to their own philosophies. It is true, of course, that medical science may someday discover new specific criteria for evaluating the functioning of a particular part of the brain or even of the functioning of the circulatory and respiratory system but this is measurement. How could medical research possibly discover that death should be pronounced when brain function rather than heart function has stopped irreversibly? Ward's proposal is really a dangerous invitation for medical professionals to exercise their philosophical judgments at the expense of nonconsenting or even unwilling patients.

Some philosophers have also expressed faith that the medical community is the appropriate body to make such decisions. Dallas High, for example, has written one of the best expositions on record of the essentially philosophical nature of the definition of death debate: He recognizes that "If . . . a philosopher or lawyer or theologian wants to claim that he has no professional business with the issue and that it is a purely medical or biological one, that too, I suggest, is to opt for a philosophical position concerning the concept of death, namely, that it is empirically decidable." He makes clear his belief that the question is not resolvable by the sciences of biology and medicine. It is disturbing, however, that what he sees as needed is a "medical-legal consensus" together with "the

5. Walter C. Ward, "Human Organ Transplantation: Some Medical-Legal Pitfalls for Transplant Surgeons," *University of Florida Law Review,* 23 (1970), p. 156. Ian Mc-Coll Kennedy, in an article "The Kansas Statute on Death—An Appraisal," *New England Journal of Medicine* 285 (1971), p. 947, argues "If one accepts, as I do, that the matters properly within the competence of a profession should be dealt with by that profession, whose views would then be accepted if it could be shown that they were informed and objectively arrived at, the intervention of the legislature is regrettable."

bona fides of the wider public," rather than a legislative determination. He concludes "I do not believe that further legislation is needed at this time. . . ." [6]

One could conceivably oppose legislation because there are
other, more effective public mechanisms for deciding: court
decisions, executive agency directives, or an informal public
consensus created without overt governmental actions. But
that means something much more than "the bona fides of the
wider public"; it requires direct public action or the action of
their agents. It may be that High simply means that the medical profession is as good at the task of philosophy and social
policy choices as the rest of humanity, and that if it is left
alone it will reach essentially the same decision that an informed public would have. If that is his position, however, it
needs to be stated explicitly.

Let us assume for a moment that the biologist or physician
may have some special skill in resolving the policy question.
Would not the consensus of the profession as a whole still be
more meaningful than the opinions of individual professionals? Individual members of any professional group may
have biases that affect their judgment. An individual physician
may have a particular attachment to the body's blood pump
going because of his childhood experiences or other extraneous factors, but should he be permitted to keep a cardiac-
functioning corpse pumping blood for months or years just
because of his own individual, and perhaps outdated, philosophy?

Thus some have proposed that in a given locality a committee of physicians, a board at the local hospital, or the medical
society as a group should have the authority to determine the
concept of death to be used. Gunnar Biorck, the prominent
Swedish physician, has called for a new definition but added,
"This may not have to be in the form of law. Better, perhaps,
would be a recommendation issued by a proper medical authority." [7]

6. Dallas M. High, "Death: Its Conceptual Elusiveness," *Soundings* (Winter 1972),
p. 456.
7. Gunnar Biorck, "Thoughts on Life and Death," *Perspectives in Biology and Medicine* (Summer 1968), p. 542. For a similar position by a lawyer see David W. Meyers,
The Human Body and the Law (Chicago: Aldine, 1970).

The *Health Law Bulletin* has proposed a statute specifying only that the method used for determining death shall be "one approved by the state medical socity." [8] This is too sweeping in at least two respects. If it meant only that the state medical society should determine the criteria to be used for measuring the presence or absence of functions in the organs associated with a particular concept of death, it would seem preferable to entrust this task to specialists—neurophysiologists, cardiologists, or others—depending on the tests to be made. But the proposal actually would place *all* authority in the hands of the medical society, not simply selection of criteria. This might effectively eliminate biases of individual physicians, substituting the consensus of the medical profession or some subgroup. But the question still remains: Why should I have to be pronounced dead or alive because there is a consensus of those trained in biology and medicine in favor of the philosophical concept of life which focuses upon fluid flow or integrating capacities or consciousness?

Laying the responsibility on the individual physician or the profession as a whole for deciding what the definition of death should be is the result of inadequate analysis, of failing to distinguish adequately between the levels of the debate. The medical professional undoubtedly has special skills for determining and applying the specific criteria that measure whether particular body functions have irreversibly ceased. Whether the Harvard criteria taken together accurately divide those who are in irreversible coma from those who are not is clearly an empirical question (although the important consideration of just how sure we want to be takes us once again into matters that cannot be answered scientifically). But the crucial policy question is at the conceptual level: should the individual in irreversible coma be treated as dead? No medical answers to this question are possible. If I am to be pronounced dead by the use of a philosophical or theological concept that I do not share, I at least have a right to careful due process. Physicians in the states that do not authorize brain-oriented criteria for pronouncing death who take it upon themselves to use those criteria not only run the risk of criminal or civil prosecution but, in my opinion, should be so prosecuted.

8. Warren, "Developing a New Definition of Death," p. 4.

A STATUTORY DEFINITION OF (WHOLE) BRAIN DAMAGE

When the Tucker case (in which the Virginia physicians defended their use of criteria for death not sanctioned by state law) reached court, it was the first case to test a *public* policy for defining death. Judge A. Christian Compton was not willing to have such a major question resolved in his court, saying, "If such a radical change is to be made in the law of Virginia, the application should be made therefore not to the courts but to the legislature wherein the basic concept of our society relating to the preservation and extension of life could be examined, and, if necessary, reevaluated." [9]

The Kansas Proposal

In 1968 Kansas was the first state to pass a law permitting the procuring of organs for transplantation.[10] The transplanters at the University of Kansas Medical Center were in a dilemma because a year earlier a court case had affirmed the traditional definition of death. With some overstatement of

9. Tucker v. Lower, No. 2831 (Richmond, Va., Law and Equity Court, May 23, 1972), p. 10. The firm tone of this call for legislative action if the definition of death was to be changed was not maintained in Judge Compton's later statements. Three days after citing the Black's Law Dictionary definition and ruling that it must be followed by the jury, he said in his instructions to the jury: "In determining the time of death, as aforesaid, under the facts and circumstances of this case, you may consider the following elements, none of which should necessarily be considered controlling, although you may feel under the evidence that one or more of these conditions are controlling; the time of the total stoppage of the circulation of the blood: the time of the total cessation of the other vital functions consequent thereto, such as respiration and pulsation; the time of complete and irreversible loss of all functions of the brain; and, whether or not the aforesaid functions were spontaneous or were being maintained artificially or mechanically." Although this seems to allow the jury to use a brain-oriented concept, it may not. To say that these factors may be considered in determining the time of death, is not to say that any one or any combination of them is what we mean by death. The instruction could be interpreted to mean that loss of brain function could be seen as a contributory cause of death defined traditionally as the stoppage of all vital functions. For a fuller discussion of the case see my comments in "Brain Death: Welcome Definition or Dangerous Judgment?" *Hastings Center Report* 2, no. 5 (November 1972), pp. 10–13.

10. Loren F. Taylor, "A Statutory Definition of Death in Kansas," *Journal of the American Medical Association* 215 (1971), p. 296.

the problem, Dr. Loren Taylor noted that they were able to procure organs at the same time case law was interpreted as precluding organ transplantation.[11]

The same year Kansas passed its organ procurement statute M. M. Halley and W. F. Harvey proposed a statutory definition of death initiating a debate about the proper statutory formulation.[12] As a result of prodding from the transplanters Kansas passed the first statutory definition of death. It is reproduced below.

> A person will be considered medically and legally dead, if in the opinion of a physician, based on ordinary standards of medical practice, there is the absence of spontaneous respiratory and cardiac function and, because of the disease or condition which caused, directly or indirectly, these functions to cease, or because of the passage of time since these functions ceased, attempts at resuscitation are considered hopeless; and, in this event, death will have occurred at the time these functions ceased; or

> A person will be considered medically and legally dead if, in the opinion of a physician, based on ordinary standards of medical practice, there is the absence of spontaneous brain function; and if based on ordinary standards of medical practice, during reasonable attempts to either maintain or restore spontaneous circulatory or respiratory function in the absence of aforesaid brain function, it appears that further attempts at resuscitation or supportive maintenance will not succeed, death will have occurred at the time when these conditions coincide. Death is to be pronounced before artificial means of supporting respiratory and circulatory function are terminated and before any vital organ is removed for purpose of transplantation.

> These alternative definitions of death are to be utilized for all purposes in this state, including the trials of civil

11. Of course even the most rigid interpretation of the old definition of death would preclude taking organs only from donors not yet dead—not even that unless one assumes that organs can be taken only from the corpse. But Dr. Taylor can be granted his hyperbole for the purposes of the political debate.

12. M. M. Halley and W. F. Harvey, "Medical vs. Legal Definitions of Death," *Journal of the American Medical Association* 204 (1968), pp. 412–15.

and criminal cases, any laws to the contrary notwithstanding.

Maryland next passed an almost identical bill.[13] Subsequently Alaska, California, Georgia, Illinois, Michigan, New Mexico, Oregon, and Virginia passed such legislation. States now considering changes include Florida, Minnesota, and New York. Others have legislators interested in new death definitions.

These statutory proposals have not gone without opposition. Probably the best focused and most widely known criticism has come from British law professor Ian McColl Kennedy.[14] "Let us have guidelines by all means. They are essential," he argues. "But let them be set down by the medical profession, not by the legislature." That the medical profession, as a profession, may have no special competence to set such guidelines is a possibility he completely misses. Like many others, he confuses medical and policy expertise. He goes on to outline six specific criticisms of the Kansas bill. Some of them seem to me more valid than others.

The first is probably the most critical and the most valid. The act, he observes, "seems to be drafted only with transplantation surgery in mind." Indeed, the bill incorporates explicit directions on this matter: "death is to be pronounced before artificial means of supporting respiratory and circulatory function are terminated and before any vital organ is removed for purpose of transplantation." As Dr. Taylor has revealed in his 1971 article, the University of Kansas Medical Center was concerned about transplants when staff members began promoting the change in the law.

The relation between a new definition of death and transplantation is complex,[15] and Ian Kennedy's first critical point

13. Maryland Sessions Laws ch., 693 (1972). The phrase "in the opinion of a physician" was deleted from the first paragraph and the phrase "and because of a known disease or condition" was added in the second paragraph following "ordinary standards of medical practice." It is not clear why the irreversible loss of brain function must be caused by a known disease or condition unless this is thought to be a protection against falsely diagnosing irreversibility in cases where a central nervous system depressant is present, unknown to the medical personnel.

14. Kennedy, "The Kansas Statute," pp. 946–50.

15. See the discussion in chapter 1.

identifies a major cause of worry: "To draft a statute on death inspired apparently by the desire to facilitate what must still be considered experimental surgical procedures must serve to disturb the man in the street. . . . The Act in its present form does not serve to reassure the person who may fear that during his last hours on earth his doctors will be less concerned with his condition than with the person earmarked to receive one of his vital organs." [16]

Don Harper Mills, physician and lawyer, does not agree that the statute is so closely associated with transplant policy. He claims that it intentionally extends to questions of when the physician can terminate resuscitive efforts or discontinue artificial maintenance.[17] Whatever the intentions of the bill's authors, both the authors and Mills may be wrong in their assumptions of what purposes such a statutory definition should serve. It is dangerous to propose a statutory definition solely for the purpose of obtaining organs, but it is equally dangerous to confuse the issue of when resuscitation should be stopped with the one of when a patient is dead. Neither considers that a statutory definition may be needed to prevent the basic indignity of treating a corpse as if it were alive—of confusing a living human with one who has lost essential humanness. Kennedy is right in recognizing that the link between transplantation and the definition of death should not be as close as in the Kansas bill.

Second, Kennedy objects that the Kansas bill seems to propose two alternative definitions of death, implying a person may be simultaneously dead according to one criterion and alive according to the other. In a law review article agreeing with Kennedy on this point, Alexander Capron, law professor at the University of Pennsylvania, and Leon Kass, professor of bioethics at Georgetown University, pose a bizarre problem.[18] A patient who meets the brain-oriented criteria for death and is a good tissue match with a potential organ recipient, is pronounced dead under a special "transplant definition." What

16. Kennedy, "The Kansas Statute," p. 947.
17. Don Harper Mills, "The Kansas Death Statute: Bold and Innovative," *New England Journal of Medicine* 285 (1971), pp. 968–69.
18. Capron and Kass, "A Statutory Definition," p. 197 n. 70.

would the patient's status be if the potential organ recipient dies before the donor organs are removed? The donor would be alive according to the heart and lung-oriented definitions but pronounced dead according to a definition no longer applicable. If it is the person who dies and not some organ or cells or function, then we need a single definition that can apply to all of us, independent of what someone may want to do with our parts. These two problems raised by Kennedy— the dangerous link with transplantation and the implication of alternative definitions of death—should be taken into account in any future bills dealing with a new definition of death.

Third, Kennedy senses something wrong with the requirement that death be pronounced before artificial means of supporting respiration and circulation are stopped. Here his instincts may be sounder than the reasons he uses to support them. The proposal that death be pronounced first is taken from the Harvard committee report. Kennedy seems to agree with the policy but feel it should not be written into the legislation. He writes that the dilemma faced by physicians is "more imagined than real" and declares that "doctors do this every day without legislative fiat and will continue to do so with impunity. . . ." I don't follow his reasoning. Does he mean that physicians declare death every day before turning off resuscitation equipment? The cry for legislative protection seems to contradict that. Or does he mean that physicians decide to stop supportive maintenance on dying patients every day? That is probably true, but an entirely different issue. Kennedy goes on to argue that the requirement that death be pronounced before stopping life support is "entirely redundant." He says, "Once the doctors decide that the conditions specified in the Act exist, and 'further attempts at resuscitation or supportive maintenance will not succeed,' death has already occurred." Indeed it has, according to the new definition, but to say that "death must be pronounced" is something else. If nothing more, this makes clear that the concept of death being used is radically new.

There is a more serious problem, which Kennedy does not mention. To say that death should be pronounced before supportive maintenance ceases (on a corpse) might imply to the

less careful reader that it is never appropriate or legal to decide to stop life support on a dying individual. If anyone were
to read that from the Kansas legislation it would be a serious
problem. The question of stopping treatment of the dying is a
separate issue to be taken up later.

Kennedy's fourth objection to the Kansas bill is that it does
not require a confirmatory judgment of a second physician
before pronouncing death according to brain-oriented criteria. He criticizes others who find this "commendable." [19]
Whether the requirement of a second judgment is reasonable
will depend upon the purpose and context of the legislation.
In the context of organ transplant practices, a second judgment may indeed control aggressive transplanters. But if Kennedy is also right that the redefinition should not be limited to
the transplantation context, then a confirmatory judgment
seems less crucial. Is his position that the brain criteria are so
much more complicated than the older heart and lung criteria
that two technically competent individual judgments are necessary? I doubt that this is true now, and surely it will become
completely unlikely, as experience is gained during the life of
the legislation. There seems no plausible reason to have two
experts involved in the general task of pronouncing death
unless the techniques used are so complex that one cannot
handle them adequately.

Kennedy's fifth criticism is that the act should require the
physician pronouncing death to be a different one from the
transplant physician. He calls for "safeguards" to protect the
patient from potential conflict of interest. This is important
and valid, particularly in the context of legislation explicitly
for transplantation. Even better would be a more general ban
on conflict of interest as part of a more general redefinition of
death. No physician who has any interest beyond the patient's
own welfare should be permitted to pronounce death.

Kennedy's final criticism is the most confusing. He claims
that the act implicitly incorporates "the detailed clinical procedures that serve to determine 'brain death'," and he is rightly

19. William J. Curran, "Legal and Medical Death—Kansas Takes the First Step,"
New England Journal of Medicine 284 (1971), pp. 260–61. See also Capron and Kass,
pp. 116–17.

concerned that the law is no place to spell out in great detail
the technical procedures for measuring whether a death has
occurred. But it is impossible to read any such specification
into the act, which simply says that the diagnosis of absence of
spontaneous brain function is to be "based upon ordinary
standards of medical practice." These standards will vary from
place to place and from time to time. New technical innovations or empirical data will change the tests to be used or the
way they are used. The length of time an electroencephalogram has to be flat may change. Virtually all others
who have criticized the Kansas bill [20] have thought that it does
avoid the trap of over-specificity. The problem seems to be
one of confusing the levels of the definition debate. Whatever
Kennedy is taking exception to, "the absence of spontaneous
brain function" certainly seems a rather general term. It specifies a function or a "locus" in the body, not empirical criteria
or tests.[21]

A Better (Whole) Brain Statute

Capron and Kass are not happy with the Kansas statute for
some of the same reasons as Kennedy: they do not like the
close link with the transplantation issue, and they are particu-

20. See Mills, "The Kansas Death Statute," p. 969; Capron and Kass, "A Statutory
Definition."

21. In order to clarify the problem of what can and should be legislated, Capron
and Kass ("A Statutory Definition," pp. 102–03) have outlined four possible levels for
legislative action. These parallel to some extent those in chapter 1 of this book. While
they also specify a purely formal definition ("the transition, however abrupt or gradual, between the state of being alive and the state of being dead"), the *basic concept* is
the most general level of the four on the list. Not unlike my use of the term *concept,*
they mean a philosophical specification of what it is that is the essential change in a
person who is no longer considered alive. This, they argue, should not be legislated. I
would agree provided it is recognized that certain assumptions at the basic conceptual
level will have to be made in order to move to the next level, which they call "the general physiological standard." They mean here something like what I called the locus:
an area of the body whose functioning is critical. Here, we all agree, is the prime area
for legislation. The third and fourth levels outlined by Capron and Kass are the operational criteria (e.g., absence of cardiac contraction and movement of the blood) and
"specific tests and procedures" (e.g., pulse, heart beat, blood pressure, etc.). All agree
that there is no place in legislation for something as ephemeral as specific empirical
tests. I also concur with Capron and Kass that "operational criteria" should not be incorporated into the law.

larly distressed at the implication that there are alternative forms of death appropriate for different situations. But they are still in favor of legislation. The questions at stake, in their opinion, are crucial matters that call for public involvement. "Physicians *qua* physicians are not expert on these philosophical questions nor are they expert on the question of which physiological functions decisively identify the 'living, human organism'." [22] The legislative route, they argue, would permit the public to play a more active role in decision making. It would also dispel both lay and professional doubt and provide needed assurance for physicians and patients' families that the new definition could be used without fear of a legal suit. They propose five "principles governing the formulation of a statute."

1. The statute should concern the death of a human being, not the death of cells, tissues, or organs, and not the "death or cessation of his role as a fully functioning member of his family or community."

2. It should move incrementally, supplementing rather than replacing the older cardiopulmonary standards.

3. It should avoid serving as a special definition for a special function such as transplantation.

4. It should apply uniformly to all persons.

5. It should be flexible, leaving specific criteria to the judgment of physicians. [23]

On the basis of these guidelines they propose a new draft statute as an alternative to the laws in Kansas and Maryland:

A person will be considered dead if in the announced opinion of a physician, based on ordinary standards of medical practice, he has experienced an irreversible cessation of spontaneous respiratory and circulatory functions. In the event that artificial means of support preclude a determination that these functions have ceased, a person

22. Capron and Kass, "A Statutory Definition," p. 94.
23. Ibid., pp. 104–08.

will be considered dead if in the announced opinion of a physician, based on ordinary standards of medical practice, he has experienced an irreversible cessation of spontaneous brain functions. Death will have occurred at the time when the relevant functions ceased.[24]

Capron and Kass have captured all of the virtues and none of the problems of the Kansas statute. Their bill fails to meet two of Kennedy's objections—it does not require two physicians to participate in determining death and it does not provide that the death-pronouncing physician be separate from the physician interested in the potential cadaver's organs—but these requirements seem superfluous for a general public policy for determining when we are dead. Nevertheless, in holding to the principle of making the definition independent of transplantation concerns, Capron and Kass may have missed an important protection for the patient potentially dead because his brain has completely and irreversibly ceased functioning. They argue, "if particular dangers lurk in the transplantation setting, they should be dealt with in legislation on that subject, such as the Uniform Anatomical Gift Act." [25] That is reasonable, but it is also reasonable that there be observed a general requirement that the physician pronouncing death should be free of significant conflict of interest (whether interest in a respiring "patient," research, continued treatment fees, or transplantation). That there must be no such conflict is obviously essential, whether or not it should be banned by the statute itself.

Critics of the proposals for statutes setting out new standards for determining death have either dealt with technical wording difficulties or made misguided appeals for vesting decision-making authority in physicians or medical professional groups. These, however, are not the only problems. In order to accept the Kansas statute or the preferable Capron-Kass revision, it is first necessary to accept the underlying policy judgment that irreversible destruction of the brain is indeed death—that individuals should be treated as dead when,

24. Ibid., p. 111.
25. Ibid., p. 116.

and only when, their brains will never again be able to function.[26] Some of us continue to have doubts about that basic judgment.

A Statutory Definition of Cerebral Death

There has been great concern that statutes designed to legalize and regularize the use of brain-oriented criteria may not be sufficiently flexible to keep up with changes in this rapidly developing area. Kennedy and others who place their faith in medical discretion fear that a statute would not permit adoption of new techniques and procedures. For the most part they are wrong, since none of the proposed statutes specifies any particular criteria, techniques, or procedures. Techniques and procedures are changing rapidly; with that the proposed laws can cope. But our concepts, our philosophical sophistication, are evolving rapidly, too. Even today most people writing in the field, including competent scientists and physicians, are careless in distinguishing between the whole brain and the cerebrum and the functions of each. Here may arise a significant problem, for under even the highly generalized statutory proposals it may not be possible to make wanted distinctions between lower brain functions, such as those that control spontaneous respiration, and those giving rise to consciousness and individual personality.

If it is decided that a person without the capacities which are thought to reside in the higher brain (cerebral) centers should really be considered dead, then an amendment to the brain death statutes might be in order. The change could be a simple one: simply strike the word *brain* and replace it with *cerebral*. This change in specifying the locus or the general stan-

26. According to both the Kansas and the Capron-Kass proposals, physicians may pronounce death without actually making measurements of brain activity. The implication of the Kansas wording is that there are really two meanings for death—at the conceptual level something like either irreversible loss of vital fluid flow centering in the heart and lungs *or* irreversible loss of bodily integrating capacity centered in the whole brain. Capron and Kass seem to lean to a single concept underlying the statute: the irreversible loss of integrating capacity. That there may be two alternate *criteria* under different circumstances for accurately predicting the loss of this essential function is not shocking. I find this explanation much more plausible.

dards for determining death may or may not have practical significance to the clinician who pronounces death. The question of criteria is an empirical one and the answer will change periodically. It may be that the only way of knowing for sure that the cerebrum has irreversibly lost its ability to function is to use exactly the same tests as for determining that the whole brain has lost its power to function, that is, the Harvard Committee criteria or something similar. But it may also be that other tests—such as EEG alone—could predict with certainty when individuals have irreversibly lost cerebral function even if they retain some lower brain functions, even if, say, they are still breathing spontaneously. The question of criteria can and must be left to the neurological experts.

There may be reasons for sticking with the old-fashioned statutes based on whole-brain conceptions of death. Only a few people will be dead according to a cerebral concept but alive according to a whole-brain concept. There may be some risk of making an empirical error in applying cerebral criteria and pronouncing someone dead who could still regain some form of consciousness. Some moral doubt may remain about the legitimacy of pronouncing someone dead who retains lower brain function. But these same problems arise with the whole-brain-oriented statutes as well. Once the judgment has been made that false positive diagnoses of life are a serious problem, serious enough to overcome any empirical or moral doubts, there is a strong case for moving on from the whole brain to a cerebral focus.

A STATUTE FOR A CONFUSED SOCIETY

There is still another option. Part of the current confusion reflects sincere and reasonable disagreements within society over which philosophical concept of death is the proper one. As with many philosophical questions, the conflict will not easily be resolved. In a democratic society, however, we have a well-established method for dealing with a diversity of religious, moral, or philosophical perspectives. It is to allow free and individual choice as long as it does not directly infringe on the freedom of others and does not radically offend the common morality.

When dealing with a philosophical conflict so basic that it is literally a matter of life and death, the best solution may be individual freedom to choose between different philosophical concepts within the range of what is tolerable to all the interests involved. There have been rare and tentative hints at this solution in the literature. In 1968 proposed by the general definition of human death Halley and Harvey had an apparent option clause:

> Death is irreversible cessation of *all* of the following: (1) total cerebral function, (2) spontaneous function of the respiratory system, and (3) spontaneous function of the circulatory system.

> Special circumstances may, however, justify the pronouncement of death when consultation consistent with established professional standards have (sic) been obtained and when valid consent to withhold or stop resuscitation measures has been given by the appropriate relative or legal guardian.[27]

They abandoned this "consent" formula, however, in later versions of their proposal.[28]

Halley and Harvey have been criticized for their "mistake in making the state of being dead (rather than the acceptance of imminent death) depend on the "consent of a relative or guardian." [29] It seems likely that they did indeed confuse the state of being dead with the state of being so close to death that a decision could justifiably be made by a relative or guardian to stop resuscitation. But I do not see that their perhaps naive formulation makes "the state of being dead" dependent upon consent of a relative. It makes the state of being *pronounced* dead dependent upon consent. Being dead or alive may be quite independent of the wishes of relatives, but the

27. Halley and Harvey, "Medical vs. Legal Definitions of Death," pp. 423–25.
28. M. M. Halley and W. F. Harvey, "Law-Medicine Comment: The Definitional Dilemma of Death," *Journal of the Bar Association of the State of Kansas* 39 (1968), p. 179.
29. Capron and Kass, "A Statutory Definition," p. 105, n. 66.

treatment of persons as if they were dead or alive can logically still be a matter of choice of a relative or even a prior choice of the individual. For those who believe that metaphysical states are to some extent independent of personal choice (as I do), this will mean that in some cases we shall continue to treat corpses as if they were alive or living people as if they were corpses, but we run that risk under any public policy alternative, whether or not it permits freedom of philosophical choice.

More recently Michael Sullivan, county probate judge in Milwaukee, had to make two critical legal decisions concerning whether patients have the right to refuse treatment. (These cases and the general issue of refusing treatment are the subject of the next three chapters.) He has explained the basis of his decisions in the *New England Law Review* [30] He writes in his article that he does not believe legislation defining death to be advisable "in this context." Since he is discussing whether dying patients have the right to refuse treatment, this attitude is perfectly plausible. But, although it is also irrelevant to his context, he goes on to state his opinion on who should decide what definition of death should be used: "The individual should decide whether he will employ the Harvard criteria, or some other definition for his death." According to Sullivan, it is the individual, not the physician, the medical society, or the state, who should have the "right to prescribe his death style" including the person's own definition of death. This obviously raises some problems, as in the cases of individuals in irreversible coma who have not recorded an opinion while conscious and competent. Some provision will have to be made for these cases.

There are two possibilities: (1) shifting decision making to the individual (or the next of kin or other legal guardians) and (2) setting up a definition to be followed unless otherwise instructed. As a practical matter both can probably be used. The law could specify a given general standard—oriented to heart or the whole brain or the cerebrum—with the proviso that the individual has the right to leave explicit instructions to the

30. Michael T. Sullivan, "The Dying Person—His Plight and His Right," *New England Law Review* 8 (1973), pp. 197–216.

contrary. Further, as with the Uniform Anatomical Gift Act, the law could provide that, in those cases where the individual has left no instructions while conscious and competent, the right would be exercised by the next of kin or guardian appointed for the purpose. Many of these issues also arise in setting up mechanisms for refusing further medical treatment for the still living patient. These will be discussed in chapter 5.

There is another problem, however. Has individualism run amok? Do we really want to be so antinomian, so anarchical, that any individual no matter how malicious or foolish can specify any meaning of death which the rest of society would be obliged to honor? What if Aunt Bertha says she knows Uncle Charlie's brain is completely destroyed and his heart is not beating and his lungs are not functioning, but she still thinks there is hope—she still thinks of him as her loving husband and does not want death pronounced for a few more days? Worse yet, what if a grown son who has long since abandoned his senile, mentally ill, and institutionalized father decides that his father's life has lost whatever makes it essentially human and chooses to have him called dead even though his heart, lungs, and brain continue to function? Clearly society cannot permit every individual to choose literally any concept of death. For the same reason, the shortsighted acceptance of death as meaning whatever physicians choose for it to mean is wrong. A physician agreeing with either Aunt Bertha or the coldhearted son should certainly be challenged by society and its judicial system.

There must, then, be limits on individual freedom. At this moment in history the reasonable choices for a concept of death are those focusing on respiration and circulation, on the body's integrating capacities, and on consciousness and related social interactions. Allowing individual choice among these viable alternatives, but not beyond them, may be the only way out of this social policy impasse.

To develop model legislation, we can begin with the Capron-Kass statutory proposal and make several changes to avoid the problems we have discussed. First, a cerebral locus for determining if a person is dead can be incorporated by simply changing the word *brain* to the narrower *cerebral*. Second, it seems to me a reasonable safeguard to insist, in general terms appropriate for a statutory definition, that there be no significant conflict of interest. Finally, wording should be added to permit freedom of choice within reasonable limits. These changes would create the following statute specifying the standards for determining that a person has died:

> A person will be considered dead if in the announced opinion of a physician, based on ordinary standards of medical practice, he has experienced an irreversible cessation of spontaneous respiratory and circulatory functions. In the event that artificial means of support preclude a determination that these functions have ceased, a person will be considered dead if in the announced opinion of a physician, based on ordinary standards of medical practice, he has experienced an irreversible cessation of spontaneous cerebral functions. Death will have occurred at the time when the relevant functions ceased.

> It is provided, however, that no person shall be considered dead even with the announced opinion of a physician solely on the basis of an irreversible cessation of spontaneous cerebral functions if he, while competent to make such a decision, has explicitly rejected the use of this standard or, if he has not expressed himself on the matter while competent, his legal guardian or next of kin explicitly expresses such rejection.

> It is further provided that no physician shall pronounce the death of any individual in any case where there is significant conflict of interest with his obligation to serve the patient (including commitment to any other patients, research, or teaching programs which might directly benefit from pronouncing the patient dead).

3

Dying Morally:
Choosing Not to Prolong Dying

There is a vast literature in the field of medical ethics on the distinct but related issues of "euthanasia," "mercy killing," treating in a way that risks life, allowing to die, deciding to cease treatment, and exercising the right to refuse treatment. The term *euthanasia* has been used in different and confusing ways, meaning at times "any good death," and "any assistance in helping dying patients in their dying (including cessation of treatments)," and "only acting directly to kill the dying patient." The fact that the term can mean both "any good death" and a "morally outrageous death" justifies a moratorium on its use, which shall be observed throughout the remainder of this chapter. Formulators of any public policy dealing with these issues will consciously or unconsciously have to make these distinctions or have a confusing policy. For thorough ethical analysis, it is vital to have these distinctions spelled out. I shall survey three of the issues in this chapter before examining the legal status of the right to refuse treatment in the next chapter and the public policy alternatives in chapter 5.

KILLING VS. ALLOWING TO DIE

Lucy Morgan is a ninety-four-year-old patient being maintained in a nursing home. She is blind, largely deaf, often not communicative and frequently only semiconscious. She does not always recognize her husband, the former president of Antioch College, when he visits. Mrs. Morgan is an educated woman, who four years previously wrote an essay entitled "On Drinking the Hemlock," in which she argued that individuals should be able to choose a dignified and simple way to die.[1] If

1. Lucy Morgan, "On Drinking the Hemlock," *Hastings Center Report* 1, no. 3 (December 1971), pp. 4–5.

the nursing home staff decide that her wishes should be honored, several courses of action are open to them. They could simply kill her by injecting an air bubble; they could decide not to begin an intravenous drip or a respirator when one was needed; they could stop intravenous feeding or the respirator if those were being used; they could wait until her weakened body was infected with pneumonia and then avoid using antibiotics; if she were in pain or unable to sleep they could give high doses of a narcotic or barbiturate with possibly fatal side effects. To clarify the moral differences in these options, let us begin with the difference between an action and an omission.

Actions and Omissions

In June 1973 Dr. Vincent A. Montemorano, the chief surgical resident at Nassau County Medical Center on Long Island, was indicted for the "willful murder" of Eugene Bauer, a fifty-nine-year-old man who had been dying of cancer of the pharynx. Mr. Bauer, according the the *New York Times* account, was in "terminal coma." [2] He was given at most forty-eight hours to live. Dr. Montemorano was the only physician on duty on the 3 to 11 p.m. shift.

According to the indictment Mr. Bauer died within five minutes of a potassium chloride injection. Potassium chloride is known to be lethal upon injection and will disappear rapidly once in the body so that autopsy does not reveal its presence. Dr. Montemorano denied any role and was acquitted. The defense in the trial argued the Bauer was already dead at the time Dr. Montemorano was called to examine him and that he could have died from a number of causes including a blood clot in the lungs.[3] The case does, however, raise some relevant questions. Is injecting potassium chloride morally different from withholding treatments that might prolong the patient's dying? Why inject potassium chloride into a comatose patient who has only forty-eight hours to live? Why did this case gen-

2. David A. Andelman, "Doctor's Alleged Mercy Killing Stirs Debate," *New York Times,* June 29, 1973, p. 42. Also see "Euthanasia: Did the Surgeon Do It?" *Medical World News* (July 20, 1973), pp. 5–6, and "Euthanasia Questions Stir New Debate," *Medical World News* (September 14, 1973), pp. 73–81.

3. Roy R. Silver, "Physician Acquitted in Patient's Death," *New York Times* (February 6, 1974), pp. 1, 44.

erate so much controversy when physicians routinely, often without authorization, withhold medical treatment from the dying?

About the same time in New Jersey, a young man, Lester Zygmaniak, was indicted for first-degree murder. Zygmaniak's brother, George, had been paralyzed from the neck down in a motorcycle accident the previous Sunday. A hospital statement described the paralysis as irreversible. According to one report the paralyzed brother begged to be killed. On Wednesday evening Lester Zygmaniak brought a sawed-off shotgun to the hospital, said to his brother, "Close your eyes now, I'm going to shoot you," and fired the gun. George Zygmaniak died of "brain injuries caused by a shotgun wound in the head." [4] His brother was tried and acquitted, but on grounds of temporary insanity.

THE LEGAL STATUS OF KILLING THE DYING

Twelve earlier cases of active killing of dying or seriously ill patients have been decided by American courts.[5] The findings are mixed. Altogether there have been nine acquittals—but seven were on grounds of temporary insanity. Standards for ruling insanity are tightening, however, and in the future it may be more difficult to get acquittal on this basis.

The other two acquittals were Montemorano's and that of Herman Sander, the only two physicians tried for active killing of dying patients where "mercy killing" might have been involved. In 1950 Dr. Sander was charged with the murder of Mrs. Abbie Borroto, who was dying of cancer. He had dictated into the hospital record the notation, "Patient was given 10cc. of air intravenously four times. Expired within ten minutes after this was started." [6] In the trial, however, there was expert medical testimony that the patient may not have died from the air bubble injections; as in the Montemorano case it was sug-

4. "Brother Held in Apparent Mercy Killing," *New York Times* (June 23, 1973), p. 35; and "Jersey Slayer of Paralyzed Brother in Hospital Called a Hero and a Villain by Shore Neighbors," *New York Times* (June 24, 1973), p. 29.

5. See summary in William H. Braughman, John C. Bruha, and Francis J. Gould, "Euthanasia: Criminal, Tort, Constitutional and Legislative Considerations," *Notre Dame Lawyer* 48 (1973), pp. 1213–14.

6. Ibid., p. 1214. Also see William J. Curran and E. Donald Shapiro, *Law, Medicine and Forensic Science* (Boston: Little, Brown, 1970), pp. 830–31.

gested that the cause of death was not clear. It was argued that
she might have already been dead at the time of the injections,
that the 40cc. of air would not have been sufficient to cause
the death (a judgment that could certainly be disputed), and
that some autopsy findings indicated death was not sudden.
The jury acquitted Dr. Sander apparently on the grounds that
the cause of death could not be determined with sufficient certainty.

It is striking that the two physicians were acquitted without
resort to an insanity defense while all the lay people's acquittals did depend on pleas of insanity. Dr. Sander had the support of a petition signed by 90 percent of his townspeople,
including the husband of the woman he was accused of murdering. The extent to which these factors played on the sym-
pathies of the jury in this and the "temporary insanity" cases is
not clear. The key conclusion from the court cases, however, is
that the courts have never found anyone responsible for actively killing a sick person, yet on the grounds of "mercy"
found the accused not guilty.

In the five other cases, four of the accused were found
guilty of manslaughter and one, an attorney named John
Noxon, was convicted of first-degree murder for electrocuting
his six-month-old mongoloid son by wrapping a lamp cord
around his neck. He was sentenced to death, a sentence later
commuted to life and then to six years. On the basis of these
cases it seems clear that no lawyer would advise that killing of
the dying, even for reasons of mercy, would be certain to go
without prosecution.

In the case of withdrawing treatment, however, the legal situation is much more complex. Among the scores of such cases
in the American courts, patterns do exist, but it will take a
much more thorough analysis to discover them. In the following discussion I shall attempt to clarify the moral differences,
if any, between these two kinds of behavior. The legal aspects
will be examined in the next chapter.

THE ETHICS OF KILLING AND LETTING DIE

The distinction between killing and allowing to die is often
debated in medical ethics. Joseph Fletcher, an ethicist at the

University of Virginia School of Medicine, recognizes that some moralists have "put great store by the distinction between 'direct' and 'indirect' " actions and states what is apparently his own position:

> To others this seems a cloudy and tenuous distinction. Either way the intention is the same, the same end is willed and sought. And the means used do not justify the end in one case if not the other, nor are the means used anything that *can* be justified or "made sense of" except in relation to the gracious purpose in view.[7]

The pragmatist may indeed ask what difference it makes whether an action is taken to cause death or a treatment is omitted so that death takes place. In either case the patient dies. Is it not philosophical obscurantism to dwell on the differences?

This "pragmatic" view is challenged by both Roman Catholic and other religious traditions that emphasize the importance of the distinction. Thus the newly revised "Ethical and Religious Directives for Catholic Health Facilities" says:

> The directly intended termination of any patient's life, even at his own request, is always morally wrong.[8]

The Roman Catholic Church stands firm on this position even though the code also says that "neither the physician nor the patient is obliged to use extraordinary means" of medical treatment.

One of the most tragic cases I have encountered occurred on a hospital floor where an elderly Catholic man was dying of widespread cancer. Reflecting on the patient's course of treatment, which had included irradiation and several operations, his clearly concerned but tough-minded secular physician remarked that proposed further surgery really could not do a thing for him. He then added, "If he weren't Catholic I

7. Joseph Fletcher, "Elective Death," in *Ethical Issues in Medicine,* ed. E. Fuller Torrey (Boston: Little, Brown, 1968), p. 148.

8. National Conference of Catholic Bishops and the United States Catholic Conference, "Ethical and Religious Directives for Catholic Health Facilities," Department of Health Affairs, United States Catholic Conference (November 1971), p. 4.

don't think I would operate." A morally concerned physician ignorant of the ethical position of a major religious group was inflicting both physical and moral injury on his patient.[9]

The distinction between the intended termination of a patient's life and withholding treatment is a complex one. At least five critical differences have been cited. Let us look at the moral implications of each.

Actions and omissions are psychologically different.   First, it is argued that actions and omissions are psychologically different. We feel differently about active killing of a terminally ill individual than we do about withdrawing treatments and letting nature take its course. These feelings are particularly relevant if we are concerned about the consequences, both psychological and legal, of our actions. Many feel that more guilt would attend the action than the omission.

But what is the origin of this felt difference? It may be that active killing actually is more wrong. Guilt feelings (according to some ethical theories) are an indication of our moral perception of rightness and wrongness. On the other hand, we may feel more guilt simply because we have traditionally *believed* that there is a moral difference between the two courses. In the latter case, it is circular reasoning to use feelings of guilt resulting from traditional beliefs as evidence that there is a significant moral difference. While we do not doubt that there has been a perceived difference, we must still determine whether that moral perception is valid.

There is another problem with the argument from psychological guilt. There may also be considerable feelings of guilt in deciding to prolong the dying process, a decision which may produce a long period of suffering and deterioration. Mrs. Morgan's family may feel guilty that they are unable to carry out her wishes. Lester Zygmaniak might have felt more guilt letting his brother lie helplessly paralyzed. If psychological feelings are to be the basis for arguing that actions and omissions are morally different, it must first be established that there are indeed consistent patterns of difference in those

9. Pope Pius XII, "The Prolongation of Life," *The Pope Speaks* 4 (1958), pp. 393–98.

feelings and then proved that the difference can be attributed
to a real moral difference, rather than to traditional but invalid moral beliefs. In short, while a psychological difference
may exist, it is probably not conclusive evidence on either
side.

1. Active killing conflicts with the role of the physician. Second, it is
argued that the duty of physicians is to preserve life. Allowing
them the role of killers—even of the dying—would conflict
with their proper role.

According to one major strand of physician ethics, the
physicians' duty is to preserve life. Sometimes it is even expressed with hyperbole—"to preserve life at all costs." It is not
clear where the "preserve life" norm, this expression of gross
biological vitalism, comes from. Francis Bacon called it a new
duty added to the physician's traditional obligation. In the
Hippocratic oath, physicians pledge that they "will neither
give a deadly drug to anybody if asked for it, nor . . . make a
suggestion to this effect." Some interpret this to forbid supplying the sick with poisons for suicide.[10] Others interpret it as a
simple prohibition on murder. However the phrase is interpreted, it is difficult to make it the basis of a moral distinction
between actively killing patients and simply letting them die.
In any event, the primary injunction of the oath is that
physicians should do what they think will benefit their patients. Another significant norm in the folk ethics of the
medical profession is the negative "first of all do no harm."
But whether stated positively or negatively, it is an open question whether refusing to hasten death will always benefit the
patient or avoid harm. The physician's duty to preserve life is
only one strand of physician ethics and not necessarily the
dominant one. Even physicians who would strive to preserve
life at all costs probably would feel obliged not only to avoid
killing actions but life-shortening omissions as well. That not
all physicians share this norm is evidenced by a study in which
18 percent of the physicians surveyed favored "positive

10. Ludwig Edelstein, "The Hippocratic Oath: Text, Translation, and Interpretation," in *Ancient Medicine* (Baltimore: Johns Hopkins, 1967), pp. 9–13.

euthanasia." [11] Another study indicated that 27 percent would practice "positive euthanasia" if it were permitted.[12]

Suppose, however, that most physicians did agree that their duty was to preserve life and somehow that led them to oppose active killing, but not omissions of treatment. Should that make any difference to the rest of us as laypeople? This sort of policy question cannot be left to the members of one profession to settle. Independent of what physicians believe, the rest of society must decide either openly or by default whether the physician's role should be kept separate from the task of hastening death. A good case can be made either way. If active killing were to be practiced at all, it would seem that the appropriate persons to carry it out would be those in the best position to know the prognosis and have access to the most humane techniques. Yet we commonly believe that it is necessary sometimes to set apart special classes of individuals to exercise unique moral duties. It may be a safer course for society to recognize that the physician *should* be in a special role oriented to the preservation of life and health, at least until contrary directions are given.

The most implied by this conclusion, however, is that physicians should not be the ones who decide to hasten death. We still have not established a general moral distinction between commissions and omissions that result in death. Even if we thought that the preserve life norm permitted omissions and prohibited commissions by physicians, it would say nothing about the more numerous cases of active killing by parents or spouses for reasons of mercy. Grounding the ethics of the commission-omission distinction on the role of the physician involves a number of presumptions: that the physician should be the one to serve as death hastener, that society sees the role of the physician as preserver of life, that commissions conflict with that principle but omissions do not, and that we would

11. Robert H. Williams, "Propagation, Modification, and Termination of Life; Contraception, Abortion, Suicide, Euthanasia," in *To Live and To Die,* ed. Robert H. Williams (New York: Springer-Verlag, 1973), pp. 90–91.

12. Norman K. Brown, Roger Bulger, Harold Laws, and Donovan J. Thompson, "The Preservation of Life," *Journal of the American Medical Association* 211 (1970), pp. 76–82. See also the views of physicians as found by Diana Crane, "Physicians' Attitudes Toward the Treatment of Critically Ill Patients," *BioScience* (1973), pp. 471–74.

not be able to set up mechanisms for releasing him from that special role in special cases. Many if not all of these presumptions seem tenuous. If commissions and omission are to be considered morally different, additional arguments are necessary.

There is a difference in intent.   A third argument is that there is a difference in intent between acts of commission and omission. The relevance of intention is perplexing, however. It is not clear that a difference in intent necessarily exists. The active injection of an air bubble or potassium chloride into a patient in order to relieve suffering has the unambiguous intention of producing death. The simple omission of treatment may have precisely the same purpose. Furthermore, some actions such as open heart surgery or treatment with high doses of a toxic drug may kill the patient when the intent was precisely the opposite.

One step in clarifying the importance of intention is to distinguish between the rightness of the act and the worthiness of the actor's motive. At least since Kant we have distinguished between worth and rightness.[13] If the physician gives what is intended to be a life-saving drug, based on previous experience with the drug at a particular dose level, and the recipient has an unusual and fatal reaction to it, the physician could be said to have done the wrong thing but would not be blameworthy unless some usual or reasonable test was omitted that might have disclosed the peculiar toxic response. The physician's intentions were good, we would say. Intention is morally significant even if the act is the wrong one.

Intention might be morally relevant even in deciding whether the act was wrong as well as blameworthy. Recently a man suffered a fatal heart attack after being assaulted. At the autopsy he was discovered to have three broken ribs, but it could not be determined whether they were suffered in the

13. Immanuel Kant, *Groundwork of the Metaphysics of Morals*, trans. and analyzed by H. Paton (New York: Harper and Row, 1964), pp. 61–67 (pages 393–99 of the edition issued by the Royal Prussian Academy in Berlin). Also see W. D. Ross, *The Right and the Good* (Oxford: Oxford University Press, 1939), p. 7. James Rachels, in his article, "Active and Passive Euthanasia," *New England Journal of Medicine* 292 (1975), p. 79, correctly makes the point that intention alone does not always separate actions and omissions. We shall see below, however, that there are problems with his analysis.

beating or in the hospital emergency room when the medical personnel attempted to revive him by pummeling his chest. The morality of the two possible reasons is radically different. It is not just that we would blame the attackers for the broken ribs, but not the medical personnel. We would actually consider the act of breaking the ribs wrong if done by the attackers but right if done by the medical personnel (because it was done for a proportionately good reason).

Intentions may thus be morally significant, at least in establishing blame or praiseworthiness, but they still may not establish an adequate basis for preferring omissions over commissions.

It can be argued that an omission differs from acts to hasten death if it results from diffuseness of responsibility or the lack of sufficient drive to make an affirmative decision. Such omission would have precisely the same result, the death of the patient. But it is dangerous to argue that an omission is morally more acceptable just because the patient gets so lost in the bureaucratic procedures of a hospital that no one is responsible for considering the alternatives for his treatment. If this reasoning is used to justify an omission for the terminal patient, would not it also justify lack of treatment for one who needs it? Indifference to patient care cannot be justified especially if death results. Omissions of treatment should be by the direct intent of someone—the physician, the patient, or the patient's agent, as we shall consider later.

Intention, then, leaves me uncomfortable. It does give grounds for making a moral distinction between some actions and omissions, at least to the extent of assigning blame. Some actions have as their direct intent the death of the patient; some omissions do not. But, as we have seen, intent does not adequately separate all actions and omissions. We need to press on.

The long-range consequences are different.   A fourth argument takes into account the long-range implications of permitting active killing. If we accept the killing of the terminally ill for humane reasons, may that not lead to the killing of the severely retarded child, the antisocial personality, or the ethnically unattractive? Leo Alexander, a physician who played a

central role in the drafting of the Nuremberg Code, fears this
may be the case. He sees a dangerous precedent in the Nazi
period. According to Alexander, the German mass murders:

> started with the acceptance of that attitude, basic in the
> euthanasia movement, that there is such a thing as life not
> worthy to be lived. This attitude in its early stages con-
> cerned itself merely with the severely and chronically sick.
> Gradually the sphere of those to be included in this cate-
> gory was enlarged to include the socially unproductive,
> the racially unwanted, and finally all non-Germans. But it
> is important to realize that the infinitely small wedged-in
> lever from which this entire trend of mind received its im-
> petus was the attitude toward the non-rehabilitable sick.[14]

Some cannot believe that this could happen in a democratic
and freedom-loving country like the United States. There is,
in fact, a significant historical debate over whether the Nazi
mass murders really began with attitudes toward the nonrehabilitable sick. Some argue that protection and purification of
the Aryan stock was the intention from the beginning.[15] A
more balanced thesis, one which may well be the most accurate, is that both the ideal of a pure race and the specific pre-
cipitating event of a plea of a father for the merciful death of
his son were necessary for the mass murders.[16]

Whether or not the Nazi historical experience required an
attitude toward the nonrehabilitable sick as a necessary condition, the critical question is whether such a shift could take
place in a contemporary state. In order to test the suscep-
tibility of educated Americans to such a trend of thought, a
psychologist, Helge Mansson, asked 570 university students to
participate in a research project. They were told that it was

14. Leo Alexander, "Medical Science Under Dictatorship," *New England Journal of Medicine* 241 (1949), pp. 39–47.

15. See Marvin Kohl, "Voluntary Beneficent Euthanasia," in *Beneficent Euthanasia*, ed. Marvin Kohl (Buffalo, N.Y.: Prometheus Books, 1975), p. 137, and Joseph Fletcher, "Ethics and Euthanasia," in *To Live and To Die*, p. 114.

16. Compare the discussion in Lucy C. Dawidowicz, *The War Against the Jews 1933–1945* (New York: Holt, Rinehart, and Winston, 1975), pp. 131–34, and also Klaus Dörner, "Nationalsozialismus und Lebensvernichtung," *Vierteljahrshefte für Zeitgeschichte* 15 (1967), pp. 121–52, especially pp. 130–31.

designed to develop ways of killing "unfit" persons as a "final solution" to problems of overpopulation and personal misery. During the presentation of the project, it was stated that mercy killing "is considered by most experts as not only being beneficial to the unfit because it puts them out of their misery or lives, but more importantly it will be beneficial to the healthy, fit and more educated segment of the population." Participants were told that the only problem was to determine which method of killing should be used, who should do the killing, and who should decide when killing should be resorted to. The students were also informed that "the findings of our studies will be applied to humans once the system has been perfected." Out of the 570 students, 326 approved of the project. When applied to minority groups the acceptance rate was even higher.[17]

When we accept active killing of the dying, we are indeed stepping onto a slippery slope. We had best know very well how to get off that slope short of crashing to the depths of moral depravity. If active killing of the suffering would lead to active killing of others, that is a relevant consequence which must be taken into account in evaluating even the first, most apparently justifiable act of this sort. If one has reason to believe that the distinctions between active killing of the terminally ill for mercy and killing of the unwanted for the convenience of society are clear or at least morally sound, then the two kinds of killing could be seen as morally different. For instance, logically one could hold that the principle that active killing for mercy is morally acceptable without also accepting the principle that active killing for the benefit of others—other individuals, ethnic groups, or the race—was also acceptable. Marvin Kohl attempts to refute the use of the wedge argument against active killing by pointing out that the appropriate rule to follow is: do not kill except in cases of voluntary inducement of painless and quick death when the intention and consequences of which are the kindest possible treatment in

17. Helge Hilding Mansson, "Justifying the Final Solution," *Omega* 3 (1972), pp. 79–87.

the actual circumstances for the recipient of the act.[18] His formula clearly separates, at least in theory, killing for kindness and killing for the benefit of others.

Arthur Dyck, in a carefully argued response to Kohl, rejects this analysis. He claims: "The injunction not to kill is part of a total effort to prevent the destruction of human beings and of the human community. It is an absolute prohibition in the sense that no society can be indifferent about the taking of human life. Any act, insofar as it is an act of taking a human life, is wrong; that is to say, taking a human life is a wrong-making characteristic of actions." [19] If the prohibition of killing per se is the underlying ethical principle rather than the prohibition of killing to benefit others, then the wedge argument is logically valid. The justification of one violation leads to the justification of another because in both cases the same underlying moral principle must give way.

At this point there seems to be two forms of the wedge argument. One is the logical form as argued by Kohl and Dyck. The other rests not on a logical point but an empirical one. Possibly tolerating active killing for mercy will lead to increase in other active killings, not because of any logical connection, but simply because those who are not careful may mistake one form of killing for another or those who want to actively kill to benefit others will rationalize their actions by claiming that they are committed as acts of kindness to the recipient. The two forms of the argument must be dealt with separately. The first form will depend upon whether acting to cause death is always inherently wrong or only wrong when it is done for reasons other than mercy. I am prepared to say that acting to cause death for reasons other than mercy can be morally more blameworthy than in cases where mercy is the motive. As will be argued below, I am even prepared to concede that there may be exceptional circumstances where active

18. Kohl, "Voluntary Beneficent Euthanasia," p. 139. Also see his *The Morality of Killing: Sanctity of Life, Abortion and Euthanasia* (New York: Humanities Press, 1974), for a fuller discussion.

19. Arthur Dyck, "Beneficent Euthanasia and Benemortasia: Alternative Views of Mercy," in *Beneficent Euthanasia*, p. 124.

killing for mercy is morally acceptable. That does not mean,
however, that I see active killings for mercy as matters of
moral indifference. Here Dyck might be right. There must be
a strong *prima facie* moral case against actively causing any
death. The nature of that case will depend in part upon the legitimacy of the distinction between *causing* a death and *permitting* one, which will be taken up next.

The second kind of the wedge argument rests on an empirical argument: that permitting active killing for mercy will lead
to more active killing for other reasons (à la Alexander's interpretation of the Nazi holocaust) whether or not there is a
logical connection between the two. Whether or not the logical
form of the wedge argument works, this empirical form seems
to me to be quite convincing. The persuasive power of the
psychologist over the American college students is troublesome. If one of the features of active killing for mercy is that it
might lead to active killing for other reasons because in general people cannot adequately make a relevant moral distinction, then that consequence must count against active killing
even for mercy.

The cause of death is different. The wedge argument presents
a potential moral difference between active killing and withholding treatment.

The fifth and perhaps the most widely intuited difference
between acts of omission and commission is that the cause of
death differs, even if the result is the same. From a Protestant
perspective, Paul Ramsey disagrees with Joseph Fletcher's
minimizing of this difference. Arguing that the difference in
cause is morally significant, he says that Fletcher "seriously
misunderstands the positive quality of the nonconsequential
'action' put forth in attending and caring for the dying. . . ."
According to Ramsey:

> In omission no human agent causes the patient's death,
> directly or indirectly. He dies his own death from causes
> that it is no longer merciful or reasonable to fight by
> means of possible medical interventions. . . . In any case,
> doing something and omitting something in order to do
> something else are different sorts of acts. To do or not to

do something may, then, be subject to different moral evaluations. One may be wrong and the other may be right, even if these decisions and actions are followed by the same end result, namely the death of a patient.[20]

Law professor George Fletcher argues that the distinction between actively assisting in the death of the patient and allowing the dying to die has a parallel in the American legal system in the different ways that culpability is assigned to "causing" or "permitting" harm to be done to others. In cases where there is an act to cause harm, liability for the proscribed harm is readily assigned once the agent who has carried out the act has been identified. In cases of omission, however, liability is not so readily assigned.[21] In the case of an omission, liability will depend upon "the relationship between the parties."[22]

Consider the parallel cases of an unknown child starving to death on the other side of the globe and one's own child starving to death through neglect. It may well be that we should bear moral responsibility for each of the deaths, yet there is clearly more direct moral culpability for the starving of one's own child. The role of parent includes specific moral duties. In Kant's phrase, there is a duty of "perfect obligation." Culpability for the omission of feeding one's own child for whom one is directly responsible is more clearly assigned.

It is true that in some cases the relationship between the parties will be such that omission that results in death will be

20. Paul Ramsey, "On (Only) Caring for the Dying," in *The Patient as Person* (New Haven: Yale University Press, 1970), pp. 151–52.

21. George P. Fletcher, "Prolonging Life," *Washington Law Review* 42 (1967), p. 1009.

22. Ibid., p. 1012. While I find this portion of Fletcher's analysis sound, he goes on to reach what to me is the totally unacceptable legal and moral judgment that whether or not it is legally permissible for doctors to turn off respirators "all depends on what doctors customarily do" (p. 1015). Even though assigning liability for an omission may very well be determined by the relationship between the parties, in this case the patient and the physician, it is by no means clear why the moral and legal obligations engendered by that relationship should be determined by the customary practices of one of the parties rather than the feelings of moral requiredness of the other party or the obligations specified by law through due process. Courts are now, I think correctly, overruling the criterion of customary medical practice in deciding liability for harms which should be evaluated by the "reasonable man" criterion.

just as wrong as actively killing. This is the argument used by James Rachels.[23] He asks us to consider two cases. In the first case Smith would gain a large inheritance if anything should happen to his six-year-old cousin. While the child is taking a bath, Smith sneaks into the bathroom and drowns the child, arranging it so it will look like an accident. In the second case Jones, who also stands to inherit if anything should happen to his six-year-old cousin, is planning to drown the child, but discovers, much to his satisfaction, just as he is entering the bathroom that the child is drowning. He merely fails to rescue him. He stands by to push the child's head back under if it is necessary—but it is not.

Rachels claims, I think correctly, that both are equally morally reprehensible in spite of the fact that one simply omitted while the other actively killed. What this proves, however, is that some omissions are morally as wrong as active killing. In this case Jones clearly had a special relationship with his cousin which obligated him to act. His failure to act is as wrong as actively drowning the child. That, of course, does not prove that all omissions are as wrong as active killings. Especially it does not prove that omission of a treatment by a physician when the physician is instructed to omit the treatment is the same as acting to cause the death of a patient (even when that action is requested).

Only if physicians caring for dying patients have a specific obligation to provide life-prolonging or death-prolonging treatments would they be responsible for an omission. If they have had that treatment requested by their patients, they may have that responsibility to act, but otherwise quite the opposite may be true. Medical treatment cannot even be rendered without the consent of the patients or their agents; how can it be claimed that physicians have a duty to offer such treatment? If treatment without consent is the crime of assault, and battery,

23. Rachels, "Active and Passive Euthanasia," p. 79. Rachels goes on to point out that this case is not the same as that of the physician actively killing for mercy. He claims, however, that in both cases "the bare difference between killing and letting die does not, in itself, make a moral difference." With that I would agree, but would add that causing a death may still be morally different from omitting a treatment in those cases when one has no specific obligation to act and in fact may have a specific obligation to not act.

then presumably the "crime" of omitting "unrequested" treatment would have to be "failure to commit assault and battery." That is not normally considered a fundamental moral wrong. On the other hand, the physician who injects an air bubble— even upon the request of the patient—has acted and would be considered responsible for that act. Thus from the standpoint of responsibility for the action or the omission, there would seem to be a difference—a difference in who is responsible for the events which follow and who "causes" the death of the patient.

In the end the case for a moral difference between actively killing the dying patient and withdrawing treatment in order that the patient may die will have to rest upon all of these arguments taken together, not on any one of them alone. The individual differences may be subtle, some more persuasive than others. Combined, however, their impact is somewhat more impressive. Of course, combining several unpersuasive arguments cannot make a persuasive one, but several possible arguments taken together can increase the probability of the conclusion. I am led to conclude that although the differences between commission and omission are much more subtle than some traditions would indicate, the wisdom of the common judgment is sound. There are significant moral distinctions between actively killing and simply omitting an action, no matter how subtle these may be in particular cases.

THE POSSIBLE MORALITY OF ACTIVE KILLING

To say that there may be subtle moral distinctions between the two types of behavior does not mean that allowing the dying patient to die by omitting treatment will necessarily be morally preferable to action which brings about death. At first glance, the moral case for withdrawing treatment may seem more attractive, but in some individual cases, active intervention may still be morally defensible. This is a possibility which the Roman Catholic tradition in medical ethics will not consider. In a case involving great pain and slow but inevitable degeneration of the body, must we maintain fastidious commitment to the general rule that withholding of treatment is acceptable, but hastening death is not? Ethical dogmatism may get in the way of both reason and compassion.

It is possible that excruciating pain is not now inevitable. Cecily Saunders, the medical director of St. Christopher's Hospice in England, claims that pain and suffering can virtually always be controlled by the proper use of painkilling drugs and sleep-inducing medication.[24] It is irrelevant to worry about making a dying cancer patients morphine addicts for the last two weeks of their lives. Recently, a special panel of the British Medical Association's Board of Science and Education has concluded that there is seldom a need for active killing in order to avoid pain. According to Dr. Phillip H. Addison, secretary of the Medical Defense Union in London, modern medicine can now overcome pain and do so even without shortening life.[25] If that is the case, the pain and suffering of a dying patient may be an empty reason justifying active intervention. This is an empirical question for which medical science is likely to give different answers for different conditions and at different points in history. In principle, though, pain and suffering may be considered as creating exceptional conditions where active killing, at least at the request of the patient and for purposes of human relief, is morally licit.

This is the conclusion reached by Paul Ramsey, a Protestant who generally agrees with Roman Catholic thought on the subject.[26] He proposes a second sort of case where active hastening of death might be tolerated morally: where the person is permanently and deeply unconscious. We assume that such patients are not suffering at all. According to Ramsey, it is "entirely indifferent to the patient" in such a condition whether his death is hastened by an air bubble or the withdrawal of treatment. This presumes that such individuals are still to be considered alive and in possession of moral claims. The point of course is that what is a matter of indifference to

24. Cecily Saunders, "A Death in the Family: A Professional View," *British Medical Journal* (January 6, 1973), pp. 30–31.

25. "Good Pain Relief Cuts Chances of Euthanasia Law in Britain," *Medical Tribune* (October 10, 1973), p. 4.

26. Ramsey, "On (Only) Caring for the Dying," pp. 161–62.

patients may be anything but a matter of indifference to the relatives; they may be suffering by the prolonged vigil over their inevitably dying family member. In this case, and only in this case, according to Ramsey, it would become moral to introduce such non-patient-centered considerations into the decision. To either omit treatment or hasten death actively for the benefit of the relatives would be a "defect of care" for patients—if this still made any difference to them—but once it is a matter of indifference to them then such secondary factors could legitimately come into play.

Unlike Ramsey, I cannot imagine that this principle could be held to the one application. Would not this emphasis on whether something is a matter of indifference to the patient also legitimate and even require giving consideration to patients' wishes if they were still conscious and competent to request active intervention? If we can justify actively hastening death when it is simply a matter of indifference to patients could we not much more readily when patients actively request the hastening of death? I would claim there is a duty to provide "appropriate care" for individuals even when they become corpses. The possible moral differences between omitting treatment and actively hastening death do not hinge upon patients' desires or patients' indifference. They presumably are rooted in more fundamental moral requirements if they are significant at all. It appears to me that this second case where active killing might be tolerated—when it is a matter of indifference to the individuals in question—either contains the seeds of a justification of hastening death by request or must be overridden by considerations extending beyond patient preference. While the first case, of hastening death to relieve intractable pain and suffering, seems plausible, the case of doing away with the comatose patient seems much less so.

In fact the case of the comatose patient may have few practical implications because virtually all such patients require active medical support which, if withdrawn, would lead rapidly to their death in any case. This is simply a hypothetical example to determine whether there is any felt moral difference between action to hasten death and omission of action to prolong life. One must ask oneself, if such a patient were before me, would it actually be a matter of total moral indifference (all other things being equal) whether I injected an air bubble or simply failed to inject penicillin to overcome a pneumonia infection? I, for one, have a strong inclination to opt for the second course.

To carry this a step further, if I were a member of the nursing staff in the institution which is "caring for" Mrs. Morgan and had decided to honor her request for a dignified and simple way to die, it seems most unlikely that it would actually be a matter of indifference which of the two courses (injecting an air bubble or simply omitting resuscitation) I would choose. All other things being equal, I have a moral preference for omitting resuscitation. It could be that my moral sense is deceived by cultural conditioning, but the difference seems to have some rational basis. The difference seems sufficiently well founded that, when we turn to consider public policy, it will be important to note whether a proposed policy legitimates action to end life or merely allows omission of action.

THE CASE FOR A DIFFERENCE: PRACTICAL CONSIDERATIONS

Even if an argument can be made for the moral acceptability of active killing and even for preferring it in the rare case, it is still an open question whether such active killing should be made legal. As we have seen, pervasive and serious consequences may attend institutionalizing the principle that it is acceptable to kill patients for whom life is not worth living. Even if we are not concerned about the extension of the principle to those other than the dying, there is reason to be cautious.

When there is an action to bring about death, barring miraculous intervention or a bungling of the job, death will most certainly occur. When action is omitted so that death may occur by the body's own disease process, however, the actual demise of the patient is taken out of the hands of human decision makers. There are two types of cases, both hopefully quite rare, when the patient might not actually die when action is omitted. The first is when there is an error in the prognosis that a disease process is irreversibly terminal. The second is when others (medical staff, relatives, government agents) decide that death should be hastened for reasons which extend beyond concern only for the patient—to dispose of a chronically ill "no-good," to gain access to a bequest, to free a hospital bed, or simply to remove an obstreperous, "problem" patient. If an air embolism is injected, one will never know for sure whether the patient really was afflicted with a terminal illness. In these two types of cases, patients would certainly be dead with death-causing action but alive if actions were omitted, even actions mislabelled "lifesaving." In a day of increasing depersonalization of medical care and grossly different standards of treatment available to different classes and ethnic groups, we must guard against the potential, if rare, abuse of this kind.

If we are really concerned about these risks and convinced that, because of the power of drugs to control pain, the need for active intervention to spare the patient suffering is extremely rare, we may want active killing of dying patients to remain illegal even in those rare cases where it might be morally justified.

This situation is inescapable in a society governed by the crude instrument of the law. Consider the "red light rule." It is really not necessary for every car to stop at every red light under every conceivable condition. There are times when one could cautiously pass through a red light when no car was in sight and save the time wasted. There can be no doubt that the rule, "always stop at every red light," is crude. A far better rule might be "stop and wait for every red light unless the road is clear." If that rule were followed scrupulously it would clearly be better than wasting valuable seconds at an empty cross street.

Yet obviously the rule, "stop unless the road is clear," will not work because too many mistakes will be made. It is better in the long run to follow the apparently less efficient rule, even if we occasionally waste time at a lonely intersection.

The situation may be similar in the rare cases where active killing of the dying might be morally justified. The courts would probably be lenient towards a parent who goes through a red light to speed a dying child to a hospital. It may be that civil disobedience is also the appropriate course in the case of the rare patient who is irreversibly dying in extreme pain. If the active hastening of death has to be justified by an appeal to civil disobedience, the courts may continue to show leniency in their judgments, but we may also continue to examine those cases carefully and thoroughly.

Other practical considerations of a much more mundane sort suggest that active killing of the dying had best be kept separate from the withdrawal of medical treatment. We have seen that among physicians only a minority (between 18 and 27 percent) favor active hastening of death, while a substantial majority (between 59 and 80 percent) favor withdrawal of treatment (negative euthanasia in the researchers' terms) for the dying.[27] Another recent study found that only 26 percent of a group of abdominal surgeons felt the terminal patient's life should be maintained as long as possible.[28] The same vast difference exists among the lay population. A 1973 Louis Harris poll asked, "Do you think a patient with a terminal disease ought to be able to tell his doctor to let him die rather than to extend his life when no cure is in sight, or do you think this is wrong?" Sixty-two percent thought it ought to be allowed while only 28 percent thought it was wrong. When asked, "Do you think the patient who is terminally ill, with no cure in sight, ought to have the right to tell his doctor to put him out of his misery, or do you think this is wrong?" only 37 percent thought it ought to be allowed while 53 percent thought it was wrong.

A Gallup poll in 1973 found a somewhat higher percentage favoring the statement, "When a person has a disease that cannot be cured, do you think doctors should be allowed by law to end the patient's life by some painless means if the patient and his family request it?" Fifty-three percent of those polled said yes while 47 percent disapproved. The question does not distinguish active killing from allowing to die as sharply as did the Harris poll. What is interesting about the Gallup poll ques-

27. Williams, "Propagation, Modification, and Termination of Life," p. 90; Brown *et al.*, "The Preservation of Life," p. 77.

28. "Surgeons Oppose Prolonging Life of Dying," *Medical Tribune* (August 15, 1973), p. 3.

tion is that it had been asked once before in 1950 when only 36 percent approved. This suggests growing acceptance of stopping "the struggle to the end," but the disagreement is still substantial in comparison with the consensus on the clearly worded withdrawal of treatment statement.[29]

The practical implications are great. First of all, if only 59 percent of physicians say they would practice "negative euthanasia" if it were authorized and requested, this means that even if you as a lay person had thought about the matter and exercised your right to refuse treatment there would apparently be four chances in ten that your opinion would not be respected and the treatment would not be stopped. It also means that both physicians and lay people sense a great difference between actively killing the dying and letting them die by withholding treatment. Especially if it is true that few if any of us would benefit in any practical way from the active hastening of our death, should we jeopardize the development of a public policy that would support our right to refuse treatment by holding out for the principle that we should also have the right to authorize death-hastening steps? From the standpoint of practical politics if not from more substantive theoretical considerations, it would seem a good idea to keep the two issues separate.

Stopping vs. Not Starting Treatments

Should Mrs. Morgan suddenly catch an infection or go into cardiac arrest, the nursing home staff would have the option of letting the ailment take its course without intervening; but the physicians treating the heroin overdose victim may not have that option for a while. He is being maintained in intensive care by the use of a respirator. Do the group of physicians, who consider the patient still alive but unable to benefit from further treatment, have the option of turning off the respirator, or do they, if they are instructed to do nothing further, have to wait until the pneumococcus finds its way into the patient's lungs?

29. "Approval of 'Mercy Killing' Rises," *American Medical News* (August 13, 1973), p. 11.

The choice in this case is not between active hastening of death and failing to start treatment but rather between active killing and stopping treatment that has already been started. This latter alternative is sometimes seen as an "action" to bring about death. For me, however, it is hard to see why there should be any moral distinction between stopping a treatment once started, and failing to start it in the first place.

From the standpoint of the five distinctions between action to end life and the simple avoidance of treatment, stopping a treatment once started has some characteristics of each. There seems to be some difference of opinion on whether the psychological impact of stopping is more akin to active killing than to not starting a treatment. We have seen, however, that the link between the psychological impact of a decision and its rightness or wrongness is difficult to establish. Paul Ramsey, for instance, observes that medical professionals tend to see stopping an ongoing treatment (like a respirator) as similar to active killing, but that ethicists and moral theologians treat it much more like not starting treatment in the first place. Stopping treatment and not starting treatment in the first place have in common that neither would open the door for policies of ending other "unworthy" lives.

From the standpoint of the immediate cause of death, stopping resembles not starting in that the body's own disease process induces death in each case, whereas in the action of injecting an air bubble, the agent introduced by the physician causes a death that would not otherwise have occurred for that reason, and might not have taken place at all.

Stopping treatment seems, at first, to most resemble active hastening of death because it requires a conscious decision by a single decision maker (or decision-making group); it can never take place by default. However, it seems that the decision to stop the machinery ought ultimately to rest with the patients or their agents in a way that the injection of an air bubble could not. Although plug pullers must make a clear and conscious decision, it is not clear that they have the responsibility for that decision in the same sense that they would if they injected an air bubble. Patients or their agents cannot command a specific "treatment" such as the air injection; for them to be treated at all, however, requires their consent and so whether or not treatment is started or continued should be under their command. From the standpoint of the patient's consent or lack thereof, stopping is much like not starting. Any public policy should deal explicitly with this ambiguous case of stopping treatments already begun. A policy will be simply vague if it fails to make clear its position on stopping treatments.

Direct vs. Indirect Killing

Another ambiguous class of actions is those which result in death although that was not the primary or "direct" intention. Consider the possibility that a patient who is being maintained is suffering from anxiety or depression. To induce sleep phenobarbitol is given, but increasing doses are required until it reaches the point where there is serious risk of respiratory depression and even death. Earlier we observed that sometimes there is an attempt to make a distinction between active killing and omission of treatment on the basis of intention. While that distinction may not always have been valid in distinguishing omissions and commissions, intention does become relevant when death is a possible side effect of a treatment, whether surgery or drugs, to relieve pain or anxiety. The newly revised "Ethical and Religious Directives for Catholic Health Facilities" states specifically:

> It is not euthanasia to give a dying person sedatives and analgesics for the alleviation of pain, when such a measure is judged necessary, even though they may deprive the patient of the use of reason, or shorten his life.

The term "indirect killing" or "indirect euthanasia" is sometimes used to refer to the omission of treatment in order to allow the dying patient to die. This language is confusing at best. At the very least it is inconsistent with traditional usage of the terms. Ramsey argues: "In omission no human agent causes the patient's death, directly or indirectly." [30] The dis-

---

30. Ramsey, "On (Only) Caring for the Dying," p. 151.

tinction between direct and indirect effect has its origins in Roman Catholic ethics. In this tradition an effect is indirect when it is really a side effect, a consequence which is secondary.

The subtlety of the distinction has always puzzled the secular world, particularly in one of the areas where the distinction has become famous.[31] Catholic moral theology, where all abortion is opposed and yet the removal of a cancerous uterus is morally licit even if it should happen to contain a previable fetus. The reasoning is that the intention is not to kill the fetus but to save the woman's life. It could be argued that even in more direct forms of abortion the intent is not really to kill a fetus but to meet a felt medical, familial, economic, or social need. The proponents of the law of indirect effect, however, will not buy this rationalization. It may be true that the intention is to help the mother or the family, but the method includes the *direct* intention of destroying the fetus. For an effect to be indirect, "the secondary effect is not sought for its own sake nor as a means toward the achievement of a further end." [32]

Now, the secular mind which finds this use of the principle of indirect effect little more than scholastic doubletalk in relation to the abortion controversy surprisingly finds a similar distinction quite plausible in the care of the dying. Intuitively even the secular man finds the accidental killing of the patient by the side effects of a high dose of narcotic less morally questionable than the overt killing of the patient. When high doses of narcotic analgesia or barbiturate are given for sedation, side effects such as respiratory depression may indeed cause death. If, however, the intention was to relieve pain or induce sleep, giving such drugs is deemed ethically acceptable. The killing of the patient is indirect.

One physician reports that he has told a patient in the final stages of an illness, "Here is a bottle of sleeping pills. Take one

31. For two of the most sophisticated critiques see Jonathan Bennett, "Whatever the Consequences," *Analysis* 26 (1966), pp. 83–102; and Philippa Foot, "The Problem of Abortion and the Doctrine of Double Effect," *Oxford Review* 5(1967), pp. 5–15.

32. Charles J. McFadden, *Medical Ethics* (Philadelphia: F. A. Davis, 1967), p. 25. See also Edwin F. Healy, *Medical Ethics* (Chicago: Loyola University Press, 1956); Bernard Haring, *Medical Ethics* (Notre Dame, Indiana: Fides Publishers, 1973).

if you need to get to sleep. Be careful—if you take the whole
bottle it will kill you." One pill would depress the body's control centers enough to aid sleep; several pills would depress
them enough to cause death. The same effect in different
degrees would be therapeutic or fatal. The intention of the
physician in making his statement is quite transparent, and
should his patient take the bottleful, the action would not differ morally from assisting the patient in turning on a gas jet or
jumping from a window. The patient as actor and the physician as accomplice would bear the full moral responsibility of
the active hastening of the death.

In the case of the indirect death from a narcotic used to
relieve severe pain, there is at least one difference from the
destruction of the fetus in a cancerous uterus. In the case of
the fetus, its destruction is completely predictable if the
woman is known to be pregnant. While the destruction may
not be "intended," it is known in advance to be inevitable. This
is not true in other cases of indirect effects, such as killing innocent civilians in bombing military targets in a "just war" or
giving terminally ill patients high dosages of needed drugs.
This may be why secular man sees the death from a drug
overdose as more acceptable than direct killing. There is good
reason, other things being equal, for finding both this indirect
hastening of death and omitting intervention so that dying can
take its course to be morally preferable to acting directly for
the purpose of hastening death.

These subtleties in the moral tradition may not be all that
helpful to the group of physicians standing around the bedside of the heroin overdose victim, or to the patient and family
trying to decide on appropriate care for the last days. What is
needed is an entirely new perspective, one which, by accident,
cuts through many of the philosophical distinctions with which
we have been dealing.

The Patient Perspective: The Right to Refuse
Medical Treatment

Although I have not always held this opinion, I now find
that I must stand morally opposed to a physician's decision ei-

ther to actively kill the dying patient *or* to omit treatment by
not starting or stopping once begun. It ought to be shocking
that the debate about acting to cause death or omitting actions
to hasten death is conducted almost entirely from the perspective of the one who acts upon the dying patient, usually the
physician. The moral question being asked is "Should we or
should we not allow the patient to die?" At times it sounds like
what we could call the "medicine man's burden" syndrome:

> There have been columns of prose, often eloquent, but
> mostly tedious in both the medical and lay literature de-
> bating the role of clergyman, law maker, judge, and fam-
> ily members in the life and death decision when to pull
> the plug in the terminal patient. But . . . the weight can-
> not be lifted from the sagging often reluctant shoulders
> of the physician.[33]

In this physician's view the patient does not even make the
list of rejected decision makers. There is, however, another
perspective: the patients' viewpoint—the rights and obligations of the potentially deceased. The right to refuse medical
treatment, for any reason, is well established in the Western
legal tradition. No competent patients (excluding prisoners)
have ever been ordered to undergo any medical treatment for
their own good by United States courts even if such a refusal
would almost assuredly lead to death. The entire next chapter
will examine the refusal of treatment, particularly the complexities that arise when patients are incompetent—when they
are children, mentally ill, or senile—or when they are people
with dependents. At the level of moral distinctions, which are
the topic of this chapter, to view the moral issue from the
standpoint of the rights and obligations of the patients rather
than from the moral alternatives of physicians, medical personnel, or other outsiders changes the character of the discussion.

From the perspective of the physician or other agent who
might decide what should be done to the patient, the ethical
issue is "When if ever is it morally acceptable for death to be
unopposed or even hastened in the patient lying before me?"

33. Robert Moser, "The New Ethic," unpublished paper written for the Foundation of Thanatology.

The patient-centered framing of the question, however, adds the ethical issue of freedom, dignity, and responsibility for decisions about the treatment of one's own person. Paradoxically, a decision rendered by another human agent would probably come at a point where human freedom, dignity, and responsibility have become no longer possible, but the mere fact that the question is put in a manner assuming the authority of another person to decide the fate of the passive patient denies these qualities, which should be respected all the more if the patient is not in a position to defend them.

Taking into account the right to refuse even life-prolonging treatment clarifies some of the other distinctions we have discussed. Many people see no real practical difference between a physician deciding to kill a dying patient and deciding to withdraw treatment. But certainly from the patients' perspective the difference is great. To grant patients the power to refuse a medical treatment that they do not want is clearly not the same as granting them the right to demand that their physician kill them. It is not even the same as granting them the right to "permit" their physicians to kill them.

Seen from the patients' perspective, the intermediate case of stopping a treatment once begun is much closer to not starting a treatment than it is to active killing. If patients have the right to refuse the beginning of a medical treatment, they also have the right to withdraw from a treatment once it has begun (subject of course to practical considerations of the possibility of stopping the treatment). But this is still far different from the right to demand or consent to a new act by the physician or any other person that is designed to kill the dying patient.

Patients routinely consent to treatments that risk the unintended side effect of death. Any surgery carries a residual risk of fatality. Consent to procedures that may be fatal, at least in cases where death is not very likely, raises no serious moral problem. This too is far different from demanding or consenting to acts to kill the patient.

REASONABLE AND UNREASONABLE TREATMENTS

Those who decide that the heroin overdose patient is alive and who also decide that they are opposed to actively hastening death must finally face the critical moral question: when, if ever, is it moral to cease treatment? Does it make any difference whether a dying patient refuses radical experimental surgery, an expensive but not experimental cardiac valve operation, a mechanical respirator, or an intravenous feeding? Does it make any difference whether the patient is in the last hours of severely metastasized cancer or the early days of a certainly fatal but not presently debilitating disease, in the prime of life or over the hill?

The distinction is sometimes made between "ordinary" and "extra-ordinary" means of medical treatment. Pope Pius XII considers the traditional moral distinction critical:

> But morally one is held to use only ordinary means—according to circumstances of persons, places, times, and culture—that is to say, means that do not involve any grave burden for oneself or another. A more strict obligation would be too burdensome for most men and would render the attainment of the higher, more important good too difficult. Life, health, all temporal activities are in fact subordinated to spiritual ends. On the other hand, one is not forbidden to take more than the strictly necessary steps to preserve life and health, as long as he does not fail in some more serious duty.[34]

This distinction has found its way into some, but not all, of the public policy proposals dealing with cessation of treatment. The terms *ordinary* and *extraordinary* are extremely vague and used inconsistently in the literature. Ramsey argues that there are three systematic differences in the use of the term by moralists and by physicians.[35] First, physicians use the term *ordinary* to mean customary as opposed to unusual procedures, where the moralists "are somewhat more likely than doctors to use these terms relative to the patient's particular medical condition." Second, moralists are likely to see the decision to stop extraordinary life-sustaining treatments as having the same moral warrant as a decision not to begin their use, where physicians are likely to distinguish between the two.

34. Pius XII, "Prolongation of Life," pp. 393–98.
35. Ramsey, "On (Only) Caring for the Dying," pp. 120–23.

Third, moralists "always understand the distinction . . . to refer decisively to morally relevant, nonmedical features of a particular patient's care" where, for physicians, the reference is more narrowly medical. Underlying the confusion are three overlapping but fundamentally different uses of these two terms.

Usual vs. Unusual

In the papal pronouncement, "Prolongation of Life," the criterion of ordinariness appears to be the "circumstance of persons, places, times, and culture—that is to say, means that do not involve any grave burden for oneself or another. . . ." This corresponds to the first half of Jesuit moral theologian Edwin Healy's definition of *extraordinary* as "whatever here and now is very *costly* or very *unusual* or very *painful* or very *difficult* or very *dangerous.* . . ." [36] That Healy includes these factors indicates that the term *extraordinary* implies more than a simple survey of frequency of use under a given condition. Nevertheless, we might expect *usualness* to correlate closely with these other factors. Thus, this first conception of the distinction may be summarized, somewhat awkwardly, as "usualness."

There are obvious problems with the notion of usualness, however. If usual treatments are morally required and unusual ones not required, the status quo defines moral requiredness. It does not seem reasonable to answer the question "What is required?" by saying "Whatever the physicians tend to be providing." It should be possible to say that even though something is not now being done, it ought to be. Adequate primary health care for urban ghettos and rural areas is unusual. That it is morally expendable because it is unusual seems preposterous. In the same light it does not seem reasonable to require a treatment simply because it is usually provided. If that were the case no change in policy could ever take place. We could never argue that a usual treatment such as a respirator for a chronically semicomatose accident victim

36. Healy, *Medical Ethics*, p. 67.

ought to be omitted. Although "usualness" may be helpful in reflecting upon requiredness, it alone cannot possibly tell us precisely what is required.

Useful vs. Useless

Gerald Kelly writes that the "standard moralists" often do not define the terms *ordinary* and *extraordinary,* but that "by ordinary they mean such things as can be obtained and used without great difficulty."[37] This formulation modifies the notion of usualness somewhat, but still is based on availability. Kelly's own definition, given elsewhere, is rather different. He defines *ordinary means* as "all medicines, treatments, and operations, which offer a reasonable hope of benefit for the patient and which can be obtained and used without excessive expense, pain, or other inconvenience."[38] The emphasis on "reasonable hope of benefit" seems to be an alternate phrasing of the concept used by Pius XII. In the "Prolongation of Life" statement, the Pope said that an anesthesiologist is not bound to use modern artificial respiration apparatus in cases that are "considered to be completely hopeless." Theologian Joseph V. Sullivan condones ceasing intravenous feeding for a terminal patient suffering great pain. He says that the feeding is "extraordinary" even though he specifically recognizes that it is a "usual" practice.[39]

To this Kelly responds in a puzzling way, saying that this might appear to be a sort of "Catholic euthanasia" to "those who cannot appreciate the fine distinction between omitting an ordinary means and omitting a *useless* ordinary means."[40] In a discussion of the use of a stimulant merely to prolong life a short time, Kelly says he agrees with Roman Catholic medical ethicist Charles J. McFadden's judgment that such use is not morally obligatory, but he rejects McFadden's argument that the stimulant is an "extraordinary means":

37. Gerald Kelly, "The Duty of Using Artificial Means of Preserving Life," *Theological Studies* 11 (1950), p. 204.

38. Gerald Kelly, *Medico-Moral Problems* (St. Louis: The Catholic Hospital Association, 1958), p. 129.

39. Joseph V. Sullivan, *Catholic Teaching on the Morality of Euthanasia* (Washington: Catholic University of America Press, 1949), p. 72.

40. Kelly, "The Duty of Using Artificial Means," p. 219.

I agree that it is not obligatory, but my analysis of the case would be somewhat different. I should prefer to say that the use of the stimulant for such a short time is an ordinary means. But since it is artificial and since it has practically no remedial value in the circumstances, the patient is not obliged to use it.[41]

In his response to Sullivan and McFadden, Kelly seems to revert to the criterion of usualness to define *ordinary*. In doing so he contradicts his definition of *ordinary* as a means which, among other things, "offers reasonable hope of success." He would be referring to a useless means (or one with "practically no remedial value in the circumstances") which nevertheless offers reasonable hope of benefit. In doing so he opens the way for his discussion of morally permissible omissions of ordinary means.

Ramsey appears to agree with Kelly's original definition rather than with these obscure references to "useless ordinary means." While he never explicitly agrees with McFadden and Sullivan that the uselessness of a procedure would be grounds for calling it extraordinary no matter how usual it was, this is clearly implied.[42]

Imperative vs. *Elective*

In his formal definition of *ordinary* and *extraordinary*, Ramsey calls imperative procedures "ordinary" and elective procedures "extraordinary." [43] But he goes on to argue that while usefulness is a central factor in determining the moral imperative, it is wrong to reduce the distinction to usefulness "without significant remainder." There are, in the first place, grounds other than uselessness for which it would be morally acceptable to omit or cease to use a medical means—repugnance of the procedure itself, cost, abhorrence of the social consequences such as separation from one's family, and the like. On the other hand, certain procedures might be useless to save or even to prolong the life of a patient, but could nevertheless be imperative for the patient's comfort.

41. Ibid., p. 219.
42. Ramsey, "On (Only) Caring for the Dying," p. 136.
43. Ibid., pp. 131, 136.

This means that the imperative procedure, the one which is morally required, is not necessarily either the usual one or the useful one. A radical mastectomy for breast cancer might, for instance, be both usual and useful in some circumstances and yet not morally required. *Ordinary* must have some relation to *usual*. That, at least, is its meaning outside of medical ethics, but reference to its common use simply confuses its meaning in the medical context today. I would propose adding *ordinary* and *extraordinary* to *euthanasia* as words that should be banned from further use. It is clearer simply to speak of morally imperative and elective means or of required and expendable means. The debate can do without the excess baggage of such ambiguous terms as *ordinary*.

What Treatments Are Required?

We are still left with the problem of distinguishing between imperative and elective procedures. I suggest that we ought to make two moves at this point. First, we ought to adopt the patients' perspective, and, second, we ought to adopt the language of reasonableness. From these perspectives, we can ask what treatments is it reasonable to refuse? From the patient-centered perspective it should be sufficient for competent patients to refuse treatment for themselves whenever they can offer reasons valid to themselves—that is, out of concern about physical or mental burdens or other objections to be discussed shortly.

For the incompetent patient, however, the standard of reasonableness must be found elsewhere. We have in our society a nebulous but nevertheless widely used "reasonable man" standard, a standard which is receiving increasing attention. Most discussion of it has arisen in the context of informed consent cases, but the principle applies directly to the subject of refusing treatment. In the debate about how much a patient or research subject must be told in order for consent to be informed, the traditional standard was what other competent medical professionals would have disclosed in similar circumstances.[44] Behind that standard was the presumption that

44. See Natanson v. Kline, 186 Kan. 393, 350 P.2d 1093 (1960) where Kansas State Supreme Court Justice Alfred Shroeder held that "the physician's choice of plausible

there was something inherently medical about deciding how much information a person would want to know. In 1969 a new standard began to emerge. It was recognized that reasonable people (the courts still use the term *reasonable man*) could judge whether they would find a piece of information sufficiently meaningful or useful that they would want to know it. The first judge to reach this decision concluded:

> We cannot agree that the matter of informed consent must be determined on the basis of medical testimony any more than that expert testimony of the standard practice is determinative in any other case involving a fiduciary relationship. We agree with appellant that a physician's duty to disclose is not governed by the standard practice of the physicians' community, but is a duty imposed by law which governs his conduct in the same manner as others in a similar fiduciary relationship. To hold otherwise would permit the medical profession to determine its own responsibilities. . . .[45]

Citing this decision, higher courts in several jurisdictions now have held that the reasonable man standard is the one that should be used to determine how much information is to be given.[46] It is the kind of question which does not need medical training to answer.

It is the same kind of question, whether it is reasonable to refuse a medical treatment once there is a particular es-

---

courses should not be called into question if it appears, all circumstances considered, that the physician was motivated only by the patient's best therapeutic interests and he proceeded as competent medical men would have done in a similar situation."

45. Berkey v. Anderson, 1 Cal. App.3d 790, 805, 82 Cal. Rptr. 67, 68 (1969).

46. For example, in Hunter v. Brown, one of the important cases in this series, Judge Jame concluded "whether or not Dr. Brown violated his fiduciary duty in withholding information is a question of fact to be judged by reasonable man standards" Hunter v. Brown, 4 Wash. App. 899, 484 P.2d 1162 (1972). For other cases see Dow v. Permanente Medical Group 90 Cal. Rptr. 747 (Cal. 1970); Cooper v. Roberts 286 A.2d 647 (Pa. 1971); Cobbs v. Grant 520 P.2d 1 (Cal. 1972); and Wilkinson v. Vesey 295 A.2d 676 (R.I. 1972); Barnette v. Potenza 359 N. Y. S. 2d 432 (1970). Cf. Martin v. Stratton 515 P 2d 1366 (Okla. 1973). For summary discussions of these developments see David S. Rubsamen, "Changes in 'Informed Consent,' " *Medical World News* (February 9, 1973), pp. 66–67; Joseph E. Simonaitis, "Recent Decisions on Informed Consent," *Journal of the American Medical Association* 221 (1972), pp. 441–42; and Joseph E. Simonaitis, "More About Informed Consent, Part 1," *Journal of the American Medical Association* 224 (1973), pp. 1831–32.

tablished diagnosis and prognosis. Answering it does not require the help of medical training at all. While it is important to have medical training to determine the diagnosis, prognosis, and alternative courses of treatment, deciding whether a particular treatment *ought* to be given (or accepted) is a normative question to be decided on the basis of ethical and other values. It is those value choices that the reasonable person can make without scientific or medical training.

For the incompetent patient—the child, the mentally incompetent, the senile, the comatose—it would seem morally acceptable for the patient's agent to refuse treatment when the refusal would seem within the realm of reason to reasonable people. We shall look in detail at cases involving refusal of treatment by competent patients and incompetent patients' agents in the next chapter.

I find then that a refusal will be morally acceptable if it is reasoned, in the case of competent patients, or if the reasonable person would find it acceptable in the case of agents acting for incompetent patients. But what exactly does the reasonable person consider a reasonable or unreasonable refusal? We have seen that usefulness is one relevant consideration. At the same time a treatment, even a usual one, ought to be dispensable if it inflicts a severe burden on the patient. I am led to this conclusion:

> A reasonable person would find a refusal unreasonable (and thus treatment morally required) if the treatment is useful in treating a patient's condition (though not necessarily life saving) and at the same time does not give rise to any significant patient-centered objections based on physical or mental burden; familial, social or economic concern; or religious belief.

This is not far from the definitions of *ordinary* proposed by Pius XII, Kelly, Healy, or Ramsey, but it avoids that ambiguous term and specifies a set of criteria together with a standard for resolving the specific case. It also eliminates two additional ambiguities. First, Pope Pius XII said that an "extraordinary" treatment is not required, leaving open at least in that paragraph the question whether physicians could morally stop a treatment they found "extraordinary" (that is, unreasonable) even though the patients or their agents might find it reasonable or might not have been consulted about its reasonableness. Actually, later in his statement the Pope asks if the physician has the right to use modern resuscitative apparatus even in hopeless cases and even when it is against the will of the family. His shocking answer is that while the physician does have the right to act in this manner, he or she is not bound to do so "unless this becomes the only way of fulfilling another certain moral duty." Only in the next paragraph does the Pope state clearly that the doctor's duties and rights are correlative to those of the patient—that the doctor has no separate or independent right and can take action only if the patient explicitly or implicitly gives permission. The "Ethical and Religious Directives for Catholic Health Facilities" simply say that "neither the physician nor the patient is obliged to use extraordinary means," thus leaving unsettled what should happen if the physician chooses not to use extraordinary means desired by the patient or vice versa. By stating the moral requirements as being what the patients would find reasonable (in cases when they are competent) and what the reasonable man would find reasonable (when the patient is not competent), I hope to avoid this dangerous confusion.

Second, in saying that treatments are extraordinary (not seen as required by the reasonable person) if they might impose a grave burden on oneself *or another,* the papal statement may dangerously depart from the patients' perspective. While it is reasonable that concern for the welfare of others could well be among patients' concerns and thus legitimate basis for patients' refusal of treatment, do we really want to say that the physician or the agent for an incompetent patient can judge a treatment unreasonable because it is a burden on persons other than the patient (including presumably the physician or agent deciding)? By emphasizing that treatments are unreasonable if they do not give rise to patient-centered objections, we can clearly eliminate such possibilities. It will obviously require careful judgment on the part of patients or their agents to determine what is a reasonable refusal in a specific instance. In some cases the judgment of the reasonable person will have to be obtained through the courts, but I think that the basis for such judgments must be that the treatment is unreasonable if it is useless in the patient's condition or gives rise to significant patient-centered objections including those based on physical or mental burdens; familial, social or economic concern; or religious belief.

ALLOWING TO LIVE VS. ALLOWING TO DIE

There is a third distinction which must be made before turning to the public policy questions involved in allowing to die. This is the distinction between decisions that, in effect, end a life which would otherwise continue until terminated by another cause, and decisions that permit the dying process to continue uninterrupted. Two contrasting but similar cases will illustrate.

A group of cases have received publicity recently involving infants born with the genetic anomaly known as trisomy-21 (Down's syndrome or "Mongolism") combined with other anatomical anomalies requiring fairly simple surgical correction. One such case involved an esophageal atresia (closing of the esophagus) which required surgical opening if the infant was ever to eat by mouth. The parents in this case decided not to have the operation performed, but not because the baby was dying. With the corrective surgery, it had a long life expectancy, albeit with the condition of Down's syndrome. They reached the decision because they felt that life in that condition was not worth living. (It might have been argued that care for the baby during its lifetime would be too inconvenient or expensive or depressing for other family members or for society. That was not the argument in this case, however.)

In contrast, another baby was born with trisomy-18, a genetic disease differing from trisomy-21 in that the abnormal chromosome is in the eighteenth rather than the twenty-first position. In this case, however, the disease was certain to be fatal. The baby was expected to die within two weeks of respiratory failure. The decision of the parents not to treat in this case was morally rather different, as it did not involve the difficult judgment that some else's life was not worth living.

Recently a physician remarked that his pulling the plug on a respirator for a dying patient is really like suicide. This seems wrong on several counts. First, suicide is normally a decision that life is not worth living rather than that dying should no longer be forestalled. Second, suicide differs from pulling a plug on a respirator in that it normally involves an action to cause death rather than simply discontinuing a treatment. Third, even if suicide were carried out by omission (such as by starvation), the means omitted would be normally considered both usual and useful in prolonging life, where stopping a respirator on an inevitably dying patient is a different matter. Finally, in suicide, it is the individual who carries out the act; the physician who pulls the plug is acting on another person.

It is a mistake to make the ethics of refusal of death-prolonging or even life-saving medical treatments stand or fall on the ethics of suicide. Especially in cases where someone other than the patient makes the decision, they are certainly different. In suicide there is a decision to take one's own life. Many who oppose suicide, including Roman Catholics and many secular moralists, find the refusal of some medical treatment morally acceptable even if that refusal will inevitably lead to death. The morality of suicide is a controversial issue on which there is much philosophical and public policy debate. It is simply not the same as the morality of refusing medical interventions. A public policy on the refusal of medical treatment should not have to carry the burden of a social judgment about suicide. The courts have, for the most part, been able to deal with them as separate policy questions. It is to this long and complex set of refusal of treatment cases that we must turn in the next chapter before dealing with the tough public policy matter of what, if anything, we should do to facilitate the patient's refusal of death-prolonging medical treatments.

4

The Right to Refuse Treatment

Upholding the right to refuse treatment may be the way out of the dilemma created by the partial success of our technological drive to prolong living. But what is the legal status of that right? Mrs. Carmen Martinez, a seventy-two-year-old Cuban woman living in Florida, may in her dying hours have left an indelible imprint on our legal system and provided an immortal service for those she left behind. In July 1971 she was dying of hemolytic anemia, a disease which destroys the body's red blood cells. Medical science, in the hands of Dr. Orlando Lopez, could not provide a cure, but it could offer continual transfusions to prolong the dying process. To facilitate the blood transfer, Mrs. Martinez's veins had to be opened surgically in a process doctors call "cutdowns." "Please don't torture me any more," she begged.[1]

Dr. Lopez, fearing that he could be charged with aiding her suicide if he granted her demands, brought the case to court. On July 2, in Miami Circuit Court, Judge David Popper ruled that Mrs. Martinez was not competent to make the decision to refuse the death-prolonging treatment. Her daughter, Mrs. Margarita Gottlieb, was appointed her guardian and the daughter also begged the judge, "No more cutdowns, no more cutdowns."

Here the court proceeding took a truly remarkable turn. A compassionate judge ruled for the first time in American legal history that the medical system may and must honor the daughter's demand that the torture be stopped.[2] He held that

---

1. *Washington Post,* July 5, 1971.
2. Palm Springs Gen. Hosp., Inc., v. Martinez, Civil No. 71-12687 (Dade County Cir. Ct., filed July 2, 1971). That the decision was rendered in a lower court may limit its use as a legal precedent. As a moral precedent, however, it could well become a decisive case.

while Mrs. Martinez still did not have the right to commit suicide, she did have the "right not to be tortured." Transfusions were stopped and Mrs. Martinez died the next day. Upon hearing of her death the judge commented, "I hope she died in peace."

Dying in peace has become difficult to achieve in the day of the biological revolution. There have been perhaps a hundred cases in American legal history where patients or their agents have tried to refuse medical treatments. Some of the cases and the rulings following them have been so complex that legal scholars have stated in law review articles that the right to refuse treatment is in doubt. If a few basic distinctions are observed, however, some clear patterns emerge. The most critical distinction is between competent patients trying to refuse medical treatments and incompetent patients or their guardians trying to refuse. Let us take up the case of the competent patient first.

THE COMPETENT PATIENT'S RIGHT TO REFUSE

The principle of freedom and self-determination especially in matters as critical as life and death is fundamental in our legal system. In the crucial legal decision which set the standards for informed consent in the 1960s, Kansas Supreme Court Justice Alfred Schroeder declared:

> Anglo-American law starts with the premise of thoroughgoing self-determination. It follows that each man is considered to be master of his own body, and he may, if he be of sound mind, expressly prohibit the performance of life-saving surgery, or other medical treatment. A doctor might well believe that an operation or form of treatment is desirable or necessary but the law does not permit him to substitute his own judgement for that of the patient by any form of artifice or deception.[3]

The fact is that no competent patients have ever been forced to undergo any medical treatment for their own good

3. Natanson v. Kline, 186 Kan. 393, 350 P.2d 1093 (1960).

no matter how misguided their refusal may have appeared.[4] Much of the case law deals with refusal of blood transfusions—often by Jehovah's Witnesses acting on their interpretation of a Biblical injunction against eating blood.[5] If one grants their assumption that the penalty for such blood eating is eternal damnation, the refusal, which merely trades off a few more earthly years, seems very plausible indeed. Although the First Amendment guarantees the free exercise of religion, "grave abuses" threatening "paramount state interests" have been held to justify infringement of religious lib-

4. There are three very special classes of exceptions to this flat rule: those who indicate they would not resist being coerced, adults with dependents, and prisoners. These special cases will be taken up at the end of the chapter.

5. Acts 15:28–29; Deuteronomy 12:33; Genesis 9:3–4, and Leviticus 17:10–14. See John C. Ford, "Refusal of Blood Transfusions by Jehovah's Witnesses," *Catholic Law* 10 (1964), pp. 212–26; also in re Estate of Brooks, 32 Ill. 2d 361, 205 N. E.2d 435 (1965). This chapter is based on numerous other law review articles summarizing the right to refuse treatment. These include: Robert M. Byrn, "Compulsory Lifesaving Treatment for the Competent Adult," *Fordham Law Review* 44 (1975), pp. 1–36; William H. Baughman, John C. Bruha, and Francis J. Gould, "Survey: Euthanasia, Criminal, Tort, Constitutional and Legislative Considerations," *Notre Dame Lawyer* 48 (June 1973), pp. 1202–60; John A. Robertson, "Involuntary Euthanasia of Defective Newborns: A Legal Analysis," *Stanford Law Review* 27 (January 1975), pp. 213–67; Robert J. Malone, "Is There a Right to a Natural Death?" *New England Law Review* 9 (Winter 1974), pp. 293–310; Gary L. Milhollin, "The Refused Blood Transfusion: An Ultimate Challenge for Law and Morals," *Natural Law Forum* 10 (1965), pp. 202–14; John C. Ford, SJ, "Refusal of Blood Transfusions by Jehovah's Witnesses," *Catholic Lawyer* 10 (Summer 1964), pp. 212–26; Norman L. Cantor, "A Patient's Decision to Decline Life-Saving Medical Treatment: Bodily Integrity Versus the Preservation of Life," *Rutgers Law Review* 26 (Winter 1973), pp. 228–64; Beverly A. Gazza, "Compulsory Medical Treatment and Constitutional Guarantees: A Conflict?" *University of Pittsburgh Law Review* 33 (1972), pp. 628–37; "Compulsory Medical Treatment and the Free Exercise of Religion," *Indiana Law Journal* 42 (1967), pp. 386–404; William P. Cannon, "The Right to Die," *Houston Law Review* 7 (1970), pp. 654–70; John D. Bonnett, "Bill of Rights of the Dying Patient," *Baylor Law Review* 27 (Winter 1975), pp. 27–33; Luis Kutner, "The Living Will: Coping with the Historical Event of Death," *Baylor Law Review* 27 (Winter 1975), pp. 39–53; Thomas A. Rutledge, "Informed Consent for the Terminal Patient," *Baylor Law Review* 27 (Winter 1975), pp. 11–21; Stephen M. Stewart, "The Problem of Prolonged Death: Who Should Decide?" *Baylor Law Review* 27 (Winter 1975), pp. 169–73; Michael T. Sullivan, "The Dying Person— His Plight and His Right," *New England Law Review* 8 (1973), pp. 197–216; Edward J. Gurney, "Is There a Right to Die? A Study of the Law of Euthanasia," *Cumberland-Samford Law Review* 3 (Summer 1972), pp. 235–61; Daniel J. Davis, "The Dying Patient: A Qualified Right to Refuse Medical Treatment," *Journal of Family Law* 7 (1968), pp. 644–59; Edward M. Kay, "The Right to Die," *University of Florida Law Review* 18 (1966), pp. 591–605; Kenney F. Hegland, "Unauthorized Rendition of Lifesaving Medical Treatment," *University of California Law Review* 53 (1965), pp. 860–77; David

erty—to require vaccination, forbid polygamy, or require school attendance, for instance.[6]

In this light it is interesting that the first court case regarding the attempt of a competent adult to refuse a blood transfusion included no explicit argument based upon religious freedom.[7] In 1962 Jacob Dilgard, Sr., was admitted to County Hospital in Nassau County, New York, with upper gastrointestinal bleeding. Dr. George D. Erickson, who later brought the case to court, claimed that an operation was necessary to halt the bleeding: "in order to offer the best chance of recovery a transfusion of blood was necessary, and that there was a very great chance that the patient would have little opportunity to recover without the blood." Mr. Dilgard was willing to submit to the operation, but refused the transfusion. His son also refused to give permission for the transfusion.

In the court debate there was never any doubt that the patient was completely competent and capable of making decisions on his own behalf. According to the judge, Mr. Dilgard understood the risks and was making a calculated decision. Judge Meyer acknowledged that a court will step in as guardian of an infant or an incompetent, but in this case he refused to intervene, arguing:

> It is the individual who is the subject of a medical decision who has the final say and . . . this must necessarily be so in a system of government which gives the greatest possible protection to the individual in the furtherance of his own desires.

J. Sharpe and Robert F. Hargest, III, "Lifesaving Treatment for Unwilling Patients," *Fordham Law Review* 36 (1968), pp. 695–706; "Compulsory Medical Treatment: The State's Interest Re-evaluated," *Minnesota Law Review* 51 (1966), pp. 293–305; Robert J. Malone, "Is There a Right to a Natural Death?" *New England Law Review* 9 (1974), pp. 293–310; James F. Hoover, "An Adult's Right to Resist Blood Transfusions: A View Through John F. Kennedy Memorial Hospital v. Heston," *Notre Dame Lawyer* 47 (1972), pp. 571–87; Arthur A. Levisohn, "Voluntary Mercy Deaths: Socio-Legal Aspects of Euthanasia," *Journal of Forensic Medicine* 8 (April–June 1961), pp. 57–79; Helen Silving, "Euthanasia: A Study in Comparative Criminal Law," *University of Pennsylvania Law Review* 103 (1954), pp. 350–89.

6. Cantor, "A Patient's Decision to Decline Life-Saving Medical Treatment," p. 238. For specific cases see Wisconsin v. Yoder, 406 U. S. 205, 215 (1972) and Prince v. Massachusetts, 321 U. S. 158, 166–67 (1944).

7. Erickson v. Dilgard, 44 Misc 2d 27, 252 N. Y. S. 2d 705 (Sup. Ct. 1962).

The court's decision may well have been influenced by the fact that it did not consider the patient's life to be in immediate danger. Still, it acted on the basic premise that a doctor who performs an operation without the consent of a competent, conscious adult patient commits an assault.[8]

There are scores of treatment refusal cases on the books, but almost all of them involve a special quirk—the patient is comatose, a child, a mental patient, or a prisoner. Usually the issue of the right of the competent patient to refuse treatment is not taken to court—it is assumed. The issue is usually whether the patient is really competent. One such case was that of Mrs. Delores Phelps.[9] Suffering from gastritis and gastroenteritis which had caused microcytic anemia due to blood loss, Mrs. Phelps needed a transfusion. But she explicitly refused on the grounds that she was a Jehovah's Witness. On July 8, 1972, she signed a "release for refusal to permit procedure." Her husband and grown son had discussed the refusal with her and agreed to support her decision. By July 11 she was comatose and her nephew, Michael Bratcher, petitioned the court to appoint him as her temporary guardian. The judge, Michael T. Sullivan, whose concern for the issues has since led him to write an article on the subject,[10] held a bedside hearing attended by Mrs. Phelp's son, the attending physician, two nurses, and eleven members of the Jehovah's Witness sect. The physician testified that he did not believe Mrs. Phelps had "the mental capacity to make her own decisions at the present time." The two nurses testified that they had spoken to Mrs. Phelps and that she had told them she wanted no blood transfusion. Judge Sullivan said that he would prefer to order the transfusion, but concluded that there was no evidence of mental illness and that Mrs. Phelps was sincere in her religious belief. He then ruled that the court could not "use the guardian device in order to foist its own personal opinions upon an adult competent citizen." Mrs. Phelps died the next day.

8. Byrn, "Compulsory Lifesaving Treatment," p. 3.
9. In re Phelps, No. 459-207 (Milwaukee County Ct., filed July 11, 1972).
10. Sullivan, "The Dying Person," pp. 197–216.

Even in this case the real fight was not over whether the hospital and the court could order treatment for a competent adult—it was assumed they could not. Rather the issue was whether the patient was really competent to make her decision and whether her decision should be respected after she became comatose. The court's decision indicates that grounds for declaring incompetency are shrinking—an important development to be taken up later in this chapter.

There seems to be a clear consensus that the competent adult has the right to refuse treatments on apparently foolish or misguided grounds, even when the treatments may be as common and clearly lifesaving as a blood transfusion. This is why so few cases are brought to court where dying patients are trying to avoid the intervention of new and partially successful biomedical technologies that will only delay the inevitable. In those few cases where a patient is still competent and strong-willed enough to put up a fight, the legal counsel for the hospital is intelligent enough to concede that efforts to get a court order will not succeed. There is one and only one case which really fits this category, and it was also decided by Judge Sullivan in Milwaukee.

On December 8, 1971, Miss Gertrude Raasch entered Doctors Hospital.[11] Now seventy-seven, she had been shuttled in and out of hospitals and nursing homes over her last seventeen years. In what was to be her last hospital ordeal, she had a left lumbar sympathectomy that same day. On January 11, her left leg was amputated below the knee. Ten days later on Friday, January 21, the physicians decided to amputate above the knee in order to keep the infection from spreading. At this point, Miss Raasch, who had no close relatives, refused to authorize surgery.

Walter Hardman, the administrator of the hospital, asked Judge Sullivan to appoint a guardian who could approve the operation. He relayed her physician's opinion that "unless the

11. Guardianship of Gertrude Raasch, County Court for Milwaukee County, Probate Division, No. 455–996, decided January 25, 1972. See also the accounts office case in Sullivan, "The Dying Person," pp. 197–98, and David Hendin, *Death as a Fact of Life* (New York: W. W. Norton, 1973), pp. 67–69.

operation is performed at 3 o'clock, which is less than an hour from now, she will not live longer than this weekend." After a hearing, the judge sent an attorney, Stewart G. Honeck, to the hospital. Honeck found Miss Raasch too weak to talk, but was able to communicate with her by having her touch his hand. She indicated that she was in pain, but able to understand him. When the question of further surgery came up, she just cried and did not respond. The attorney concluded that the statutory criteria required to demonstrate incompetence had not been met.

By the following Monday Miss Raasch had not died and the attending physician had filed a letter with the court agreeing that she "is competent to decide whether she wishes to submit to further surgery." In the meantime, Judge Sullivan had made contact with Helen Krause, the administrator of a nursing home where Miss Raasch had previously stayed. She said she was a friend of Miss Raasch and thought she could talk with her. According to one report, she tried earlier to call Miss Raasch at the hospital, but the hospital, deluged with calls about the case, had hung up on her.

Early Monday morning Judge Sullivan went to the hospital with the friend for supplemental hearings. According to the judge, Miss Raasch seemed alert at the hearing and recognized her friend. The woman had brought a picture of a Yorkshire terrier Miss Raasch used to play with at the nursing home and Miss Raasch smiled in recognition. Her friend tried to persuade her to have the operation and offered to go up to surgery with her and remain with her afterward. At this suggestion Miss Raasch's face tensed. Judge Sullivan decided, "There is absolutely no evidence of incompetence"; Miss Raasch knew what was being asked and she did not want the operation.[12] He then dismissed the hospital administrator's petition for a guardian. Judge Sullivan was quoted in a wire service news story as saying, "I'm positive we're doing the right thing." He said he would leave her "to depart in God's own peace." She died some six weeks after the physician had predicted she would not live through the weekend.

12. Sullivan, "The Dying Person," p. 198.

Children and Incompetent Adults

Unfortunately, not all judges are as understanding as Judge Sullivan; not all patients have friends as persistent as Helen Krause in penetrating the hospital bureaucracy to help them insist on their own wishes. To some judges and hospital personnel, the will to refuse death-prolonging medical intervention is a sure sign that patients must be "crazy," and if they are crazy they can then be declared incompetent so they cannot refuse treatment. The situation is worse for an incompetent patient—a child or an adult who lacks the legal capacity to make decisions—in their case, there is no consensus that a guardian has the right to reject medical treatments.

The day before Judge Sullivan's initial decision in Milwaukee, Clarence Bettman, a seventy-nine-year-old former investment banker, was transferred to the Manhattan facility of New York Hospital–Cornell Medical Center from its Westchester County division to have a the battery replaced in his implanted cardiac pacemaker, which maintained his heartbeat. The physicians who wanted to do the rather simple surgical procedure were reported in the only published account of the case to have described him as factually incompetent, unaware of his condition, and incapable of making the decision.[13] His wife had repeatedly refused permission. She described him as "turning into a vegetable." According to Dr. William A. Gay, Jr., assistant attending surgeon at the hospital, a court order was sought because Bettman's wife had repeatedly rejected requests from the hospital for permission to operate. Angrily criticizing the hospital and the court she asked, "What has he got to live for? Nothing. He knows nothing, he has no memory whatsoever. He is turning into a vegetable. Isn't death better?" New York State Supreme Court Justice Gerald P. Culkin after a hearing named Dr. David D. Thompson, the hospital director, as guardian for Mr. Bettman, authorizing the hospital to "perform whatever medical and surgical procedures" were "necessary to protect or sustain [his] health and life." It

13. Walter H. Waggoner, "Court Overrules Wife on Surgery," *New York Times,* January 28, 1973, p. 40.

was never answered why the judge saw fit to appoint the hospital director, with his special moral positions and lack of
knowledge of the patient, rather than the wife whose commitment to her husband's interest was never in question and who
normally would have both the moral and legal familial obligation to act in her husband's behalf. After the court order she
commented, "I resisted as long as I could and then I gave in."
She was able after the operation to see that her husband was
not sent back to the same nursing home.[14]

Refusal of Treatment for Children

Before advocating that guardians should automatically have
the right to refuse treatment, we should look at the dangers
involved. Some of the most difficult cases involve children,
with whom the first assumption is that the consent of the
parents is necessary for medical treatment. In the case of one
infant born with mongolism and duodenal atresia or blockage
similar to the case discussed in chapter 3, the parents refused
permission for the surgeons to correct the intestinal blockage.
The medical staff decided not to try to get a court order to
override them because, according to one report, they were advised by their attorney that they would not be able to get such
an order.[15] Whether they could or not we do not know for
sure because the case never reached the court.

The refusal of treatment for the child with mongolism combined with the intestinal blockage is a terribly difficult matter.
It is a decision that the dying process could be interrupted but
should not be because it would not be worth it either because
of the burden to others of the continual care needed by the
child, or because of the burden to the child himself. Before

---

14. A second New York case follows the same pattern. A patient had sought medical attention from a hospital and then become comotose. His wife refused to consent
to surgery for reasons she felt were justified, but which were judged "medically unsound." The court ruled that once the patient had come to the hospital seeking care,
it was the responsibility of the hospital and its doctors to heal him. The court distinguished the case from those in which the patient was completely competent (Collins v.
Davis, 254 N. Y. S. 2d 666, 1964).

15. Andre Hellegers, "Problems in Bioethics: The Johns Hopkins Case," *Obstetrics
and Gynecology News* 8 (June 15, 1973), pp. 40–41.

discussing this most difficult problem, we should first get clear the legal situation in some cases where the courts have been clear.

UNREASONABLE PARENTAL REFUSAL

The most clearly established principle is that of a child who is dying, but who can be restored to something approaching normal health by a fairly routine medical intervention.

In 1952 two similar cases occurred in Illinois and Missouri. In both, infants were suffering from erythroblastosis fetalis (Rh incompatability). They needed transfusions to save their lives. In the Illinois case, a court appointed a guardian to authorize the administration of blood to eight-day-old Cheryl Labrenz after her Jehovah's Witness parents had refused. The judge had to declare the child a "neglected dependent." [16] In doing so he conceded the sincerity of the parents, but declared that there exists no parental right to make martyrs of one's children. The courts reached a similar conclusion in Missouri.

One of the cases cited most frequently occurred in New Jersey in 1972.[17] The parents of a baby with a congenital malformation objected to a transfusion on religious grounds, but the Supreme Court held that freedom of religion did not give parents the right to risk the life of their children. According to the judge's ruling, the First Amendment embraces two concepts—freedom to believe and freedom to act. The first he held was absolute while the second could not possibly be:

> The right to practice religion freely does not include the liberty to expose . . . a child . . . to ill health or death. Parents may be free to become martyrs themselves. But it does not follow they are free, in identical circumstances,

16. People ex. rel. Wallace v. Labrenz, 4, 1 Ill. 618, 104 N. E. 2d 769 (1952). For other relevant cases reaching similar conclusions see Morrison v. State, 252 S. W. 2d 97 (C. A. Kansas City, Mo., 1952); Hoener v. Bertinato, 67 N. J. Super. 517, 171 A.2d 140 (1961); In re Santos, 16 A. D. 2d 755, 227 N. Y. S. 2d 450, appeal dismissed 232 N. Y. S. 2d 1026 (1962); Application of Brooklyn Hospital, 45 Misc 2d 914, 258 N. Y. S. 2d 621 (1965); In re Clark, 21 Ohio Op. 2d 86, 185 N. E. 2d 128 (C. P. Lucas 1962); In re Vasko, 238 App. Div. 128, 263 N. Y. S. 522 (1933).

17. State v. Perricone, 37 N. J. 463, 181 A.2d 751, cert. denied 371 U. S. 890 (1962).

to make martyrs of their children before they have reached the age of full and legal discretion when they can make that choice for themselves.

It is not only Jehovah's Witnesses who have chosen religious faith over faith in modern medicine. As far back as 1903 a father was convicted for allowing his infant daughter to die of pneumonia after he refused on religious grounds to obtain medical services.[18]

A recent case is one of the most bizarre. On May 26, 1972, the *New York Times* reported that eight-year-old girl, Kalete Tole, suffering from systematic lupus erythematosus, an autoimmune failure where the connective tissue becomes allergic to itself, [19] was rushed to the intensive care unit of Long Island Jewish Hospital. She needed massive doses of phenobarbitol and steroids as well as blood transfusions to combat the disease. The doctor said immediate treatment was essential. Her father, Bendriis Tole, a member of an African sect, the Gheez Nation, refused the treatment, saying, "The medication may change her life. . . . I lean on divine healing more than on drugs. Once they start drugs, the body relies on them. God will intercede on my behalf."

Justice B. Thomas Pantano apparently had more faith in man's medicine than God's intervention. He ordered the transfusions and medications for the girl, on the grounds that the court had "an obligation to protect the interests of the infant child who is a ward of the court and it is our obligation to see to it that whatever steps can be taken to save the child's life be taken."

The state may have a clearly established right to intervene to save the earthly life of a child from the religious fervor of its parents, but where the child's life is not at stake the issue is much more complicated. In eleven such cases that I have been able to compile, opinion seems nearly divided. In six, parents or guardians were not permitted to refuse the treatment and in five they were. This does not mean that legal opinion is sim-

18. People v. Pierson, 176 N. Y. 201, 68 N. E. 243 (1903).
19. David A. Andelman, "Parents Who Refused Treatment for Girl, 8, Overruled by a Judge," *New York Times*, May 26, 1972, p. 39.

ply in a state of chaos, however. Although the state is generally not permitted in common law to take custody of children
to provide medical care even in an emergency, modern statutes throughout the United States do permit the court to take
custody based on either explicit statute, like the pioneering
1881 New York law, or general statutes providing for custody
of a child who is "neglected" or "dependent," or for whom the
parent has failed to provide the "necessaries." [20] Even so in
every case the presumption is that the parents have the right
to refuse until the court determines that the refusal is so unreasonable that it constitutes neglect. The reasonableness of
the refusal on the part of the guardian is the key point.

In the six cases where the court intervened to order treatment the court overrode parental judgments—often apparently in good faith, but based on aberrant religious or qua-
sireligious views. A father lost custody of two children, five
and eight, to their maternal grandmother after his wife and
his other three children had died of diphtheria within a few
months of each other. He had treated them all himself by the
"Bannscheidt system," not calling a doctor until "death was at
the door." His system "consisted of pricking the skin of the patient on different parts of the body with an instrument composed of about 30 needles, and operated by a spring, and then
rubbing the parts thus pricked with an irritating oil." The father explained his failure to call the doctor by stating he "had
not entire faith in the infallibility of the old school of physicians." [21]

The mother was not permitted to rely solely on home remedies and faith healing to treat a twelve-year-old boy with pain
and impaired movement from arthritis and complications following rheumatic fever.[22] Another mother was able to get a
court to charge a father with neglect for refusing to permit an
operation for their ten-year-old child to correct and prevent

20. James A. Baker, "Court Ordered Non-emergency Medical Care for Infants,"
Cleveland/Marshall Law Review 18 (1969), pp. 297–98. See also Stephen Grant Young,
"Parent and Child—Compulsory Medical Care Over Objections of Parents," *West
Virginia Law Review* 65 (1963), pp. 184–87.

21. Heinemann's Appeal, 96 Pa. 112, 42 Am. Rep. 532 (Ct. of App. 1880). The
case is described in Baker, "Court Ordered Nonemergency Medical Care," p. 303.

22. Mitchell v. Davis, 205 S. W. 2d 812 (Tex. Civ. App. 1947).

extension of a leg deformity induced by poliomyelitis.[23] A woman who objected only to a blood transfusion was charged with neglect when she refused to permit surgery for her fifteen-year-old son suffering from neurofibromatosis. The disease had caused a massive deformity on one side of his face and neck so severe that he had not attended school since he was nine. Tests showed that with surgery the boy had a reasonable chance of being educated and becoming partly self-sufficient, but without it he had little chance of living a normal, useful life.[24]

In another case, parents were found guilty for refusing an operation for removal of adenoids which were causing "mental dullness, impaired breathing, deafness, and some anemia." Although the operation was not serious, it required anesthesia, and it was this to which the parents objected.[25]

In a case described as "the farthest reaching of 'neglect'," [26] the court ordered a psychiatric examination of a child over the objections of its parents. The judge's ruling was:

> A failure to care, to look after, to guide, to supervise, and I might even go just one word beyond that—to direct the activities of a child . . . when a parent is apprised of the conduct of the child . . . and does nothing about correcting that conduct that would constitute neglect.

In the ruling ordering treatment of the child with adenoids the judge was the reasonableness of the parents' refusal the explicit criterion of whether neglect exists. In defining neglect he said:

> The question is one of fact to be decided in each case on the evidence, and the Justices in deciding that question must take into consideration the nature of the operation and the reasonableness of the parents' refusal to permit it.

23. In re Rotkowitz, 175 Misc. 948, 25 N. Y. S. 2d 624 (Dom. Rel. Ct. 1941).

24. In re Sampson, 328 N. Y. S. 2d 686, 278 N. E. 2d 918 (Ct. App. 1972).

25. Oakley v. Jackson, 1 K. B. 216 (1914) cited in Baker, "Court Ordered Non-emergency Medical Care," p. 304.

26. In re Carstairs, 115 N. Y. S. 2d 314 (Dom. Rel. Ct. 1952), cited in Baker, "Court Ordered Non-emergency Medical Care," pp. 306–07.

REASONABLE PARENTAL REFUSAL

In these six cases the refusals seem perverse, but in the other five cases, the refusals are much more plausible. There seem to be three acceptable grounds for refusing treatment. The earliest case illustrates the principle that a refusal is reasonable if the proposed treatment itself carries substantial risk. A seven-year-old boy suffering from rickets was destined to remain a cripple for life unless he had an operation. It was conceded, however, that "there was some probability that the child could die from the operation." The parents, who had already lost seven of their ten children, were supported in their judgment that they did not want to risk the boy's life.[27]

The same principle of "substantial risk" is crucial in a bizarre and famous case in which an eleven-year-old girl, Patricia Hudson, had been born with a grossly abnormal left arm. It was so much larger and longer than the right arm that it was useless. The physicians recommended that it be removed since it was enormously heavy, her heart was burdened by having to pump blood to it, and her chest was becoming deformed from the enormous weight. The greatest burden, however, was probably psychological. The girl and her father favored removing the arm, but her mother, who was the "dominating parent," objected—wanting to wait until the girl could better make up her own mind. The operation itself involved substantial risk, which apparently figured in the court's decision that the state had no authority to interfere with non-emergency medical care by requiring risky treatments.[28]

A second ground for finding refusals reasonable is the lack

27. In re Tuttendario, 21 Pa. Dist. 561 (Quar. Sess., Phila. Co. 1911). This decision also emphasized that "neglect" required "malicious intent" which was clearly lacking. "We have not yet adopted as a public policy the Spartan rule that children belong not to their parents, but to the state. As the law stands, the parents forfeit their natural right of guardianship only in cases where they have shown their unfitness by reason of moral depravity." Now, however, it is clear that we also have not adopted the equally Spartan rule that children do belong to their parents. Malicious intent (clearly lacking in the blood transfusion cases) must be abandoned as a required condition for neglect.

28. In re Hudson, 13 Wash. 2d 673, 126 P. 2d 765 (1942).

of a clear need for treatment. That the removal of the girl's
arm could wait a few years was obviously relevant. Certainly
an excessively paternalistic physician who attempted to get a
court order for minor treatment of a child against the parents'
wishes—say to get a boy to take his vitamins—would find little
sympathy in the courts. If the court has a responsibility to exercise a parental role (as *parens patriae*), it may still in some cases
reach the decision that the proposed treatment is too trivial or
too controversial to be necessary. Perhaps that was a contribut-
ing factor in another case where a parent was permitted to
refuse treatment for his child. The father was charged with
neglecting to get proper care for a speech impediment in the
child. The maternal grandmother sought and was given custody, but the judgment was reversed in appeal on the ground
that the father had no obligation to furnish medical assistance
in this case.[29]

A third ground for a reasonable refusal is that in non-
emergency cases, particularly those involving older minors,
the treatment can wait until the minor becomes competent to
be consulted. This consideration played a part in the Patricia
Hudson case, as well as in two others. A nineteen-year-old
with a massive harelip and cleft palate probably should have
had surgery when he was an infant, but his father had refused
because of his belief in "mental healing." The boy had been
influenced by his father to the point that he also opposed the
surgery. The court ruled that if the case had been brought to
it before the boy had formed his own convictions, it would
have had no hesitation in ordering the treatment, but now,
since the boy's cooperation would be necessary in postoperative rehabilitation and no further harm would result from
waiting, it would not intervene.[30] The appellate court reversed
the decision against intervening only to be in turn reversed by
the Supreme Court of the State of New York on a split decision, four to three.

This disagreement among the judges suggests that reason-

29. In re Frank, 41 Wash. 2d 294, 248 P. 553 (1942).

30. In re Seiferth, 127 N.Y.S. 2d, rev'd., 284 App. Div. 221, 137 N.Y.S. 2d 35
(1955). The case is also discussed in Baker, "Court Ordered Non-emergency Medical
Care," p. 302.

able people may well disagree about the state's right to intrude on the family relationship in this case. If the criterion for justifying a guardian's refusal is that it be reasonable at the time the decision is to be made, then there will naturally be borderline cases and split opinions. Nevertheless, in situations that are not a matter of life and death, the right of the parent or guardian to refuse will depend upon the reasonableness of the refusal.

REASONABLE REFUSALS IN LIFE AND DEATH CASES

So far it is clear that treatments that will save a child's life, restoring that child to reasonably normal health, will be ordered by the courts. Important treatments in cases that are not matters of life and death will also be ordered if the benefits are much greater than the risks. If, however, the risk is relatively great, the treatment is trivial, or the minors can wait to make up their own minds, the parental refusal may be judged reasonable. We are left with two kinds of cases in which the courts are not very clear: cases where the child is inevitably dying, and cases where a dying child's life could be saved, but at a burden that some would consider too great. Neither type of case has had a full hearing in court.

Of the two types of cases, the case of the inevitably dying child seems easier to handle.

Each year over 150,000 persons under twenty years of age die in the United States. Except in rapidly fatal accidents or the now rare case of illness where death comes before medical technology has a chance to prolong the dying, someone, somewhere must make the decision that no further treatment should be tried.

The case of the dying child arises daily in hospitals. The physician, parent, nurse—someone acting for a helpless, never competent human being—decides to stop the epinephrine for the asthmatic, to forego the surgery on the baby's malformed heart, to take the child without an immune system out of its sterile environment cell. That not one of those decisions has ever been reviewed in court is itself important, but it means we shall not get much guidance in handling the case of the dying, no longer competent adult.

The papers carry tragic stories of parents deciding to stop prolonging dying. "Parents Let Injured Son, 20, Die So His Kidneys May Aid Others," read one headline concerning a youth critically injured in an automobile accident whose parents ordered doctors to let him die.[31] "Mom's Agonized Decision: Let My Boy Die," was the headline a few months earlier after a ten-year-old boy had been hit by a pickup truck.[32] Doctors had been keeping him breathing artificially for nine days; there was no hope for recovery. No one has suggested the parents be tried for neglect. Deciding to stop prolonging the dying in these cases seems very different from the fervent refusal of blood in the Jehovah's Witness cases.

In an unusual case reaching the courts, a sixteen-year-old Cincinnati girl dying of an osteogenic sarcoma (bone cancer) refused, with the support of her mother, to have her leg amputated. This case is not really relevant because the girl's own decision was crucial. It can be seen as indicating the rapidly expanding scope of the legal definition of competency. We shall take up this important development along with the details of this case later in the chapter.

While the court cases have not really clarified whether parents may reasonably refuse treatment for a child who is inevitably dying, legal, medical, and ethical debate is beginning to focus on the problem.[33] Some are arguing that treatments that prolong dying are required; that letting babies die is homicide.[34] Others reject this conclusion.[35] There is ample evidence that some physicians participate in decisions to let inevitably dying babies go ahead and die.[36]

31. *New York Times,* August 31, 1973, p. 14.

32. *New York Post,* May 8, 1973, p. 2.

33. John A. Robertson, "Involuntary Euthanasia of Defective Newborns: A Legal Analysis," *Stanford Law Review* 27 (January 1975), pp. 213–67; Chester Swinyard, ed., *Decision-making and the Defective Newborn* (forthcoming).

34. Robertson, "Involuntary Euthanasia."

35. See Philip B. Heymann and Sara Holtz, "The Legal Leeways for Medical Decision-making," and my "Abnormal Newborns and the Physician's Role," both in Swinyard, *Decision-making and the Defective Newborn.*

36. R. S. Duff and A. G. M. Campbell, "Moral and Ethical Dilemmas in the Special Care Nursery," *New England Journal of Medicine* 289 (1973), pp. 890–94; Anthony Shaw, "Dilemmas of 'Informed Consent' in Children," *New England Journal of Medicine* 289 (1973), pp. 885–90.

Certainly not all treatment refusals are considered illegal. The courts specifically authorize refusals by competent adults. They would not similarly authorize homicides or even suicides. Precedent, however, should not determine the ethical question, one way or the other. The question is should parents or other agents for inevitably dying children be permitted to let their babies die—should those judgments be considered reasonable? If the standard for deciding whether the parents are being reasonable in their refusal is whether the treatment is greatly burdensome or useless to their child, it seems clear that many treatments of the inevitably dying could be reasonably refused on the grounds of uselessness. In fact, such decisions are made routinely, so routinely that they have not been challenged in court. If relatively high treatment risk in comparison to possible benefits is a reasonable ground for refusing treatment, then any treatment from which no good can come must be classed as reasonably refusable, even if it means that a child may die some hours or days earlier. Of course, some treatments would still remain obligatory, treatments that relieve pain and suffering or treatments rendered until there is certainty of the prognosis.

I now return to the most difficult of all the problems, the situation where a dying child's life could be saved, but with a burden which some would consider too great. This is the case of the mongoloid child or the baby born with a severely impairing case of spina bifida. In the case of the mongoloid child with an intestinal blockage, which was discussed at the first of this section, it is difficult to argue that the intestinal surgery would be useless. The child would still be mongoloid, but the surgery would allow it to live. In fact, some mongoloid children are long lived. The refusal arises from the underlying mongolism. If the refusal cannot rest on grounds of the uselessness of treatment, then it would have to be on the basis of grave burden. One kind of burden would be burden on others—on the parents, on other children, or on the state which would have to provide a lifetime of institutionalized care. In the last chapter, however, I rejected the general argument of burden to others as a legitimate reason for refusing treatment for one who is incompetent. That leaves the crite-

rion of burden to the patient. While the evidence seems to indicate that mongoloid children do not generally suffer any abnormal burden (they may be generally happier than more
nearly normal children), there may well be cases where burden to the child would justify the refusal. The most obvious
case would be one where, in addition to the mongolism and
intestinal blockage, there was something like a congenital
heart malformation which would require repeated surgery.
This and other burdens anticipated for the child, might, it
seems to me, justify the parental refusal even when the child
could survive for a reasonably normal life span.[37]

In the case of the spina bifida infant, similar questions arise.
The most severely afflicted infants have an abnormality high in
the spinal cord which protrudes from the baby's back. In such
cases there is certainty of paralysis, at least below the waist,
lack of control of bladder and bowels, and serious risk of
blocked flow of cerebrospinal fluid. This produces hydrocephalus, a condition in which fluid trapped in the ventricles
of the brain produces swelling and eventual mental retarda-
tion. Hydrocephalus can be corrected by a shunt providing a
passageway for the cerebrospinal fluid from the ventricles of
the brain. A tube is placed below the skin from the skull, down
the neck, draining into the heart or the peritoneal cavity
around the intestines.[38] If these operations are not performed, the severely affected baby will almost certainly die. If
the cord abnormality is corrected surgically the baby in many
cases will live, but with possibly serious physical and mental
handicaps which predictably can be severe. In some cases,
countless operations may be necessary to correct problems
with the shunt, and other difficulties may arise. What then is
the position of the parents who wish to refuse the initial
surgery to repair the spinal abnormality?[39] Robertson argues,

37. Cf. "Judge Orders Care for Mongoloid Child," *New York Times*, Oct. 2, 1973.

38. See Chester A. Swinyard, *The Child with Spina Bifida* (New York: Institute of Rehabilitation Medicine, 1971), pp. 17–18.

39. For examples of the debate about care of spina bifida infants, see J. Lorber,
"Results of Treatment of Myelomeningocele," *Developmental Medicine and Child Neurol-
ogy* 13 (1971), pp. 279–303; John Lorber, "Selective Treatment of Myelomeningocele:
To Treat or Not to Treat?" *Pediatrics* 53 (March 1974), pp. 307–08; John Lorber,
"Early Results of Selective Treatment of Spina Bifida Cystica," *British Medical Journal* 4

"The parental decision to refuse consent to a medical or surgical procedure necessary to maintain the life of a defective infant quite clearly falls within the bounds of homicide by omission." [40] He believes, "Parents undoubtedly have a legal duty to provide necessary medical assistance to a helpless minor child." [41]

I am convinced that the legal evidence at the present time simply does not support this conclusion. While it is clear that the courts would require lifesaving treatment that would restore or improve the child's health to a relatively normal state, there is virtually no case law giving clear guidance in situations where the treatment would save the life of the child, but leave it with severe mental and physical burdens.[42] Especially where

---

(October 27, 1973), pp. 201–04; G. Keys Smith and E. Durham Smith, "Selection for Treatment in Spina Bifida Cystica," *British Medical Journal* 4 (October 27, 1973), pp. 189–97; Sherman C. Stein, Luis Schut, and Mary D. Ames, "Selection for Early Treatment in Myelomeningocele: A Retrospective Analysis of Various Selection Procedures," *Pediatrics* 54 (November 1974), p. 556; Richard C. Cook, "Spina Bifida and Hydrocephalus," *British Medical Journal* 4 (December 25, 1971), pp. 795–99; R. B. Zachary, "Ethical and Social Aspects of Treatment of Spina Bifida," *Lancet* 2 (1968), p. 274; John M. Freeman, "The Shortsighted Treatment of Myelomeningocele: A Long-Term Case Report," *Pediatrics* 53 (March 1974), pp. 311–13; Report by a Working Party, "Ethics of Selective Treatment of Spina Bifida," *Lancet* (1975), p. 88; Herbert B. Eckstein, "Severely Malformed Children: The Problem of Selection," *British Medical Journal* (May 5, 1973), p. 284; and especially Swinyard, *Decision-making and the Defective Newborn*.

40. Robertson, *Involuntary Euthanasia*, p. 213.

41. Ibid. Robertson is imprecise in his definition of the term *involuntary euthanasia*. He makes no use of the moral and legal differences between active killing and simply letting die, nor of the cases where treatment may acceptably be refused on grounds that it is not sufficiently reasonable. The grounds for approving the refusal may be in Robertson's own wording. When he says that there is a legal duty to provide necessary medical assistance to the helpless minor, the implication is that it is not required to provide "unnecessary" assistance. That opens the debate about the definition of *necessary*. It is my contention that grave burden to the patient should be sufficient to classify the treatment as unnecessary. Clearly there is no homicide for failing to provide unnecessary treatment. This argument Robertson fails to take up. Also see the debate between Robertson and me in Swinyard, *Decision-making and the Defective Newborn*.

42. One very similar case is that of the newborn son of Sgt. and Mrs. Robert B. T. Houle who was born with several severe deformities, including a tracheoesophageal fistula, as well as the prospect of permanent physical and mental damage. The physician is quoted as saying the infant's "probable brain damage has rendered life not worth preserving." See Richard A. McCormick, "To Save or Let Die: The Dilemma of Modern Medicine," *Journal of the American Medical Association* 229 (1974), pp. 172–76. Upon the parents' refusal of treatment, the court ordered treatment for the infant, but the child died after the surgery. *New York Times*, Feb. 25, 1974, p. 13.

repeated surgery for shunt correction is anticipated, I am convinced that such treatments, which would be gravely burdensome to the patient, would not be morally required and possibly would not be required legally either.

Incompetent Adults

The long record of cases involving children may be of some guidance in deciding when guardians should be able to refuse treatments for incompetent adults. The medical journals were confused by the case of a twenty-two-year-old Jehovah's Witness for whom blood was ordered. A "Doctor and the Law" column headlined "Court-Ordered Blood Transfusion Upon An Adult Patient," implied a break with precedent of other adult patients.[43] In a column headed, "Adult Jehovah's Witnesses and Blood Transfusions," it was implied that the court decision contradicted the earlier cases where adults have been able to refuse even lifesaving blood.[44] The confusion may be traced to a less-than-clear decision written by Judge Weintraub, the Chief Justice of the New Jersey Supreme Court, when he confirmed the order to administer blood to the young woman, but the facts are quite consistent with the pattern we have already seen.

Delores Heston was unmarried and twenty-two when severely injured in an automobile accident.[45] She was rushed to John F. Kennedy Memorial Hospital in Stratford, New Jersey, with a ruptured spleen. Her mother, a Jehovah's Witness, signed a release of liability for the hospital and medical personnel. According to Chief Justice Weintraub, the patient was in shock on admittance to the hospital, and "in the judgment of the attending physicians and nurses was then or soon become disoriented and incoherent." At 1:30 in the morning the hospital applied to a judge of the superior court for the appoint-

43. George E. Hall, "Court-Ordered Blood Transfusion upon an Adult Patient," *The New Physician*, Feb. 1972, pp. 89–90.

44. Edwin J. Holman, "Adult Jehovah's Witnesses and Blood Transfusions," *Journal of the American Medical Association* 219 (1972), pp. 273–74.

45. John F. Kennedy Memorial Hospital v. Delores Heston and Jane Heston, 279 A. 2d 670, N.J. Sup. Ct. 1971.

ment of a guardian. The court complied "for the preservation of the life of Delores Heston." At 4 A.M. surgery was performed. Blood was administered. Delores Heston was saved.

There are as noted confusing elements in the judicial opinion, but the result really is not surprising. A mother does not have the right to refuse lifesaving blood for her daughter when she is acting as guardian. That her daughter is twenty-two is irrelevant, at least if the young woman has not expressed her own views in a manner the court can accept.[46]

While it is plausible that a mother should not be permitted by the courts to refuse a blood transfusion for her incompetent daughter when that transfusion would restore the daughter to something resembling normal health, it is dangerous to generalize from that one case to those of other incompetent adults.

Karen Quinlan is the twenty-one-year-old woman maintained for months in a respirator after a prolonged respiratory arrest produced irreversible brain damage. She could breathe spontaneously for only short periods. After six months her father petitioned the court to be appointed her guardian for the purpose of authorizing the discontinuance of "all extraordinary means of sustaining the vital processes of his daughter." [47]

The case, which received extremely wide publicity, was unfortunately tried in the same state where the Heston case had been decided. Citing the Heston case, the lawyers for the physicians and the hospital argued that there was a compelling state interest to preserve human life.[48] Influenced by the reasonable judgment in the Heston case that the court should

---

46. A similar case has already been mentioned (Collins v. Davis, 254 N.Y.S. 2d 666 [1964]). A patient sought medical attention and then became unconscious. He needed an operation or he would die. With the operation there was a good chance of saving his life. The patient's wife refused to give her consent for unspecified reasons which she felt justified refusal, but in the opinion of the court were unsound. The case did not involve a person who for religious or other reasons had refused to seek medical attention. The court ruled that once the patient came into the hospital, it was the responsibility of the hospital and its doctors to treat him. Like the mother of Delores Heston, this patient's wife was not permitted to refuse the life-saving treatment.

47. In re Quinlan Superior Court of New Jersey, Chancery Division, Docket No. C-201-75 (Nov. 10, 1975), p. 1.

48. Ibid., p. 20.

order treatment for the incompetent patient that would restore her to normal health, Judge Robert Muir concluded, er-
roneously in my opinion, "There *is* a duty to continue the life-
assisting apparatus, if within the treating physician's opinion it
should be done." [49] Judge Muir directed, "the determination
whether or not Karen Ann Quinlan be removed from the respirator is to be left to the treating physician. It is a medical
decision, not a judicial one." [50] He added, "There is no constitutional right to die that can be asserted by a parent for his incompetent adult child." [51]

I think the opinion written by Judge Muir, undoubtedly
with an agonized and dedicated conscience, is a tragically
faulty analysis. In the first place, Mr. Quinlan did not ask for
his daughter the right to die; he asked for the right to refuse
medical treatment. The difference between the two has a long
legal and moral history.[52] Second, the opinion simply misunderstands the nature of the decision the court was asked to
make. It takes the question as one that the medical professional ought to decide on the basis of professional standards
and skills. This confuses the technical questions, which the
physician clearly ought to have a special competence in deciding, with the policy question. It is one thing to ask the physician or the medical community what Karen Quinlan's prognosis was. It is quite another to ask what ought to be done in
her case, given that prognosis. The former question is one
which physicians should be able to answer; the latter is one in
which they have no special skills.

The opinion was self-contradictory. While at some points
the decision is to be left to the individual physician, at other
points Judge Muir makes the standard to be used that of the
practice of the medical profession as a whole.[53] We were at

49. Ibid., p. 29.
50. Ibid., p. 31.
51. Ibid., p. 38.
52. See the recent discussion of the distinction in Byrn, "Compulsory Lifesaving
Treatment," pp. 17–19.
53. In re Karen Quinlan, p. 29. Both these views are in turn inconsistent with the
statement in the opinion, "The judicial power to act in the incompetent's best interest
in this instance selects continued life. . . ," ibid., p. 37.

least left with the question unresolved of what should be done
when individual physicians disagree with their colleagues.

More fundamental is the question why the secular courts
should be bound at all to the standard values of the medical
profession. What if a guardian wanted the treatment to continue while the physician, with or without the support of colleagues, wanted to stop? Would the court still hold to the
opinion that the treatment is to continue "if, in the opinion of
the physician, it ought to go on," implying it need not if the
physician wanted to stop? What if a competent patient were
sitting up in bed demanding that the treatment continue and
the physician was maintaining that in his opinion it was in the
best interest of the patient to stop treatment so the patient
could go ahead and die? If a single physician or physicians as
a whole favor continuing or stopping treatment, that is certainly relevant—just as any other moral views are relevant—
but such a narrowly-based opinion should not be decisive in a
court of law. The burden of deciding whether it is reasonable
for Karen Quinlan's father to refuse further respirator treatment for her is one that the court ought not to have shirked.
It is its job to decide whether he was being reasonable. It
would have been understandable—wrong, I believe, but understandable—had Judge Muir decided that Karen Quinlan's
father was proposing an unreasonable course of action. The
judge did not do that, however; he held that the question was
for the physicians to decide. In that he must be wrong. I
wonder what he would have said if, on the day following the
decision, the physicians had announced a decision, "based on
their medical judgment," that the treatment ought to stop.

On March 31, 1976, the New Jersey Supreme Court, in effect, rejected this logic. It built its new decision primarily on
the constitutional right of privacy.[54] The court, explicitly rejecting the Heston case as a precedent, began by saying:

> We have no doubt, in these unhappy circumstances, that
> if Karen were herself miraculously lucid for an interval

54. In re Quinlan, Supreme Court of New Jersey, A-116, September Term 1975
(March 31, 1976), pp. 33–49.

(not altering the existing prognosis of the condition to which she would soon return) and perceptive of her irreversible condition, she could effectively decide upon discontinuance of the life-support apparatus, even if it meant the prospect of a natural death.[55]

The court goes on to argue in that case "no external compelling interest of the State could compel Karen to endure the unendurable, only to vegetate a few measurable months with no realistic possibility of returning to any semblance of cognitive or sapient life." [56] The state has a legitimate interest, according to the court, in the preservation and sanctity of human life and defense of the right of the physician to administer medical treatment according to his best judgment (a point I shall come back to),[57] but it also recognizes that "the State's interest *contra* weakens and the individual's right to privacy grows as the degree of bodily invasion increases and the prognosis dims." [58]

Thus far the court has followed a line of argument emphasizing privacy and self-determination of the competent patient much like the argument earlier in this chapter. The court moved on, however, to more controversial virgin territory. It begins by recognizing that "the sad truth, however, is that she is grossly incompetent." [59] Then comes the key sentence: "Nevertheless we have concluded that Karen's right of privacy may be asserted on her behalf by her guardian under the peculiar circumstances here present." [60]

This recognition of the right—I would say the responsibility—of the guardian to exercise the right of privacy on behalf of the incompetent patient is an exciting departure and, I think, a key insight for future resolution of similar cases of incompetent patients.

The court also had to deal with the physician's claim of a right or responsibility to administer medical treatment accord-

55. Ibid., p. 34.
56. Ibid., p. 35.
57. Ibid., p. 36.
58. Ibid., p. 37.
59. Ibid., p. 38.
60. Ibid., p. 38.

ing to his best judgment. At various points in the lower court opinion, Judge Muir said or implied that the physician had either the right or the obligation to use his own judgment or, at other points, to follow the tradition of the medical profession.

With one exception the supreme court found that neither the physician's best judgment nor the tradition of the medical profession were sufficient reasons for the state to cede responsibility holding:[61]

> Such notions as to the distribution of responsibility, heretofore generally entertained, should however neither impede this Court in deciding matters clearly justifiable nor preclude a re-examination by the Court as to underlying human values and rights.

The opinion contains admittedly confusing language in which the court says that "the medical obligation is related to standards and practice prevailing in the profession." [62] This is confusing on two counts. First, it seems amply clear that treatment stoppage in Karen Quinlan's condition is not contrary to the prevailing practice of the profession. Second, and more critically, it ought not to matter what the consensus of the profession is, once the guardian decides it is in the patient's interest to have the treatment stopped and the court finds it can accept such a decision.

In spite of this confusing language the supreme court opinion goes on to make just this point:[63]

> However, in relation to the matter of the declaratory relief sought by plaintiff as representative of Karen's interests, we are required to reevaluate the applicability of the medical standards. . . . The question is whether there is such internal consistency and rationality in the application of such standards as should warrant their constituting an ineluctable bar to the effectuation of substantive relief for the plaintiff at the hands of the court. We have concluded not.

61. Ibid., p. 42.
62. Ibid., p. 44.
63. Ibid., p. 45.

In other words the standards of the profession are not sufficiently consistent and rational that the court felt obliged to
apply them to Mr. Quinlan's request—a great victory for patient and public responsibility. With two possible exceptions
the supreme court in this opinion has consistently recognized
the right and responsibilities of patients and their agents to
make treatment refusal decisions.

The two exceptions are the declaratory judgment where the
court says that after Mr. Quinlan has selected a physician and
with the guardian's and the family's concurrence:

> should the responsible attending physicians conclude
> there is no reasonable possibility of Karen's ever return-
> ing to a cognitive, sapient state and that the life-support
> apparatus now being administered to Karen should be
> discontinued, they shall consult with the hospital "Ethics
> Committee" or like body of the institution in which Karen
> is then hospitalized. If that consultative body agree that
> there is no reasonable possibility of Karen's ever emerg-
> ing from her present comatose condition to a cognitive,
> sapient state, the present life-support system may be with-
> drawn. . . .[64]

In order to see the two potential problems it is necessary to
isolate precisely the tasks given the physician and the so-called
ethics committee. The physician is given two tasks. First, he is
to determine if there is any reasonable possibility of Karen's
ever emerging from her present comatose condition to a cognitive, sapient state. That is entirely plausible. Her prognosis
should be confirmed before the final decision is made, and a
physician is clearly the one with the expertise to do it. But the
court then adds a second task for the physician. It says that he
should also decide "that the life-support apparatus now being
administered to Karen should be discontinued." That seems to
me to be a mistake. Once the prognosis has been determined,
once Mr. Quinlan has been given the right to exercise privacy
on her behalf, and once the court has recognized in general
that a treatment refusal by a guardian for such a patient is ac-

64. Ibid., pp. 56–58.

ceptable, why should the physician then have the second task of determining whether life-support apparatus should be discontinued?

As a practical matter this mistake may not make much difference. Presumably if things developed to the point where the selected physician determined that there was not only no reasonable hope of recovery but also that the life-support apparatus should not be discontinued, Mr. Quinlan would select a new physician. But as a matter of clear thinking, there is no reason why the physician should be given that second task. Perhaps there should be an understanding between guardian and physician ahead of time to avoid the possibility that the physician would have to participate in treatment decisions that violate his conscience, but the decision to stop must remain with the guardian under the supervision of the court.

The second difficulty is in the ethics committee proposal. In fact the so-called ethics committee is given one and only one job: to confirm that there is no reasonable possibility of Karen's ever emerging from her present comatose condition to a cognitive, sapient state. In other words their single job is entirely a technical, neurological one requiring no ethical judgment whatsoever. There is no provision for the committee to confirm the ethical judgment of the guardian and no veto power should they disagree with his decision. The ethics committee has no ethical tasks at all, only neurological ones. I fear that the court opinion will lead to a proliferation of committees and confusion over their task. The dangers of the use of committees to make ethical rather than neurological and other technical jugments will be discussed in chapter 5.

I began this chapter with the optimistic claim that Mrs. Martinez may have led the way for a new policy for dying because, though she was incompetent, her daughter was permitted to refuse painful surgical procedures. The way is still open, I trust, but the present situation is that we do not now have a clear public policy that refusal of death-prolonging treatment by a guardian acting in good faith should be decisive. Such a new, humane policy for the dying is desperately needed.

Karen Quinlan and Clarence Bettman, the man needing his pacemaker battery recharged, differed from the children and

Delores Heston in that treatment could not save their lives but only prolong their dying. The Bettman case presents two other considerations that are important for public policy development. Mr. Bettman may not really have been incompetent at all, but a victim of the catch-22 reasoning that if a man refuses medical treatment he must be crazy and if he is crazy he can't refuse treatment. The criteria by which one can be judged incompetent, however, are shrinking. This is a revolutionary, exciting development having far-reaching consequences, which will be discussed next. Then we shall take up a final way in which the cases of Karen Quinlan and Clarence Bettman may differ from those of Delores Heston and especially from the children's—he was formerly competent and may have expressed his wishes while competent, while the children had never been in that position.

The Shrinking Circle of Incompetency

The decision that Mr. Bettman was not competent to refuse his treatment may have overridden his refusal; a similar decision may have required the appointment of a guardian for Mrs. Martinez, but the number of those who are treated as incompetent is shrinking. Declaration of incompetency was once a humane act, intended to protect wrongdoers from punishment for acts for which they were not responsible and to protect the mentally ill from performing foolish acts to their detriment. But labeling someone legally incompetent can be dangerous. It is a fundamental assault on personal dignity. In the case of the dying patient, it can and has been used to infringe the right to a humane, dignified death free of suffering. But on at least three fronts, individuals who once would have been treated as incompetent are now being found competent. It seems both true and good that incompetency will be a harder label to apply in the future.

INCOMPETENCY AND THE DYING

Obviously, not all dying patients will be declared incompetent when they refuse death-prolonging treatment. The sensitivity of Judge Sullivan, which led him to Gertrude Raasch's bedside to determine that she was competent even though she could not speak, may indicate that in the future decisions will be more discriminating.

A remarkably confusing case shows the legalistic morass that results when questions of competency are confounded with questions of the reasonableness of the treatment and its refusal. Sadie Nemser, an eighty-year-old widow, had lived at the Jewish Home and Hospital for the Aged in New York City for over two years.[65] She was now suffering from arteriosclerotic heart disease and had suffered at least three strokes and three attacks of pneumonia. In August 1966 she was admitted to Beth Israel Hospital, her condition diagnosed as "diabetic and arteriosclerotic gangrene with infection." Her physician recommended amputating her right foot above the ankle, stating that the operation was "distinctly a matter of the difference between life and death." But Mrs. Nemser wanted no amputation. As many of us would, she said that she wanted both to live and to retain her limb. The attending psychiatrist at the hospital said she was not capable of understanding the nature of the surgery and the consent she was being asked to give.

Mrs. Nemser's closest relatives, three sons, made matters more complicated because they could not agree. There were long-standing differences among them over the support of their mother and over the adequacy of her medical care. Two of the brothers sought to be appointed temporary legal representatives for the specific purpose of executing the consent. The third brother, however, sided with his mother in refusing to go along—and he was a physician. He raised doubts about the effectiveness of the procedure and, indeed, about whether his mother could survive the operation and its consequences. After a complicated interchange the court ruled that it would not intervene to order the surgery.

Three grounds that were relevant in the other cases discussed may have gone into this refusal. The procedure itself may have seemed unreasonable in view of Mrs. Nemser's condition. The court may have sided with the physician son, functioning in a guardian's role. The judge may have decided that Mrs. Nemser herself was competent to refuse. Reading the

65. Petition of Nemser, 51 Misc. 2d 616, 273 N.Y.S. 2d 624 (Sup. Ct. 1966).

opinion does not shed a great deal of light, and it may be that all three grounds played a part. Despite the first physician's opinion that the surgery was a matter of life and death, two other consulting physicians, in addition to the physician son, averred that the procedure as proposed was not lifesaving and might in fact hasten death. In addition, the court may have been listening to other relevant parties. One son was actively resisting the surgery. There was also a court-appointed guardian *ad litem* who interviewed all the parties and reported, "I do not believe that intervention on the part of the Court is indicated." If the court was honoring this opinion or that of the physician son, it would be another case, like Mrs. Martinez's, where guardians were able to refuse treatment for what seemed to be a dying patient.

But there is a third, intriguing interpretation. The opinion notes that the court-appointed psychiatrist never categorically stated that Mrs. Nemser was mentally incompetent for all purposes, but rather limited his opinion to the question of consent for this particular operation. He reported she was unable to understand the situation or to render an informed decision, but also noted there was a difference of opinion concerning the patient's mental status. At least one judge seemed to imply that Mrs. Nemser retained her right foot because she was judged competent. Judge Sullivan, who ruled Miss Raasch competent to refuse her amputation and accepted Mrs. Phelps's refusal of a blood transfusion, says of the Nemser decision, "noting the woman was not adjudicated incompetent, the court refused to invoke *parens patriae*." [66]

There is a clear right of the competent patient to refuse treatment for any reason, but the right not to be declared incompetent while exercising that refusal is only beginning to emerge. This is one of the public policy areas where action is called for.

THE COMMITTED BUT COMPETENT

The circle of incompetency is also shrinking for the mentally ill. Now even those who are involuntarily committed to a mental hospital may, at least in some jurisdictions, be compe-

66. Sullivan, "The Dying Person," p. 206.

tent to make financial commitments, marry, execute a will, or refuse medical treatment. In July 1972, Paula Stein was found by a court to be suffering from chronic schizophrenia with acute flare-ups and was committed to Bellevue Hospital in New York City where the psychiatrists decided that electroshock therapy was necessary.[67] The treatment involves passing a current of 70 to 130 volts through the subject's brain, causing a convulsion similar to an epileptic seizure. It is effective in treating some forms of depression; however, it is traumatic and has been known to cause bone fractures, pulmonary edema, and, in rare instances, even death. Mrs. Stein's mother had consented to the shock treatments, in fact she had "consented to the doctors doing whatever they believe might help. . . ." Mrs. Stein, however, refused. The court produced conflicting testimony, but the independent psychiatrists permitted by the court to examine Mrs. Stein concluded, "she has the mental competence to consent or withhold consent for her treatment and to participate with her physicians in the choice of appropriate treatment modalities." On the basis of this advice the judge concluded that Mrs. Stein could indeed refuse the treatment. This did not mean she was free to leave the hospital. She was still, according to the court determination, "sufficiently mentally ill to require further retention"—in spite of her capacity to consent or refuse the electroshock therapy.[68] The judge concluded by saying "It does not matter whether this Court would agree with her judgment; it is

67. New York City Health and Hospitals Corporation v. Paula Stein, 335 N.Y.S. 2d 461 (1972).

68. This case is rather complicated by the change in the New York State Mental Hygiene Law about the same time. A new regulation was scheduled to take effect on January 1, 1973. This would expressly permit mental patients to refuse not only electroshock treatments, but also "surgery . . . major medical treatment in the nature of surgery, or the use of experimental drugs or procedures." It was apparently significant that in July 1972 when this case was being considered, the parties were aware of the new regulation and the hospital chose "to proceed in accordance with the spirit of the new recodification." This is somewhat puzzling since the new codification expressly grants *all* mental patients the right to refuse these four specific classes of treatment presumably including those who are not competent to exercise the refusal. Yet the decision granting Mrs. Stein's refusal was not based on a general right to refuse these treatments, but on a specific determination that she was competent to refuse and that the therapy "is not clinically indicated." Under the new regulation it would seem that finding Mrs. Stein to have the capacity to consent knowingly or withhold her consent would be extraneous.

enough that she is capable of making a decision, however unfortunate that decision may prove to be."

In Mrs. Stein's case the treatment was not a matter of life and death. In Maida Yetter's case, a Pennsylvania court was willing to find a committed mental patient competent to refuse a treatment that could very well jeopardize life.[69] Mrs. Yetter was committed to Allentown State Hospital in June 1971, diagnosed as having chronic undifferentiated schizophrenia. Late in 1972 in connection with a routine physical examination, she was discovered to have a breast discharge possibly indicating the presence of breast cancer. The doctors recommended a surgical biopsy together with any additional corrective surgery that would be indicated by the pathology of the biopsy. Mrs. Yetter refused to consent, saying "she was afraid because of the death of her aunt which followed such surgery." In response to questions in the court she also said she was afraid "the operation would interfere with her genital system, affecting her ability to have babies, and would prohibit a movie career." Mrs. Yetter was sixty years old and without children.

Her brother finally asked to be appointed her guardian for the purpose of consenting to the biopsy. A caseworker said Mrs. Yetter was "lucid, rational and appeared to understand that the possible consequences of her refusal included death."

The judge concluded:

> It is clear that mere commitment to a state hospital for treatment of mental illness does not destroy a person's competency or require the appointment of a guardian. . . .
>
> In our opinion the constitutional right of privacy includes the right of a mature competent adult to refuse to accept medical recommendations that may prolong one's life and which, to a third person at least, appear to be in his best interests; in short, that the right of privacy includes a right to die with which the State should not interfere where there are no minor or unborn children and no

69. In re Appointment of a Guardian of the Person of Maida Yetter, an alleged incompetent, 62 Pa. D. & C. 2d 619 (C.P., Northampton County Ct. 1973).

clear and present danger to public health, welfare or morals. If the person was competent while being presented with the decision and in making the decision which she did, the Court should not interfere even though her decision might be considered unwise, foolish or ridiculous.

The court would not let her brother consent on her behalf. Thus a person can now be competent to refuse treatment even if committed to a mental hospital.

Recently in Wisconsin, Judge Richard W. Bardwell was not even willing to grant that a hospital could administer drugs to a mental patient against his will after he was judged incompetent. The case was one where Thorazine (a major tranquilizer) had been administered to a patient in spite of his protest that it was producing an adverse reaction. He was being held for a thirty-day observation period during which, according to the state's attorney, the administration of drugs was authorized under Wisconsin law. The judge disagreed, saying, "As far as this circuit is concerned, there is precedent that a mental hospital cannot forcibly administer drugs to a voluntary patient who doesn't want them." In that jurisdiction patients committed under the thirty-day observation statute were considered "voluntary" until adjudicated otherwise. This would make the patient competent to refuse drugs although he was committed. When asked whether a patient who has been adjudicated mentally ill could have the right to refuse drugs, Judge Bardwell said that it was "questionable." [70]

COMPETENCY IN OLDER MINORS

A third class of people gaining the right to be considered competent is older minors. There is general confusion about the proper age of majority for making critical decisions. "If we are old enough to be drafted, we are old enough to vote," the slogan goes. But maybe older minors are old enough to consent or refuse consent to some things even before they are old enough either to vote or be drafted. Venereal disease treat-

---

70. Richard G. Sharp, "Wisconsin Court Acknowledges Patients' Right to Refuse Drugs," *Psychiatric News* (Dec. 12, 1973), pp. 1, 8.

ment and contraceptive services are available in many states without parental consent.[71]

But there are are real dangers in a general move to lower the age of medical treatment without parental consent. Do laws legalizing minors' access to contraceptives include sterilization for a fourteen-year-old? Some may. The age for competency to refuse lifesaving treatment may not be the same as the age for refusing trivial, experimental, or death-prolonging treatments. The courts are beginning to grant that older minors can, in some cases, refuse at least death-prolonging treatments. I have already mentioned the case of a sixteen-year-old girl suffering from an osteogenic sarcoma.[72] Although her chances of surviving, according to an independent surgeon, were 2 to 3 percent without the amputation of a leg and 20 to 30 percent with it, the girl refused to consent to the operation. The case resembles those where guardians might be permitted to refuse, because of the chance that the girl would not survive even with the operation. The mother agreed with her daughter's decision. But Judge Benjamin Schwartz emphasized the girl's own refusal, not that of her mother: "The girl testified in court that she would rather take her chances without the operation. She said if her leg was removed she would be a charity case the rest of her life. . . . She wouldn't be able to enjoy life, get married or even afford an artificial leg. . . ." Whether anyone should have to refuse treatment because she could not afford it is a separate question, but in this case the judge ruled, "I am not going to play God." The court would not impose its will on the unwilling girl.

In another case, sixteen-year-old Ricky Green had had two attacks of poliomyelitis, leaving him obese and with paralytic scoliosis with a 94 percent curvature of the spine. The boy was unable to stand or walk. Doctors said that if nothing was done he could become a bed patient. They recommended spinal fusion, involving moving bone from his pelvis to his spine. Although there was admitted danger in this type of operation,

71. Harriet Pilpel, "Minor's Rights to Medical Care," *Albany Law Review* 36 (1972), pp. 462–87.
72. *New York Post*, July 9, 1971.

Ricky's mother consented to the surgery, but with the condition that, as a Jehovah's Witness, she would permit no blood transfusion. The director of the State Hospital for Crippled Children in Elizabethtown, Pennsylvania, sought a declaration that Ricky was a neglected child and the appointment of a guardian.

When the case reached the Supreme Court, Chief Justice Jones, writing for the majority, observed that since the operation itself was dangerous, the state did not have sufficient interest to outweigh the parent's religious belief since the child's life was not immediately imperiled. They went beyond this, however, to declare that "the wishes of this sixteen-year-old boy should be ascertained." They cited a dissenting opinion in the case of the boy with the harelip in concluding, "we believe that Ricky should be heard." [73] The case was sent back to the lower court to determine the boy's wishes.

This case, then, differs somewhat from the earlier case where the decision was made that the boy's harelip operation could wait until he was of age. Here the judges determined that the boy at sixteen was already sufficiently mature to understand the issues and therefore to play a role in the decision. This tendency to lower the age of competency to decide is an important development in the refusal of treatment cases.

These cases in which older minors have had their own opinions recognized are rather special instances where reasonable people may differ about what is appropriate. In other cases the court has decided that it was cruel to place the burden of decision on an older minor. The case of Kevin Sampson was one in which it was decided that the parents' refusal of a blood transfusion was unreasonable.[74] At fifteen he was suffering from Von Rechlinghausen's disease, which caused a massive deformity on the right side of his face and neck. He had not attended school since he was nine. Physicians had recommended delay until the boy was old enough to decide for himself. The family court judge ruled against this and also against letting him participate in the decision. They decided that such a difficult choice should not be placed on the boy, fearing psy-

73. In re Green, 292 A. 2d 387 (Pa. Sup. Ct. 1972).
74. In re Sampson, 37 A.D. 2d 668, 323 N.Y.S. 2d 253 (1971).

chological harm if he was forced to choose between his parents' wishes and his own health.

Older minors are not always judged capable of competently deciding to refuse treatment, but there is clearly an increased willingness to consider them able to make a judgment. In another case, a sixteen-year-old was permitted to refuse an abortion demanded by her mother.

Perhaps the reasonable course is to lower the general age of majority to a more realistic figure, say eighteen, and then to make specific exceptions. Some exceptions may be made legislatively—for reversible contraceptive aid or venereal disease treatment—when it seems that bypassing parental consent will often be in the minor's best interest. Other cases will have to be decided individually so that courts can determine in each instance if the minor has sufficient understanding of the situation to make an informed and voluntary judgment.

Regardless of the decisions in specific cases, it is clear that the circle of incompetency is shrinking rapidly. It is no longer assumed that patients are incompetent simply because they want to refuse a death-prolonging treatment, because they are committed to a mental hospital, or because they are minors.

The criteria for reasonable refusal of treatment by guardians for incompetent adults may be similar to those for guardians of children. Treatments involving substantial risk in comparison with the potential benefits may be refused, but those offering great benefits at small risk may not be. As a general rule, refusal of death-prolonging treatments seems more reasonable than refusal of lifesaving ones. We need a clearer authority for refusals for incompetent and dying patients. What we are now learning is that many patients who were thought incompetent may be judged competent to make their own decisions, thus altogether avoiding the difficult issue of guardians.

The Never Competent vs. the Formerly Competent

Although in general it seems reasonable to treat incompetent adults like incompetent children in accepting refusal of treatment on their behalf by guardians, there is at least one crucial difference. This difference has been almost never recognized until now and it could become the basis for a major public policy innovation.

While children and some mental patients have never been competent at any point in their lives to express a reasoned judgment about what kind of treatment accords with their own moral and religious convictions, terminally ill adults have normally been competent at previous periods in their lives.

There are dangers in honoring a wish made while the patient was competent. The will to live even for a few days may be greater at death's door than in the middle of life. A refusal expressed in advance may be too vague to stand or, because of new biomedical breakthroughs, may have radically different implications at the time of death. This problem arose in Karen Quinlan's case. There was some evidence that at twenty she had expressed to her mother and others the wish not to be kept on a respirator if she were not going to regain consciousness. Judge Muir rejected the relevance of this, arguing that she did not reject the specific treatment but had merely held "theoretical" conversations. He held that "the vigor of youth that espouses the theoretical good and rightness" and the "absence of being presented the question as it applied to her" were in his opinion "not persuasive to establish a probative weight sufficient to persuade this Court that Karen Quinlan would elect her own removal from the respirator." [75]

It seems wrong that such "theoretical conversations" should be considered irrelevant. True, in this particular case, the opinions were voiced at a relatively young age and were not conveyed in formal documents, but they are, nevertheless, the best evidence available of her views. It is in some sense an affront to her memory that someone else's estimate of what she would want in her present condition is taken as more reliable than her own, albeit casual, expressions made in the vigor of youth.

There are some cases where the formerly competent may have left a clearer message. A fifty-nine-year-old woman named Winters had a chronic schizophrenic reaction of a

75. In re Quinlan, pp. 30–31.

paranoid type when brought to the hospital by an emergency ambulance.[76] Compelled to take "rather heavy doses of tranquilizers" against her will, she protested, citing the Christian Scientist convictions which she had held for ten years. In her suit for damages it was argued that there was no contention that the current alleged mental illness in any way altered these convictions. The appeals court found that the case had to be tried on its merits, implying that the convictions arrived at while competent would remain valid.

In a clearer case where the same conclusion was reached, Mrs. Bernice Brooks entered McNeal Hospital in Illinois in 1964, suffering from a peptic ulcer.[77] She had informed her physician repeatedly over a two-year period that she was a Jehovah's Witness and that her religious and medical convictions precluded receiving blood transfusions. She and her husband had signed documents releasing the physician and hospital of all civil liability and were assured that there would be no further effort to persuade her to accept blood. Nevertheless, as Mrs. Brooks's condition weakened, the physician petitioned the court, obtaining a guardian (or conservator) for her who gave consent for her to be given the transfusion. After her recovery Mrs. Brooks sought to have the conservatorship proceedings expunged and the petition dismissed.

Justice Underwood explicitly framed the question of the rights of a formerly competent patient with a known history of refusal of a specific treatment:

> When approaching death has so weakened the mental and physical faculties of a theretofore competent adult without minor children that she may properly be said to

76. Winters v. Miller, 446 F. 2d 65 (N.Y. 1971).

77. In re the estate of Bernice Brooks, 32 III 2d 361, 205 N.E. 2d 435 (1964). A similar case is being decided in Illinois. A twenty-year-old married man needed blood after an automobile accident. While fully conscious and competent he refused because of his religious convictions. His wife, brother, sister, and parents all also refused and he and his wife both signed releases. Without adequate notice to the family, the hospital had a guardian appointed who consented to the transfusion. Later the wife brought suit, charging violation of First Amendment rights. The guardian was found not liable for his action since he was acting under the protection of the court, but the court refused to dismiss the charges against the hospital and the physicians. The court found that the ruling in Brooks, that the wishes expressed while competent must continue after the patient is incompetent, should be applied. Holmes v. Silver Cross Hospital of Joliet, Illinois, 340 F. Supp. 125 (D.C. N.D. Ill. 1972).

be incompetent, may she be judicially compelled to accept treatment of a nature which will probably preserve her life, but which is forbidden by her religious convictions, and which she has previously steadfastly refused to accept, knowing death would result from such refusal?

After a lengthy examination of the limited nature of the right to free exercise of religion, the court ruled that the answer was no; a patient may not be forced to undergo lifesaving treatment she has previously refused simply because she has become incompetent.

The implications of this decision for formerly competent terminally ill patients may be great. If such a patient's wishes for refusal of even lifesaving treatment are to be honored, then a death-prolonging treatment refused while competent must not be foisted upon a now incompetent patient. The formerly competent patient is different from the never competent child in this one crucial way. Our public policy must recognize that all of us who are competent are potentially formerly competent and that our wishes must continue to be respected even after we are in no condition to continue to express them. Whether this needed protection can be given without statutory intervention will be discussed in the next chapter.

Competent Adults: Three Special Cases

One of the main principles established in this chapter is that the competent individual may legally refuse any medical treatment for any reason whatsoever. No rule is truly exceptionless, however, and in the vast collection of cases in the American judicial record, I find three special cases.

Willing to Be Coerced

The first exception to the general rule is really only a semantic distinction between consenting and being coerced. Some individuals, objecting to receiving blood on religious grounds, are unwilling to consent but let it be known that they would not resist an order to be treated. On December 22,

1965, Mrs. Willie Mae Powell was in Ward 16C of Columbia-Presbyterian Hospital bleeding to death after a Caesarian section, about to be survived by a husband and six children.[78] She was critically ill and placed on the danger list. She had signed a release of liability, and the hospital took the view that it had fulfilled its obligations under the circumstances.

Mrs. Powell, however, apparently would not actively resist the transfusion. She did not even object to the treatment. She simply found herself, because of her religious convictions, unable to sign a prior written consent. Was she to die over a moral technicality? Her husband sought injunctive relief, trying to get an order for the blood transfusion.

Judge Jacob Markowitz, in a rare moment of passion in the history of court opinions, condemned the "legalistic minded" society we live in:

> I was reminded of "The Fall" by Camus, and I knew that no release—no legalistic absolution—would absolve me or the court from responsibility if I, speaking for the court, answered "No" to the question "Am I my brother's keeper?" This woman wanted to live. I could not let her die!

Nine months earlier a Connecticut court reached a similar decision. A Mr. Elishas George, suffering from a bleeding ulcer, signed a release while rational and coherent for refusing a blood transfusion on the grounds that he was a Jehovah's Witness. However, he indicated he would not resist a court order directing the transfusion, and the court so ordered.[79] Although the patient did indicate he would not resist, it is not clear in this case whether that was the basis of the legal opinion.

Competent Adults with Dependents

In the case of Mrs. Powell, the judge apparently did not base his decision on the fact that she had six children. How-

78. Powell v. Columbian [sic] Presbyterian Medical Center *et al.* 49 Misc. 2d 215, 267 N.Y.S. 2d, 450 (Sup. Ct. 1965).
79. U. S. v. George, 33 U. S. L.W. 2518 (D.C., Conn., March 24, 1965).

ever, in the case of Mrs. Jesse E. Jones, responsibility to dependents was apparently a significant factor.[80] Mrs. Jones was brought to the hospital by her husband for emergency care, having lost two-thirds of her blood from a ruptured ulcer. At twenty-five, she was the mother of a seven-month-old child. Having no personal physician, she was under the direct care of the hospital staff. When death became imminent, the hospital sought permission to administer blood. After an initial denial the request was appealed to Judge J. Skelly Wright of the United States Court of Appeals. In a rapidly arranged bedside hearing, all he could understand her to say was "Against my will." In ordering the transfusion, he offered five reasons, some of which are perplexing and will be discussed below. One reason cited, however, was that the state, as *parens patriae*, will not allow a parent to abandon a child.[81] Mrs. Jones "had a responsibility to the community of care for her infant." According to Judge Wright, "The people have an interest in preserving the life of this mother." [82] Thus one clear ground for ordering a competent adult to undergo medical treatment is that it is in the interest of a dependent.

That dependent may be an unborn child. In 1964 in New Jersey a pregnant woman "quick with child" (that is, in the late stages of pregnancy) attempted to refuse blood necessary to save her life. The trial court ruled, following the usual pattern, that it could not order treatment for a competent adult.

---

80. Application of the President and Directors of Georgetown College, Inc., 331 F. 2d 1000 (D.C. Cir. 1964).

81. Another reason was that because Mrs. Jones was *"in extremis"* and "hardly *compos mentis"* she was "as little able competently to decide for herself as any child would be." For this reason Judge Wright felt justified in applying the analogy of the cases involving parental refusal of blood for children where, as we have seen, the court will routinely order the transfusion. Since Mrs. Jones was a known Jehovah's Witness who had expressed her refusal of the blood transfusion before she lost competency, it would appear that she was really a "formerly competent adult" and not in the same position as a child. Thus it is not certain that this argument of Judge Wright should remain valid. However, the argument is consistent with the view that wishes stated while conscious and and competent may be overridden if the patient rejected treatment before knowing that death would be the result.

82. The state may have a twofold interest: preventing psychological harm to the child from loss of its mother, and preventing expense that will ensue if the child becomes a public charge. See Cantor, "A Patient's Decision to Decline Life-Saving Medical Treatment" pp. 251–54.

In a reversal upon appeal, the court unanimously ruled that the unborn child is entitled to the law's protection. The authority to transfuse was given.[83]

This denial of the right to refuse treatment when there are dependents is not unlimited, however. A remarkably sensitive Judge Bacon had her ruling sustained recently in the District of Columbia Court of Appeals. Charles P. Osborne, a thirty-four-year-old Jehovah's Witness, desperately needed whole blood if he was to survive internal bleeding caused when a tree fell on him.[84] In hearings held at the bedside, the court first determined that the patient was conscious, understood the consequences of his decision, and "had with full understanding executed a statement refusing the recommended transfusion and releasing the hospital from liability." The court also considered the possibility that, like Mrs. Powell and Mr. George, Mr. Osborne might consider himself blameless if forced to undergo the blood transfusion. Mr. Osborne, however, expressed the belief that "he was accountable to God, in the sense of a loss of everlasting life, if he unwillingly received whole blood through transfusion." His blunt response: "It is between me and Jehovah; not the courts. . . . I'm willing to take my chances. My faith is strong. . . . I wish to live, but with no blood transfusions. Now, get that straight." As his grandfather put it, "He wants to live in the Bible's promised new world where life will never end. A few hours here would nowhere compare to everlasting life." Mr. Osborne made a prudent choice, given the assumptions on which he worked.

Judge Bacon raised the possibility of the state's overriding interest because the patient had two young children.[85] Here, however, the result was different from that in the Jones case. The patient's wife made the statement:

> My husband has a business and it will be turned over to me. And his brothers work for him, so it will be carried

83. Raleigh Fitkin–Paul Morgan Memorial Hospital v. Anderson, 42 N.J. 421, 201 A. 2d 537 (1964) cert. denied, 337 U. S. 985 (1964). Also see Robert M. Byrn, "An American Tragedy: The Supreme Court on Abortion," *Fordham Law Review* 41 (1973), pp. 844–49.

84. In the matter of Charles P. Osborne, 294 A. 2d 372 (D.C. Cir. 1972).

85. Sharpe and Hargest, "Lifesaving Treatment for Unwilling Patients," p. 699, notes that the state might have a stronger interest if it were the life of a sole surviving parent at stake.

on. That is no problem. In fact, they are working on it right now. Business goes on.

As far as money-wise, everybody is all right. We have money saved up. Everything will be all right. If anything ever happens, I have a big enough family and the family is prepared to care for the children.

The court was persuaded and did not intervene.[86] It was faced with a man who "did not wish to live if to do so required a blood transfusion, and who had, through material provision and family and spiritual bonds, provided for the future well-being of his two children." The strength of that religious conviction may be reflected in a footnote added later: "We are also advised that the patient has recovered though his chances were very slim and that he has been discharged from the hospital."

Prisoners

There is a final group of competent adults for whom treatment may be ordered: prisoners. Among the many rights currently denied the incarcerated is apparently the right to refuse medical treatment. In this strange world, some prisoners, like some mental patients, are fighting for their right to get medical treatment,[87] while others are struggling to avoid the physician's meddling medicaments. Whether or not it should be, at the moment prisoners do not have the same right to control their medical treatment that their guards do. There are at least six cases where prisoners have demanded that right, but in none of them has it been granted. None of the decisions,

86. In "Constitutional Law: Transfusions Ordered for Dying Woman Over Religious Objections," *University of Pennsylvania Law Review* 113 (1964), p. 294, it is also argued that the interest of the state is difficult to defend when the surviving parent does not object to the spouse's decision.

87. See addendum in Ramsay v. Ciccone, 310 F. Supp. 600 (Mo., 1970): "A prisoner in need of medical treatment (including medical attention and surgical treatment) cannot, without leave and assistance of his keepers, at will go to a public or private facility to secure medical treatment and cannot at will call in a practitioner to treat him in prison. (If he is indigent he might not be able to secure medical treatment in or out of prison with leave of his keepers.) Having custody of the prisoner's body and control of the prisoner's access to medical treatment, the prison authorities have a duty to provide needed medical attention."

however, seems to be based on a clear case of a reasonable refusal on grounds unrelated to prison confinement. None is
based upon long-standing religious convictions (such as those
of a Jehovah's Witness or Christian Scientist). None involves
death-prolonging treatments.

One set of cases denies the prisoner's right to refuse tranquilizers and other psychoactive drugs. One prisoner with a
confused and chaotic religious history—he had once claimed
to be a "messenger of love" with a secret prophecy for the
Pope and his attempted conversion to Judaism was rejected by
the prison rabbi—was not permitted to refuse Thorazine and
Permitil tranquilizers.[88] Another was not permitted to refuse
Prolixin (a potent antipsychotic agent) on the ground that it
violated his will and unspecified religious belief.[89] Another
court decision found administration of drugs acceptable if
sanctioned by any substantial, recognized medical authority.[90]

A prisoner being held at the medical center for federal prisoners claims he is "arbitrarily and capriciously" declared mentally incompetent.[91] Another claims that certain medical treatment administered to him, without his consent, constitutes
corporal punishment.[92] In the latter case the judge claims that
"petitioner argues in effect that he, and he alone, should determine whether he should receive certain medical treatment,
and that 'forced medical treatment is corporal punishment
and cannot be legally inflicted upon anyone confined under
sentence that calls for less than capital punishment.' " This
argument, the judge says, is "obviously without merit."

The last case involves a prisoner's attempt to refuse treatment for his diabetes mellitus. Although his refusal seems to
result from a misunderstanding of what constitutes reasonable
treatment for diabetes rather than religious objection or an attempt to avoid a behavior-controlling drug, the case is of interest because the opinion spells out at great length the constitutional rights of federal prisoners related to medical

88. Peek v. Ciccone, 288 F. Supp. 329 (W.D. Mo. 1968).
89. Smith v. Baker, 326 F. Supp. 787 (W.D. Mo. 1970).
90. Veale v. Ciccone, 281 F. Supp. 1017 (W.D. Mo. 1968).
91. Petition of Baptista, 206 F. Supp. 288 (W.D. Mo. 1962).
92. Haynes v. Harris, 344 F. 2d 462 (8th Cir. 1965).

treatment. After affirming the duty of the prisoner's "keeper" to provide needed medical attention, the argument is advanced that "*intentional* denial to a prisoner of *needed* medical treatment is cruel and unusual punishment." Even treatments which are "unusually painful" or cause "unusual mental suffering" may be administered to prisoners without their consent "if it is recognized as appropriate by recognized medical authority or authorities." Obviously the right and duty to consent to medical treatment is not a generally recognized principle in the prison setting. In fact, it is striking that the only grounds for argument in the opinions seem to be that the treatment is "cruel and unusual punishment," a rather different case from that of the free, competent adult. The possibility of rejecting treatment because it violates religious or ethical convictions or the right of privacy rather than because it is medically wrong seems not to have been considered in these cases. The religious objector or the morally motivated refuser of death-prolonging treatments in a prison setting may be in for a very hard time at present.

Conclusion

There is no paucity of cases in American courts dealing with the refusal of treatment. The cases we have discussed or referred to at first seem to present a maze of confusing and contradictory opinions. Yet, examined carefully in the light of common sense, they seem to reduce to a consistent pattern that can be summarized in a few general principles.[93]

---

93. This is not to say that the actual judicial opinions upon which these decisions were made reduce to an equally simple set of principles. This is not a legal treatise examining the juridical justifications for refusal of treatment decisions. That is the task for a lawyer. It may well be that some of the reasons for the opinions discussed here may not really be consistent with the general principles which we seem to find. In particular, there are two principles in decisions ordering treatments for incompetent patients or patients with dependents that would seem to apply equally well to patients who are adult and competent.

One is the argument that no one has the legal (or moral) right to commit suicide. This argument was made explicit in the case of Mrs. Jones where it was cited, along with her incompetency and her obligation not to abandon her seven-month-old infant, as a reason why she should have to receive a blood transfusion. Likewise, it was used in the case of Delores Heston, the incompetent twenty-two-year-old whose

First, competent individuals may refuse any medical treatment they desire for whatever reason they desire (unless they are prisoners) if the treatment is offered for their own good. Second, among incompetent patients (children, incompetent mental patients, and those medically incapable of making any decision) guardians may not refuse a clearly lifesaving treatment that would restore reasonably normal health. If treatment is not a life-and-death matter, the acceptance of the refusal will depend on whether the refusal is seen as being sufficiently reasonable. A refusal will be reasonable if (1) the risk of the proposed treatment is substantial in comparison to benefits (2) there is a lack of a clear need for treatment, or (3) the treatment can wait until the incompetent is in a position to make a personal decision.

---

mother was not permitted to refuse blood for her. But at least two other cases specifically reject this argument. The judge in Mr. Dilgard's case rejects it on the somewhat trumped-up ground that "it is always a question of judgment whether the medical decision is correct" and therefore the individual should have the final say. Mrs. Martinez's judge was more to the point and philosophically more subtle.

Her doctor feared he would be aiding her suicide if he permitted her to refuse the blood vessel cutdowns necessary to prolong her dying. Judge Popper said he did not mean Mrs. Martinez had the right to commit suicide, but that she had the "right not to be tortured" and she could refuse treatments which produced pain.

The other argument used in Mrs. Jones' case could also be applied to competent patients. Judge Wright argued that the hospital and physicians were given an "impossible choice" by Mrs. Jones's refusal: They could either provide proper treatment or honor her demand for no transfusion. Judge Weintraub, in Delores Heston's case, followed Wright closely. He argued, even more explicitly, that the medical and nursing profession are "consecrated to preserving life" and that "when the hospital and staff are thus involuntary hosts and their interests are pitted against the belief of the patient, we think it reasonable to resolve the problem by permitting the hospital and its staff to pursue their functions according to their professional standards." This opinion is, in fact, a violation of their medical professionals' own code of ethics. Their duty is not to "preserve life" but rather to do what is in the patient's interest. To opt for their own interests rather than the patient's cannot possibly be morally acceptable. They may, of course, on grounds of conscience, withdraw from the case, but to impose their own professional ethics on a patient in violation of her religious convictions cannot be tolerated.

Perhaps our intuitions are sounder than our carefully articulated legalistic opinions. Although these two arguments—the prohibition on suicide and the obligation to permit physicians to act on their own ethical systems—could equally apply to competent patients, they never have been so applied. Perhaps judges looking for reasons to order treatments where there was a good intuition that treatment should be ordered went searching for a ground and happened to find in these cases two rather short-sighted arguments.

These patterns seem established, but a few areas remain in which public policy is still very uncertain. These are the areas needing more attention by individuals, the courts, legislatures, and other policy-making bodies. First, it must be made clear that refusal of a death-prolonging treatment is not in itself grounds for declaring a person incompetent. Second, especially for incompetent patients, refusal of death-prolonging treatments should be seen as radically different and normally more reasonable than refusal of lifesaving treatments. Third, a clear distinction is needed between the never competent (or those who have never expressed themselves while competent) and the formerly competent. It is an assault on human dignity to impose treatment on adults despite wishes they clearly and knowledgeably expressed while coherent and competent. They should not be regarded as children who have never made moral judgments of their own just because they have passed into a semiconscious or unconscious state.

Finally, we need to clarify conditions under which it is reasonable for guardians to refuse treatments, especially lifesaving treatments, for the incompetent patient. Whether a death-prolonging or truly lifesaving treatment may be refused on the grounds that it is unreasonable—because of its uselessness or the burden it generates—is the one issue really not clear in the courts. There seems to be a substantial moral consensus that merely death-prolonging treatments for incompetents ought to be refusable as unreasonable by guardians. That no cases are available suggests that such judgments are not often questioned. The case of the lifesaving but gravely burdensome treatment for the incompetent is the most difficult one of all. While no legal consensus has yet emerged, if we concede that burden generally can be a legitimate grounds for refusing treatment in a competent patient and that guardians are charged with serving the interests of their wards, then it seems plausible that guardians might on some occasions reasonably refuse treatment for their wards on the grounds of burden. The next chapter will look at the series of public policy proposals now being debated that deal with these gaps in our present policy.

5

Dying Morally: The Formation
of a Workable Public Policy

(Although the laws permitting refusal of treatment are much clearer than many realize, there is still confusion in the practical day-to-day decisions about the care of the seriously ill and dying—confusion brought about by the same powers and the same people who have brought new hope to a humanity long afflicted with sickness, suffering, and the tragedy of untimely death.) What steps are needed to resolve this confusion and bring about a workable public policy? What are the options of individuals who know they too will someday be among the dying? What choices can and should be made by family members, friends, clergymen, lawyers, and medical professionals?

This chapter will face these practical questions. It will survey the public policy options now being debated heatedly in hospital halls, congressional caucus rooms, research institutions, and bedrooms throughout the nation. Before looking at four major public policy alternatives, it is important to see what any policy would have to do—what variables are critical. The theoretical ethical distinctions discussed in chapter 3 will have to be dealt with. Should a policy include active killing of the dying or only the withdrawal of treatment? Should it permit any treatment to be withdrawn or only "extraordinary" or "unreasonable" treatments? Should the policy apply to those who are "better off dead"—in someone's judgment—or only to those whose dying process is out of the hands of man?

A policy will particularly have to come to terms with the remaining legal ambiguities discussed in the last chapter. How is the decision to be made whether the individual is personally competent to decide a treatment, and should refusal of treatment be a ground for declaring incompetency? Do previously expressed views on terminal care by a now clearly incompetent patient make any difference? Who should make the inevitable decisions about the care of the incompetent?

ISSUES IN THE PUBLIC POLICY DEBATE

In addition to these theoretical questions concerning what is ethical and what should be legal, other variables arise primarily at the policy level rather than in the context of the earlier discussions. Three such variables will be crucial in our public policy analysis, and I will examine their application in each case.

Vagueness and Specificity

One distinguished physician has drafted an informal letter which he, or someone in his position, might write to his own physician. It includes the sentence:

> I find it hard to think of any circumstances in which I would regard it as sound practice to employ artificial respiration to prolong my life if I had lost the ability to breathe for more than two or three (not five or six) minutes.[1]

This specification to the minute is an illustration of how precise instructions can be in defining when one wants to be allowed to die. At the other extreme, a bill introduced into the Florida legislature by Walter Sackett merely provides that any person may "execute a document directing that he shall have the right to death with dignity and that his life shall not be prolonged beyond the point of a meaningful existence." [2] The vagueness of the term *meaningful existence* could hardly be greater, and nowhere in the bill is there any effort to make it any more specific.

---

1. The letter is by Robert S. Morison, Professor Emeritus, Department of Sociology, Cornell University.

2. The legislation carried the title "Death With Dignity." This wording was in the 1970 version.

Anticipatory or ad hoc Decision

In addition to how specific a policy proposal is, there is the related matter of whether it requires individuals to take action before the onset of a terminal condition or whether it can be applied in crisis situations. In both the proposals above, individuals are expected to contemplate their fate calmly in advance and initiate some action which presumably would guide others at some future time to decide that they should be allowed to die.

On the other hand, some proposals being offered can be called, for lack of a better label, "ad hoc." They do not require signing any formal document or writing any letter in advance. The vagueness of the Sackett proposal stems in part from the requirement that lay people write an understandable document which can apply to all possible conditions when life might become "no longer meaningful," and which would not lead to unacceptable actions should future technology provide remedies not yet contemplated.

Ad hoc proposals eliminate these problems. They simply provide ways in which decisions can be made on the spot about whether treatment is morally appropriate at this particular time, with this particular patient, in this particular condition. Current policy, whereby the individual physician considers each case and then makes a decision day-by-day whether to go on, is an ad hoc type of policy. To be sure, any plan ahead policy will require supporting ad hoc decisions. If a physician is authorized to cease treatment when the patient cannot regain consciousness, then the physician will have to decide at some point that the time has come. The real distinction is between policies where the initial directive is given ahead of time (with some subsequent decision making required to determine when the specified conditions have been met) and those where the initial directive is given on the spot.

The Line of Authority

One of the major functions of any public policy in this area will be to clarify the lines of authority in making the decisions on allowing the dying to die. There is currently a working assumption that physicians have the authority to make such decisions. Some quarters espouse the extreme view that it is the "medicine man's burden" to assume this responsibility and that it cannot be abandoned.

There are other candidates for the decisive role, however. I shall discuss the line of authority with the following possible major contenders in mind:

> the potentially deceased person
> the members of the family
> the person's agent
> the physician caring for the person
> some hospital authority (committee, board, etc.)
> the courts or other government agency

Any policy will have to distribute authority among such possible candidates or others added to the list.

As important in its way as who exercises the authority is the kind of mandate given to them. Will the agents be permitted discretion within certain limits or will they be obligated to carry out particular directions? In the most obvious case the patients may have written documents granting their physicians leave to cease treatment or not initiate it at the physicians' discretion. Alternately, patients might be given the authority to direct their physicians to cease treatment, thus placing them under a specific obligation and removing physician discretion. It is apparent that when one agent is given discretion, other agents in the list may and in many cases will have their freedom in decision making restricted. If the physician has discretion, the family may not. One of the major differences in policy proposals is the permissive tone of some and the obligatory terms of others.

POLICY ALTERNATIVES

With these theoretical and policy distinctions spelled out, we are finally ready to review some of the major alternatives for developing a more explicit and consciously formulated public policy to deal with the problems of the dying patient. Some of the policies under discussion might, by the way, also permit decisions which will terminate the living of a living patient as well as terminate the dying of the dying patient. It will not be our intention, however, to offer a thorough review of proposals of this type. Such problems may well be directly or indirectly affected by policies designed to facilitate responsible care of the dying. Here, we will deal with four basic groups of proposals. The first is our unacknowledged status quo—permissive, ad hoc decision making by personal physicians.

Permissive, Ad Hoc Decision Making by Personal Physicians

Some will say that we should have no public policy at all to facilitate dying. The fact is that we do have a public policy— unexamined and not thought out but nevertheless a policy— and I would say that it is the second worst of all possible ones. That policy is that individual physicians should, using their knowledge of their patients and the patients' condition, consider the alternatives carefully and then, perhaps after consultation with others based on their view of the best interests of the dying, decide when certain treatments will no longer be attempted.

/There are a small number of physicians and an even smaller proportion of the public who hold, at least in principle, that the physician should never decide to omit or stop a treatment that is at all relevant to the patient's condition. They argue, with a strong moral tradition behind them, that the physician's duty is to preserve life at all costs and that no compromise with that moral imperative is possible. More realistically, however, most people would recognize that there are some conditions for which some possible treatments are not morally obligatory even though it might conceivably be relevant to the patient. We shall assume for our purposes that such omission may at least occasionally be justified, for example, when a terminal, deeply comatose patient could be the subject of some new experimental procedure which would require flying the patient, the medical staff, and perhaps the family, around the country or around the world.

The injunction "preserve life at all costs" exists primarily within the professional fraternity of physicians: it does not derive, at least in its stark form, from a universally legitimated source. It is possible that a commitment to preserve life can be derived from an ethic committed to maximizing good consequences on the presumption that life is always a good thing regardless of its burden. It might also be derived from a Kantian ethic of treating the person always as an end, never only as a means. Neither position would support a claim that life should be preserved at all costs. It is especially implausible for an ethic of ends. It is important that there is no evidence that the physician maxim, when stated in this extreme form, is grounded in a more universal principle. The other Kantian implications of treating man as an end—telling the truth independent of the consequences, for instance—are generally not present in the more specific maxim of the group of physicians who are committed to preserving life per se.

If, in fact, virtually all physicians do omit some theoretically relevant treatments for at least occasional patients, we do not judge them in all cases to be morally culpable. Thus there is already a public policy regarding allowing the dying patient to die. It is for the most part limited to omitting means that are thought useless or that would impose grave hardship on the patient and to hastening death indirectly by giving drugs to relieve suffering. The policy is extremely vague; it is ad hoc; it is certainly permissive rather than mandatory (with the complicating exception that the patient has the right to withdraw from treatment and therefore from the responsibility of the physician involved); and it places the physician first in the line of authority. What practical and moral problems are raised by the current policy? I see two.

First is the difficulty of judging patients' interests. This may not be immediately apparent. Current practice places decision making in the hands of one who knows the patient's medical condition and one who, at least in principle and by tradition, is committed to caring for the patient. In the Hippocratic Oath, the physician pledges to work "for the benefit of the sick according to my ability and judgment." The first objection is that not all physicians do, in fact, always work for the benefit of the sick even according to their ability and judgment. This is a very real problem, but rather than emphasize it, we shall limit ourselves to those cases where we assume the physician is indeed striving to work for the benefit of the sick according to his ability and judgment. Then we can see if in the real world the problem of failure to work in the patient's interest is truly significant.

One of the first reasons that dying patients should be concerned about this norm is that it calls for physicians to work for the benefit of the sick according to their judgment rather than simply "doing what will benefit the patient" or "doing what is right in the case." It has been shown that there are serious deviations between what physicians see as being in their patients' interests and what patients see as being in their own interests.

In the next chapter we shall see how physicians and patients differ radically in their judgment about whether patients would be better off if told about a terminal cancer diagnosis. Either physicians are better predictors of what is in the best interests of the patients than the patients themselves, or their judgment of the patients' own interests is not very good.

The explanation may be that physicians judge what they think would be in their own interests if they were in the patient's condition. This is a particularly dangerous moral principle, sometimes called "the Golden Rule," It is dangerous when there are systematic differences between what two groups (e.g., physicians and laymen) might want in a specific situation. Feifel,[3] Kübler-Ross,[4] and others have suggested that physicians as a group have unusually high anxiety in the face of death. This may be in part because individuals with a high fear of death choose to enter a death-conquering profession and in part because of socialization after entering the profession. If physicians do tend to have a greater than normal desire to conquer death, they may then tend to misjudge what is in the patient's best interests.

In any event, it cannot be denied that there are random variations in physicians' judgments on the subject. Under the

3. Herman Feifel et al., "Physicians Consider Death," *Proceedings of the American Psychological Association* (1967), pp. 201–02.

4. Elisabeth Kübler-Ross, *On Death and Dying* (New York: Macmillan, 1969), p. 20.

present policy, whether a treatment is omitted or stopped or indeed whether death is actively hastened is to a large extent a matter of luck, depending on which physician happens to be assigned to the patient when he happens to stumble into the potentially death-producing condition. If the patients are fortunate enough to be under the care of their personal physicians, this randomness may be reduced somewhat, but even then many patients do not pick their physicians primarily on the basis of their attitudes about termination of treatment.

Second is the problem of special ethical norms for physicians. As well as having a different attitude toward death, physicians may feel they have a special moral duty, a duty not understood by the layman. Perhaps it is this duty that is codified in the medico-moral folk tradition already discussed, "Life is to be prolonged at all costs." In fact, in spite of the fact that this is bluntly stated by many physicians, to my knowledge it is not incorporated into any more formal code of medical ethics. The Hippocratic Oath does, as we have noted, specifically forbid giving "a deadly drug to anybody if asked for it." For one who does not distinguish between actions and omissions and between direct and indirect killing through drugs, this Hippocratic requirement might be extended to the general problem of caring for the dying. If medical professionals feel bound by such a special ethical norm in their medical roles, then it is quite possible that physicians will systematically reach different conclusions about what is ethically required of them even if they overcome the social and psychological problems involved in calculating how to advance their patients' interests in matters like anxiety, pain, and suffering.

Lord Brock, in a particularly blatant example of ethical special pleading, has argued:

> As an ordinary citizen I must accept that the killing of the unwanted could be legalized by an Act of Parliament, but as a doctor I must know that there are certain things which are part of the ethics of our profession that an Act of Parliament cannot justify or make acceptable.[5]

5. Lord Brock, "Euthanasia," *Proceedings of the Royal Society of Medicine,* (July 1970), pp. 661–63.

He concludes, "We may accept the need for euthanasia on social grounds but we cannot accept that doctors should implement it." [6]

Lord Brock's position is that the morality of "euthanasia" is an open question in a more general or universal moral perspective, but that "as a doctor" he knows as only doctors can that they have a special moral norm: never deliberately kill a patient.

Let us bracket this conclusion and examine his ethical argument. His claim that physicians as a class have a special moral norm which can only be known by and relevant to physicians is a strong reason why the decision to allow dying patients to die or actively bring about their deaths should never be left to the individual physician. This mode of special ethical reasoning is particularistic. It cannot be universalized in the Kantian sense. There is no claim that all reasonable persons should agree that anyone in the physicians' position should act as physicians claim they do. Knowledge and applicability of special norms is limited to one social group.

If one special group (physicians) makes judgments based on a set of moral norms different from those of their clients, predictably what is done will reflect a different perception of what is morally required. Thus if it is widely held within the medical profession that special moral norms apply to physicians, and I think it is, it will be very dangerous if individuals—patients or healthy laymen—cede moral decision making to their physicians. The physician may misjudge what patients would consider to be their best interest, and he may be operating with a special set of moral norms which lead to systematic differences in judgment about what is morally required. But let us assume that the problems of the physicians' special outlook and particular professional code can be overcome so that medical personnel reach exactly the same decision that the patients personally would have reached if they had made the decision. Better still, say the physician reaches the "morally right" decision even if the patient would not have. The pragmatic arguments are thereby ruled out.

6. Ibid., p. 663.

The moral problem still remains. Even when exactly the same decision would be reached (which I believe would not happen often), patients' freedom to control their own bodies and to make decisions which affect them personally is violated.

Dying with dignity may be inherently impossible. It certainly will be if the critical decisions surrounding one's own dying are taken away. Too often, the patient is treated as a thing, or at least as a child in need of careful "management." The parent-child metaphor for the physician-patient relationship is a favorite of establishment medical sociologists. Such an assault on patient freedom and dignity is dehumanizing. It is probably also illegal in the United States. The Declaration of Independence proclaims the unalienable rights not only of liberty and the pursuit of happiness, but life as well. This right is protected in the Constitution and in specific laws granting individuals the right to self-determination, including self-determination in the treatment and control of medical interventions into their bodies. A decision by another individual to continue or terminate treatment without consent of patients or their legal agents would appear to violate this right rather explicitly. Thus even if physicians should, by chance, reach the same decision that patients would have reached (or even a morally superior one), they are in the process assaulting their patients' humanity, their freedom and dignity.

(Medical) Committee Decision Making

In choosing a public policy to facilitate allowing dying patients to die, an alternative proposal would have a hospital committee of medical personnel reach the decision to omit or cease treatment. In my opinion, this is even worse than the individual physician model. Such committees have been used in experimental programs for deciding who will have access to scarce medical resources such as artificial kidney machines. When Ernie Crowfeather walked away from the dialysis program at the Northwest Kidney Center in Seattle, a committee had already decided that he could not continue in treatment under their auspices and financing. The presumed advantage of committees is that they will not be subject to random and inevitable variations among physicians, thus avoiding the effects of any bizarre beliefs at either extreme. There is greater probability of knowledge of relevant data and greater likelihood of impartiality. There are also three very serious problems with committee responsibility.

First, if there is any merit in the ad hoc, permissive decision making by the individual physician, it is that the individual physician may know the patient personally, may be committed to giving personal attention, and may even have discussed the alternatives with the patient. The committee mechanism bureaucratizes death, destroying the one possible advantage of individual physician decision making.

Second, while the committee may reduce random biases of individual physicians, it in no way eliminates the systematic biases of the medical community as a whole. If physicians as a group tend to exhibit peculiar psychological responses to death or to operate on moral norms peculiarly their own, then the committee would still reflect these biases. The assumption that a collection of expert opinions will eliminate bias could be called the fallacy of consensus of expert opinion.

Third, even if both random and systematic bias were eliminated, the committee approach would still depend upon and reinforce the misconception that physicians as a group have expertise in making moral decisions about when, if ever, treatment should be omitted or stopped. This assumption of moral expertise assaults patient freedom and dignity perhaps to an even greater degree than the ceding of decision-making authority to individual physicians. If a committee mechanism is to be used at all, and I believe it should not be, it would be preferable to have the committee made up of randomly picked citizens, peers of the patient, rather than of members of a group with a particular type of technical knowledge. In short, not a panel of technocrats, but rather a jury of peers.

The support of the use of committees for making such decisions is likely to increase as a result of the decision by the New Jersey Supreme Court in the case of Karen Quinlan. The opinion explicitly calls for what was termed an "ethics committee." [7] Great danger and serious confusion is likely to result.

7. In re Quinlan, Supreme Court of New Jersey, A-116, September Term 1975 (March 31, 1976), pp. 57–58.

Actually the declaratory judgment if taken literally poses no real problem. It says that if Karen Quinlan's father (acting as guardian) and the physician he selects agree that the treatment is to be discontinued on the grounds that there is no reasonable possibility of her ever emerging from her present comatose condition to a cognitive, sapient state, then the ethics committee should be consulted. The judgment is clear, however, that the committee has one and only one function: to confirm that there is no reasonable possibility of Karen's ever emerging from her present comatose condition to a cognitive, sapient state. In other words, the committee called an ethics committee is given only a technical neurological task of confirming the prognosis. They have no responsibility for approving or disapproving of the ethical decision that the life support apparatus should be disconnected. The committee should really be called a neurology committee and be made up only of neurological experts.

The court seemed somewhat confused, however, because it took the idea from one of several articles proposing that ethics committees make or share in the ethical decisions. Karen Teel, a pediatrician and Director of Pediatric Education at Brackenridge Hospital and Central Texas Medical Foundation, proposed rather casually in a law review article appearing shortly before the court acted that such a committee might be an appropriate forum for reviewing ethical dilemmas in order to provide assistance and safeguards for patients and their medical caretakers.[8]

Even in her offhanded proposal she recognized some of the problems I have mentioned with using such committees to make or even advise about treatment stopping decisions: problems of logistics and imposition on the freedom of patients or their agents. She does not pursue the analysis at a very deep level, however. She does not take up the difference between confirming a medical prognosis, which is a task for medical experts, and making ethical judgments about the prognosis, which is not properly a task of medical experts at all. We have seen that it is simply illogical to give such authority to privately constituted committees, even if those commit-

8. Karen Teel, "The Physician's Dilemma—A Doctor's View: What the Law Should Be," *Baylor Law Review* 27 (1975), pp. 6–9.

tees happen to include lay people as she proposed. If anyone is to override the patient or the guardian in making the ethical judgment, it must be a public agency such as the court. On the other hand it is illogical to give such a committee which includes lay people the task of making a purely neurological judgment.

The New Jersey court, in giving an "ethics committee" a purely technical task specified the correct job for a neurological committee, but in calling it an ethics committee and connecting their instructions to a not very carefully analyzed proposal for committees to perform a different task, the court may lead us to confusion.

Personal Letters and Documents

To correct the difficulties arising when physicians attempt to make the decision to omit or cease treatment on their own or in committee, several mechanisms have been proposed to provide guidance. These attempt to shift the locus of decision making to the patient himself so that he has control over what happens to him. Four such proposals will provide examples.

A PHYSICIAN'S INSTRUCTIONS FOR HIS OWN CARE

At least some physicians worry about how they will be cared for themselves should they become terminally ill. Robert S. Morison, a distinguished New York physician, has given considerable thought to the problem of deciding to stop treatment for the dying. He has written a set of instructions for his own care:

> Now that I have reached the age of 65, I would like to reach some understanding with you about the principles which should guide my medical care. It is my understanding that physicians normally act on the principle that an individual life is of such value per se that it should be preserved at almost any cost. Certainly in most circumstances an individual who consults a physician does so in the hope and expectation that both of them will work together to preserve health and life. A physician is expected to be dedicated to his patient's welfare and the

presumption must normally be that an individual's welfare is crucially dependent on his continuing existence. During one's active years, one's "welfare" may be defined as including not only the opportunity to experience a large variety of sensations, but actively to discharge his obligations to give material and emotional support to his family and to the larger society of which he is a part. All these considerations argue for closely identifying "welfare" with life during this period.

As one grows older, however, the situation changes. The flow of stimuli from both the internal and external environment gradually comes to arouse fewer and fewer enjoyable sensations and more and more painful and undesirable ones. Finally subjective consciousness may disappear entirely leaving only a vegetable existence. More or less concomitantly, one's abilities to discharge one's obligations to those around him decline and give place only to burdensome demands upon them. In such circumstances, what I think of as the patient's welfare reverses its relationship to the preservation of his life. What I am asking you to do in conducting my medical care during my declining years is to have primarily in mind a responsibility to my "welfare" defined so as to include the possibility that I may be better off dead than alive.

Specifically, I attach a negative value to a state of being in which I could no longer read, think, and talk intelligently to those around me. Therefore, I specifically ask you not to attempt to prolong my life in such circumstances. I understand the normal concern of a physician that such states may be temporary and likely to be followed by satisfactory recovery, but at my age I regard the small chance that I might again enjoy life and contribute something of value to others as so slight as to be completely outweighed by the much larger possibility of losing all human dignity and becoming only a burden to myself and others.

Thus, I find it hard to think of any circumstances in which I would regard it as sound practice to employ artificial respiration to prolong my life if I had lost the ability to breathe, for more than two or three (not five or six) minutes. In any circumstance in which I remain unable for more than a day or two to communicate with others and make decisions for myself, I should regard it as wrong to resort to artificial feeding either by mouth or by vein or to control infection with specific drugs. On the other hand, I would hope that I would be helped to be quiet and comfortable by the use of narcotics if necessary, without regard to their other effects.

In writing this letter, I not only intend to relieve you of any implied legal obligation to engage in any form of treatment designed to prolong my life, but I also regard this expression of my desires as a simple and direct extension into the future of my present rights as an individual to accept or refuse any medical treatment that may be offered to me.[9]

His letter is designed to be addressed to his personal physician (perhaps with copies going to members of his family and others concerned). The recognition that "physicians normally act on the principle that an individual life is of such value per se that it should be preserved at almost any cost" agrees with my observation that this summarizes many physicians' perceptions of their primary moral obligation although patients may not accept it or believe that physicians should act on it. In this case a physician himself cannot accept it. The letter states the author's moral perspective: "I attach a negative value to a state of being in which I could no longer read, think, and talk intelligently to those around me. Therefore, I specifically ask you not to attempt to prolong my life in such circumstances. . . ." For him this means omitting any use of artificial respiration after there has been a loss of "the ability to breathe for more than two or three (not five or six) minutes."

1. Vagueness and specificity. Such instructions could hardly be more specific. Perhaps they are too specific—let us hope that he really does not mean the loss of "the ability to breathe" but rather the loss of oxygenation whether or not he main-

9. The statement by Robert S. Morison was presented to a meeting of the Research Group on Death and Dying at the Institute of Society, Ethics and the Life Sciences.

tains any of his own ability to breathe. And in saying "In any circumstance in which I remain unable for more than a day or two to communicate with others and make decisions for myself, I should regard it as wrong to resort to artificial feeding either by mouth or by vein or to control infection with specific drugs," he creates two problems for anyone else who might want to use this letter as a guide. First, another individual might not accept the same conclusions about the value of prolonging life when there is no longer the ability to think, read, or talk intelligently. For some, at least, loss of the latter two abilities would not make life utterly valueless.

Second, and even more of a problem, very few individuals and virtually no nonphysicians would be capable of specifying how many minutes without oxygen they would find acceptable or the chances of recovery after a day or two of inability to communicate with others. A letter this specific can be written only by people with medical knowledge. Even then they would have to be careful to make sure that the empirical data and technology incorporated in the instructions would not change.

Yet, although the letter is extremely specific, it is at the same time vague. What is meant, for instance, by "I find it hard to think of any circumstances in which I would regard it as sound practice" to employ artificial respiration? Does that mean never use it, use it only in extemely special cases, or use it only if you think you should? Terms such as "communicate with others" and "think intelligently" also are vague. The attending physician may not obtain as much guidance for the tough cases as the writer intended.

2. *Anticipatory or ad hoc decision.* Vagueness is perhaps inevitable in any attempt to plan ahead. While the author is now clearly of sound mind and body and able to anticipate some of the conditions under which he would not want to be treated, he cannot possibly be specific enough to cover all eventualities.

3. *The line of authority.* The letter attempts to deal with the line of authority by shifting some of the responsibility for decision making to the patient (who in this case happens to be a physician). Yet secondary decision making will clearly be needed, and may land in entirely different hands. The letter will require two types of decisions by the physicians who must

interpret it. They must decide when the patient can no longer read, think, and talk intelligently or when he has not communicated with others or made decisions for himself for a day or two. This is open to a broad range of interpretation, and the physicians involved will be influenced heavily by their own values as well as those of the patient. But first of all, the attending physicians must decide how or even whether to honor the letter. It is permissive in tone: "What I am asking you to do . . ." "I specifically ask you not to attempt . . ." "I find it hard to think of any circumstances . . ." "I would hope that I would be helped . . ."—all of these leave the ultimate decision to the attending physicians. Thus the decision-making authority—at least at the level of specific actions at the time of dying—still remains with the treating physicians. Even if the letter were not so permissive, it would stand without legal authority or sanction. It assumes a close relationship between a patient and trusted personal physicians.

Realistically, how often does such a relationship exist? Many patients have no personal physician at all, and if they do, the relationship is not necessarily one of trust. Even if it is, there is no guarantee, in this age of mobility, that one will do his dying under the care of that physician. Finally, even if one does do one's dying with a personal physician, few patients have the self-confidence and status to discuss the matter with the physician in a relationship of equality in which the patient's values will be forcefully expressed and seriously regarded.

Informal instructions are often nothing but wishful thinking, but the existence of such a letter might help to guide one's last physician whether or not one knows him or her. It would probably help more, however, if it were sent to and discussed with one's family. But beyond providing guidance, a policy that depends on informal letter writing faces all the problems of the present ad hoc decision making by physicians. Authority over the life and death of one individual is still ultimately placed in the hands of another.

A PHYSICIAN'S INSTRUCTIONS ON FINAL CARE

Medical World News has published a copy of a letter by Eugene Stead, a noted Duke University professor of medicine.

It is in many respects comparable to Robert Morison's instructions:

> If I become ill and unable to manage my own affairs, I want you to be responsible for my care. To make matters as simple as possible, I will leave certain specific instructions with you.
>
> In event of unconsciousness from an automobile accident, I do not wish to remain in a hospital for longer than two weeks without full recovery of my mental faculties. While I realize that recovery might still be possible, the risk of living without recovery is still greater. At home, I want only one practical nurse. I do not wish to be tube-fed or given intravenous fluids at home.
>
> In the event of a cerebral accident, other than a subarachnoid hemorrhage, I want no treatment of any kind until it is clear that I will be able to think effectively. This means no stomach tubes and no intravenous fluids.
>
> In the event of a subarachnoid hemorrhage, use your own judgment in the acute stage. If there is considerable brain damage, send me home with one practical nurse.
>
> If, in spite of the above care, I become mentally incapacitated and have remained in good physical condition, I do not want money spent on private care. I prefer to be institutionalized, preferably in a state hospital.
>
> If any other things happen, this will serve as a guide to my own thinking.
>
> Go ahead with an autopsy with as little worry to my wife as possible. The anatomy crematory (at the medical school) seems a good final solution.[10]

Again, there is a specificity that could come only from a physician. Yet as an anticipatory document it also has large areas of vagueness: "If I become ill and unable to manage my own affairs, I want you to be responsible for my care." What is

10. Eugene Stead, "A Physician's Instructions on Final Care," *Medical World News*, April 7, 1972, p. 47.

the meaning of "unable to manage my own affairs" or "think effectively?" The area for secondary decision making is very broad and remains in the hands of the treating physician. While the patient appears to be exercising some authority over decisions which affect his own fate, the crucial decisions will still be made by the physician. Even more explicitly than in the earlier letter, Stead's letter is permissive: "I want you to be responsible for my care . . ." "In the event of a subarachnoid hemorrhage, use your own judgment in the acute stage . . ." "If any other things happen, this will serve as a guide. . . ." The letter is clearly written as guidance to a trusted medical colleague. As such it must face all the problems already discussed.

THE "LIVING WILL" OF THE EUTHANASIA EDUCATIONAL COUNCIL

Guidance can be provided with more formal documents. The Euthanasia Educational Council has drafted a model letter, called the "Living Will":

To my family, my physician, my clergyman, my lawyer:

If the time comes when I can no longer take part in decisions for my own future, let this statement stand as the testament of my wishes:

If there is no reasonable expectation of my recovery from physical or mental disability, I, _____, request that I be allowed to die and not be kept alive by artificial means or heroic measures. Death is as much a reality as birth, growth, maturity and old age—it is the one certainty. I do not fear death as much as I fear the indignity of deterioration, dependence and hopeless pain. I ask that medication be mercifully administered to me for terminal suffering even if it hastens the moment of death.

This request is made after careful consideration. Although this document is not legally binding, you who care for me will, I hope, feel morally bound to follow its mandate. I recognize that it places a heavy burden of responsibility upon you, and it is with the intention of sharing that responsibility and of mitigating any feelings of guilt that this statement is made.

(Signed)_____

Date_____
Witnessed by:

_____
_____

As with the two former letters, authorization is limited to omissions and cessation of treatment despite the troublesome word *euthanasia* in the title of the sponsoring society. The first physician's instructions and the Living Will, however, specifically distinguish between direct and indirect hastening of death by condoning the use of drugs. (The Living Will states, "I ask that drugs be mercifully administered to me for terminal suffering even if they hasten the moment of death." Morison's instructions specify, "I hope that I would be helped to be quiet and comfortable by the use of narcotics if necessary without regard to their other effects.")

The Living Will makes an additional distinction when it excludes only "artificial means or heroic measures." No effort is made to explicate the complexities of these terms.

This proposal is even more vague than the other anticipators letters. This "will," in contrast to the other two letters, is written for the layman. It is devoid of technical medical terms. Treatment is to be stopped "If there is no reasonable expectation of my recovery from physical or mental disability . . ." This represents the extreme generality.

As with the earlier prospective proposals, a secondary decision-making process is generated. Who is to decide when there is no longer reasonable expectation of recovery and what criteria of reasonable expectation and recovery are to be used? Since the letter is addressed to a number of parties the answer is vague, but the physician seems to be implied. If this is the case, then authority is once again handed to an individual who has no special competence for this kind of decision making.

More than the other letters, the Living Will is explicitly permissive: "Although this document is not legally binding, you who care for me will, I hope, feel morally bound to follow its mandates. I recognize that it places a heavy burden of responsibility upon you, and it is with the intention of sharing that responsibility and of mitigating any feelings of guilt that this statement is made."

The responsibility is "shared;" there is moral urging, but hardly anything more than hope that the physician will follow the patient's request.

A LEGALLY BINDING INSTRUCTION

If all such informal letters and instructions lack the power to relieve those who fear they may not do their dying in the care of a physician they can trust, it may be possible under present legal authority to create a more forceful instrument. Although the Living Will does not attempt to be legally binding, it is not clear whether a document designed to have legal force would stand up. A possible device would be giving power of attorney to designate someone (a spouse, grown offspring, or friend) as an agent for the purpose of making decisions about medical care should you become incompetent to make those decisions yourself.

Such a power of attorney could begin with a general statement about the importance of receiving medical care that would preserve social, psychological, and spiritual wholeness rather than merely physical, vitalistic signs of life. Instead of acknowledging that the document has no legal weight, it could designate the individual who should be responsible for medical decisions should the writer become incompetent. By clearly indicating that it is the responsible agent of the patient whose judgment is decisive, the specific decisions can be made in an ad hoc fashion when necessary. The vagueness of the anticipatory letter is thus overcome. Following a statement of the individual's religious, moral, and philosophical convictions, the operative paragraph might read:

Draft Treatment Refusal Instructions

I, _____, while of sound mind, hereby authorize my wife (husband, or other designated individual) _____ to act as my legal agent for the purposes of accepting or refusing specific medical treatments, if I am ever judged incompetent or otherwise incapable of expressing myself, with the expressed specific instructions that she (he) refuse treatment if in her (his) opinion it is not appropriate.

I instruct her (him) to seek remedy in the court if my refusal expressed while I was competent to express such refusal or her (his) refusal made on my behalf under circumstances stated above is not being honored by any other individual including all medical personnel.

Signed _____

Witnessed by:

_____

_____

Some may want to spell out more specifically when treatment should be refused. After the words "if in her (his) opinion it is not appropriate," more specific guidance could be added as in the letters of the two physicians discussed above. Some of the "euthanasia" legislative proposals to be discussed next have included a fairly refined description of the conditions under which dying should not be prolonged. This kind of description might be included here as a way of designating when the agent might consider refusing treatment. These conditions could include suffering from (1) an illness thought to be incurable and progressive and expected to cause severe distress, (2) a grievous physical affliction involving immediate and serious disability, or (3) a condition of physical brain damage or mental deterioration such that normal faculties are severely and irreparably impaired.

While these conditions are still ambiguous, they are offered here only as guidelines and so are, less critical than in the legislative proposals. There is no real need to include them at all.

Although several lawyers who have examined this form believe that it would give legal force to a treatment refusal, others are not sure. There is some doubt that a power of attorney would remain in force after the individual signing it had become incompetent. A will remains in force, of course, as does a donation of body parts (which we shall explore in the final chapter), but both of these occupy a special position in the law.[11] No one should assume that a power of attorney would necessarily stand up and be legally binding, at least without the advice of his own attorney. Until there is a court test of such a document, we cannot know for sure. But the power of attorney may be one way of moving beyond the clearly nonbinding living will and relieve some of the anxiety of those who fear they will not be able to die in accordance with their own ethical convictions.

Legislative Proposals

If even this last proposal for personal action cannot completely resolve the confusion of the present situation then, as some are suggesting, legislation may be the only answer. As early as 1936 the British House of Lords considered legislation to permit "voluntary euthanasia" under certain conditions. In 1947 the General Assembly of the State of New York considered a bill with similar intentions. It would have permitted sane persons over twenty-one who were "suffering from painful and fatal disease" to petition a court for "euthanasia." The court would have appointed a commission of three, two of them physicians, to investigate the case and determine whether the patients understood what they were doing and whether they came under the provisions of the act. If the court accepted the report, then a physician or other person chosen by the patient or commission could have "administered euthanasia."

The bill failed and the legislatures were dormant on the issue until the late 1960s when a new flurry of activity began.

11. In some jurisdictions, but not others, consent of an individual while living for an autopsy remains valid after death. See David W. Meyers, *The Human Body and the Law* (Chicago: Aldine, 1970), p. 103.

The Euthanasia Society of England prepared a draft bill which was considered in Parliament in 1969. It has become a model for one of the three main types of bills. Since then no fewer than twenty bills have been introduced into the legislatures of at least fourteen states. Two of these simply call for a commission (Florida, 1971) or hearings (Hawaii, 1972) to study the matter. The others fall into three broad groups which we will now explore.

BILLS TO PERMIT INSTRUCTIONS ON TERMINAL CARE

Walter Sackett, a state representative and a physician, has long been concerned with dignified death. He has made several attempts to have the Florida state legislature act on the subject—at various times with a constitutional amendment, a bill or the establishment of a committee to investigate the matter. The 1970 bill would have been the first to legitimate (anticipatory) statements and set up mechanisms for deciding when patients cannot decide for themselves:

> Any person, with the same formalities as required by law for the execution of a last will and testament, may execute a document directing that he shall have the right to death with dignity and that his life shall not be prolonged beyond the point of his meaningful existence.

The proposed bill is mute on the question of causing and permitting death to occur with dignity. The affirmation of the "right to death with dignity" does not specify whether actively assisting death is included or even indirectly causing death through the use of drugs, although it is possible to assume from the language that they are. Certainly there is no distinction made between ordinary and extraordinary means. It is not even clear whether the bill facilitates only ending the dying process; the ending of living may be included as well. Some people might try to argue that they are "beyond the point of meaningful existence" when they are not dying at all. With this interpretation the bill might legitimate medically assisted suicide in the nonterminal patient.

Vagueness and specificity.   One of the most serious problems with the Sackett bill of 1970 is its extreme generality. Most sig-

nificant is the vagueness of the term *meaningful existence.* The
legislative proposal, in contrast to the two physicians' letters,
must apply to laymen and must be general enough to cover
virtually all who might want to take advantage of its provisions. Controversial conceptions of meaningful life such as the
ability to read and communicate with others must be excluded. The vagueness of the bill is a serious deficiency.

Anticipatory or ad hoc decision. The 1970 Sackett bill is like
all three of the letters discussed in that the decision to execute
the document will be made while of sound mind and body in
anticipation of some future event. While this permits reflection at one's leisure, it does not permit the specificity needed
to really control decision making and raises problems about
changing one's mind.

The line of authority. The Sackett bill appears to represent a
significant shift in authority over the decision to stop treatment. Any person may execute the document, thus reserving
"the right to death with dignity." Beyond that the bill provides:

> In the event any person is unable to make such a decision
> because of mental or physical incapacity, a spouse or per-
> son or persons of first degree of kinship shall be allowed
> to make such a decision, provided written consent is ob-
> tained from:
>
> (1) Spouse or person of first degree of kinship or . . .
> (2) In the event of two persons of first degree kinship,
>   both such persons . . .
> (3) In the event of three or more persons of first degree
>   kinship the majority of those persons.

With regard to the primary decision to execute the document, the relatives of the patient are thus placed second in
line of authority. The bill goes on to specify that if there are
no relatives, "death with dignity shall be granted any person if
in the opinion of three physicians the prolongation of life is
meaningless." Thus the physician, or rather three physicians,
are next in line for the primary decision. This is the first pro-

posal in which the family has been given any role whatsoever (although the Living Will is directed to the family as well as the physician and others).

There are four political theories represented in the various proposals. We have already discussed a technocratic theory centering authority in the professional cadre. (Subordinating the individual to the decision-making authority of the state would be possible in an authoritarian state but fortunately this is not being seriously considered.) The informal letters represent the development of modern Western philosophical individualistic voluntarism. The patient, alone, shall control his or her own destiny with no subordination to a professional cadre, the state, or to the kinship system. This is perhaps one of the deficiences of the letter proposals. They make no provision for ongoing familial responsibilities. Yet obligations to one's kin are among the most fundamental in a society. This is seen in the legal responsibility parents bear for the actions and welfare of their offspring and in the quasi-property right and the concomitant responsibilities of the kin for the body of a deceased family member. The family is obligated to care for the welfare of its members and to do what is morally required for them.

A conflict exists between the rights and obligations of the individual and the family especially when the dying person wants treatment stopped and the family members do not. In fact, in all societies the kin have a centrol role in decisions about the care of the dying.[12] The kinship nexus is deeply rooted in even the modern Western individualistic society where the extended and perhaps even the nuclear family are not as crucial as they once were. At the time of crisis—at first word of a serious illness or death—it is normally the family who gather from across the country to care for the afflicted member and the spouse and children. This strength of commitment and loyalty cannot be matched by the professional medical cadre. The commitment of the family to its members

12. Talcott Parsons and Victor Lidz, in *Essays in Self-Destruction*, ed. Edwin S. Shneidman (New York: Science House, 1967), pp. 141–42; Michael T. Sullivan, "The Dying Person: His Plight and His Right," *New England Law Review* 8 (1973), p. 203.

gives rise not primarily to rights but to responsibilities—responsibilities for the care and protection of the welfare of the clan.

Any policy will have to cope with the occasional family
where there is reason to doubt the responsibility will be fulfilled, but usually the concern of the family will provide the
best guarantee for the individual. Some would argue that this
familial obligation should take precedence over a radical individualism. I reluctantly side with the right of individuals to
control their own fate, but in those cases where the individuals
have not expressed themselves—in the case contemplated in
the Sackett proposal—it seems ethically imperative to follow
the Sackett order (with qualifications to be discussed below),
placing the obligation, as well as the right, for decision making
with the family. The second in line of authority must be the
next of kin rather than a medical professional.

But what if there are no kin? Sackett calls for three physicians to make a decision. The problems with placing a physician, or worse yet a troika of physicians, in the position of
moral decision maker over the life and death of a patient seem
to me so grave that in that rare case where the patient has no
available kin, I would prefer that the courts appoint a guardian. Nor should the guardian be a hospital administrator or
physician involved with the case. There is room for errors
with either alternative. I feel it is far better to chance the
errors of the state-appointed guardian. The alternative would
be open to abuse when an irresponsible physician merely
wants to dispose of a nuisance case. If there is a guardian,
however, and the physician in charge believes the guardian is
acting irresponsibly, there is the alternative of appealing to the
court to get a new guardian appointed just as is done now in
refusal of treatment cases.

Since the Sackett proposal is anticipatory, it will generate a
secondary line of authority. The bill states that an individual
has a right not to demand death with dignity, but to "execute
a document that he shall have the right to death with dignity
and that his life shall not be prolonged beyond the point of a
meaningful existence." The question still remains who shall
decide when existence is no longer meaningful and when shall

treatment be omitted or stopped. The bill is vague on this point, but in many readings this secondary authority, which is crucial for the bill to be effective, would continue to rest with the physician. If this is the case, the Sackett proposal still has all the problems of the informal letters, which are permissive. The real authority does not rest with the patient or the patient's relatives but with another individual citizen who has none of the particular responsibilities and knowledge of the patient's value system that the relatives do. On these grounds I feel that, while the Sackett bill goes beyond the informal documents, it still does not correct any of the difficulties or put aside the fears of patients who believe that they might not do their dying under the care of the personal, trusted physician who has been convinced of the patient's wishes and has agreed to follow them.

Since the Sackett proposal of 1970, other states have considered bills closely following the Florida model. In 1971, Wisconsin considered a bill that followed it almost verbatim. It did, however, specify that the person shall have the right not only to execute a document expressing his desires, but also "refusing and denying the use or application by any person of artificial, extraordinary, extreme or radical medical or surgical means or procedures calculated to prolong his life." Attorney E. H. Snyder, author of the bill, has avoided the vagueness of "meaningful existence," but in its place used the complex notion of "artificial, extraordinary . . . means" and at the same time has implied that the dying patient does not have the legal right to refuse "ordinary" means, however that may be defined. The Wisconsin bill also provides that those who act or refrain from acting shall be immune from any liability that might otherwise be assigned.

In 1972 Sackett introduced another version of his 1970 bill. This was similar, but included a few changes. It now permitted an individual to execute a document "directing that medical treatment designed solely to sustain the life process be discontinued." He has now, like the Wisconsin version, avoided the vagueness of his earlier bill, but limited its relevance to a narrow group of treatments. The new bill also requires that two physicians declare an individual "terminally ill," and adds a provision exempting a physician acting in accordance with the instructions in good faith and without negligence from criminal or civil liability.

In 1973 the Oregon legislature considered a proposal of the same type. It is virtually identical to the 1972 Florida proposal, applying to an individual "at such time as he suffers a terminal illness." Both also contain an explicit provision that the person executing such a document may revoke it at any time.

In addition to the bills in those states which permit guardians to act on behalf of the incompetent patient, there are at least three proposals which apply only to the patient personally. The first was introduced in the Wisconsin legislature in 1971 along with the bill mentioned above. It is identical to the other Wisconsin bill except that it excludes the paragraph on decisions on behalf of incompetent patients. In 1973, two bills were considered. One was introduced by Walter Sackett in Florida. Evidently giving up on his earlier proposal which had authorized guardians to make decisions, he introduced a simple proposal which would give anyone over eighteen the right to execute a document directing that "medical treatment designed solely to sustain the life processes be discontinued," provided that two physicians certify the patient to be terminally ill. The document is apparently still anticipatory—that is, it can be written before becoming terminally ill—and still applies only to treatments designed solely to sustain the life processes in the terminally ill.

With all of these compromises, on May 25, 1973, the Florida house became the first state legislative body to approve a statute dealing with "death with dignity," a name Sackett has now dropped from his legislation. The senate, however, did not go along.

Another 1973 bill was introduced in Delaware; it was similar to the Florida proposal. Like the earlier Sackett bill, the author limited its applicability to individuals without reference to guardians. In the Delaware version, if a person is "unable to execute such a document because of mental or physical incapacity, such person may make an oral request to three physicians, all three being present at the time, that further treatment cease." This rather strange formulation presumably applies only to patients who are sufficiently competent to refuse treatment but not competent to put it in writing. The wording implies that if patients vigorously want to refuse but can reach only one or two physicians at the same time, they will be subjected to compulsory treatment. Since the right of the competent patient to refuse treatment is already well established, it is hard to see what would be accomplished by such legislation.

The Florida version, and possibly the Delaware one, would apparently make the "Living Will" continue to be valid even after the signer had lapsed into incompetency, but that is not clearly stated. The Delaware bill may contradict that by specifying, "If the patient is in fact dying, with no expectation of recovery, the physicians may cease further medical procedures." That the bill says that even in the case of the dying they *may* rather than *shall* cease treatment suggests the provision is still permissive to the physician. If so, we are really no better and possibly much worse off than we are now. There is very little comfort in this group of bills designed to give some legal weight to the informal letter arrangement. They probably create more problems than they solve. To the extent that they suggest that the final choice is in the hands of the physician (or the unanimous approval of three physicians), they may jeopardize the already existing legal right to refuse any medical treatment.

BILLS TO PERMIT ACTIVE HASTENING OF DEATH

A rather different sort of bill was introduced into the Idaho legislature in 1969. Introduced by Representative H. R. Koch, it was patterned almost word for word after the British bill debated in Parliament the same year. This bill unambiguously included actively assisting the dying process. It defined *euthanasia* as the painless inducement of death and stated "euthanasia shall be administered to a patient in accordance with the terms of his declaration." Once the all-inclusive nature of the bill is made clear, there is no need to explore the distinction between ordinary vs. extraordinary means.

Vagueness and specificity. Among the proposals which are basically anticipatory in character, the Idaho bill and its British equivalent are perhaps the best in striking a balance between the vagueness of the Sackett bill's "meaningful existence" and the specificity of the physicians' letters. The bill specifies four conditions for euthanasia:

> A. If I should be at any time suffering from a physical illness thought in my case to be incurable and progressive and expected to cause me severe distress, I request the administration of euthanasia at a time or in circumstances to be indicated or specified by me or, if it is apparent that I have become incapable of expressing wishes, at the discretion of the physician in charge.

> B. If I should at any time suffer from a grievous physical affliction involving immediate and serious disability thought to be permanent and expected to cause me severe distress, I request the administration of euthanasia at a time or in circumstances to be indicated or specified by me.

> C. If I should at any time suffer from a condition of physical brain damage or deterioration such that my normal mental faculties are severely and irreparably impaired, I request the administration of euthanasia as soon as it is apparent that I have become incapable of leading a rational existence.

> D. In the event of my suffering from any of the conditions specified above, I request that no active steps should be taken, and in particular that no resuscitatory techniques should be used, to prolong my life or restore me to consciousness.

Some real effort is made to specify the nature of illnesses and afflictions under which euthanasia may be practiced. This is particularly important since the bill includes action which could cause the death of the not otherwise dying. The conditions are general enough to include virtually all conceivable legitimate reasons for ending the dying process and at the same time are specific enough to exclude trivial, nonterminal cases.

Anticipatory or ad hoc decision.   From the above it can be seen that the bill is basically anticipatory in character. The document is executed ahead of time. But patients may still be involved in the ad hoc decision to cease treatment or hasten death actively. They request euthanasia "at a time or in circumstances to be indicated or specified by me . . ." or, if they suffer from a condition of physical brain damage, "as soon as it is apparent that I have become incapable of leading a rational existence." One would prefer that the last clause read "permanently incapable," but otherwise the bill seems to permit a maximum of patient ad hoc decision making.

The line of authority. The primary line of authority is clear. The patient retains decision-making authority as long as possible, and then it passes to the physician. There is no provision for relatives to be involved. I have already argued that as individuals with special knowledge of the patient's values and special responsibility for family members' welfare, relatives should remain higher on the line of authority than the physician. In this respect the bill is deficient.

The bill is in places clearly permissive rather than mandatory. The patient "requests" euthanasia and presumably the physician decides if and when "it is apparent that I have become incapable of expressing wishes," so that the decision is made "at the discretion of the physician in charge." More significantly, the document concludes:

> I ask and authorize the physician in charge of my case to bear these statements in mind when considering what my wishes would be in any uncertain situation.

Thus, in spite of the retention by the patient of primary authority, the physician in fact has a great deal of control. Even if the active killing provisions were removed from the bill, this would remain a problem.

LEGAL PROTECTION OF THE PHYSICIAN

Like some of the better bills which simply authorize documents, the Idaho bill offers strict legal protection of the physician who ceases treatment or in this case actively hastens death according to the policy proposal:

A physician who in good faith administers euthanasia or other treatment to a qualified patient in accordance with what the physician believed to be the patient's declaration or request under this act shall not be guilty of any offense.

Fear of prosecution is reported to be one of the reasons that physicians refuse to cease treatment. Such a provision must be included in any policy if it is to be effective in facilitating the dying patient's freedom and dignity.[13]

The Idaho bill includes another important provision, the right of the professional to withdraw:

No physician or nurse who is opposed on principle to euthanasia shall be required to take any steps in furthering its administration.

Assuming that this would not exempt physicians from their obligation to inform patients that their condition met the requirements of the bill (or to withdraw so that another physician can), this provision is vital to any proposal that would facilitate the death of dying patients. If the moral integrity of medical professionals is to be preserved, then they cannot be required to participate in what they deem to be an immoral act. They must be given the opportunity to withdraw from the case.

After the resounding defeat of the Idaho proposal in 1969 and the more publicized defeat of the British version the same year, there was a slackening of activity. Then in 1973 two more states, Montana and Oregon, considered bills on the British model to permit active hastening of death. There are slight differences in wording. In the Montana version, the declaration would have to have been filed with the county clerk at least fifteen days before "euthanasia administration."

---

13. The Idaho bill also gratuitously states that physicians and nurses shall be deemed not in breach of any professional oath or affirmation. This reflects a basic confusion about the nature of a professional code. Since the state did not create it, it is hard to see how the state can grant exemption. In fact it is included only because physicians' licenses (granted by the state) can be revoked if they are in violation of the professional code. This illustrates the foolishness and danger of making conformity to a professional code one of the requirements for licensure.

All three states' versions contained strong penalties for wilful violation of the intent of the bill. In Idaho the draft states, "a person who wilfully conceals, destroys, falsifies, or forges" a declaration is guilty of first-degree murder. In the Montana version, the penalty is life imprisonment. It is strange that in both states concealing the document, which is really refusing to go along with the requested euthanasia, is punishable in the same way that forging the document is. This represents either very bad writing or a strong conviction that individuals have the right to have their death hastened. In the Oregon version there are different penalties—life imprisonment for falsifying a document to suggest a patient does desire euthanasia, but only ten years or $5000 fine or both for falsifying the document to state a patient does not want it.

In part because of the ethical and political problems discussed in chapter 3, the likelihood of these active killing statutes becoming law seems very small. There is a third type of proposal, however, which is intermediate between the active killing bills and those giving physicians permission to act on a Living Will.

BILLS BASED ON THE RIGHT TO REFUSE TREATMENT

A bill was introduced in the Illinois legislature in 1973 which closely resembles the bills from Florida, Wisconsin, and Delaware that simply legitimate the individual's decision. While these other bills would have permitted the individual to write a document ahead of time, the Illinois bill was designed to permit individuals over eighteen to refuse a specific medical treatment presumably on an ad hoc basis after they become terminally ill. This avoids the serious problem of the anticipatory proposals, which can never really be specific about when the individual would or would not want a treatment.

For this reason the Illinois bill is better, but it offers real problems. First, it still applies only to individuals where "in the opinion of the attending physician or physicians treatments cannot effect a cure or rehabilitation and are administered solely to prolong life." This means that refusals of treatments even in terminal patients are not supported by this bill if the physician concludes that treatments could possibly contribute

to rehabilitation or even that they are not solely to prolong
life. Second, and an even more serious problem, the bill recognizes only part of a right that clearly exists in broader scope already. Competent patients now have the right to refuse any
medical treatment, but could jeopardize that right even to
consider a law which would grant it only where a physician
decides the treatment could not effect a cure and is administered solely to prolong life. Third, the bill does nothing for
the real problem cases which proliferate today—the cases
where patients are incompetent to make their own decisions.
Are we to continue letting the physician make decisions in
those cases on an ad hoc basis or is there a workable alternative?

Based on the discussion of the philosophical distinctions we
have discussed and the criticism of other policy proposals, I
have developed a proposal for legislation which I think deals
most equitably with the competing moral, legal, and pragmatic
issues at stake. Before presenting a draft bill and a defense of
it, I shall outline the principles that I feel should guide any
such policy, the guidelines for an allowing to die policy:

1. The emphasis should be on the patient's own perception of
   what is morally required to preserve dignity and humanness. This can best be attained by basing any legislation on
   the well-established principle of the right to refuse treatment, rather than on some other agent's actions or omissions.
2. While it may not always be moral to refuse treatment, the
   principle of individual freedom requires that it should be
   legal for any competent dying patient to do so. Refusal of
   treatment as such should not be considered evidence of
   legal incompetency in a patient or a patient's agent.
3. The decision to refuse treatment as much as possible
   should be made on an ad hoc rather than an anticipatory
   basis to minimize difficulties arising from vagueness in individual expression.
4. The policy should be limited to allowing to die because of
   three factors: the theoretical ethical differences between

the positive active hastening of death and the omitting or stopping of treatment, the increased danger of abuse with allowing the direct and active hastening of death, and the rarity of cases in which there would be a moral preference for active hastening of death. (This should not exclude providing treatment to relieve suffering which might indirectly hasten death.)

5. The line of authority should place decision making as much as possible in the hands of the individual. The next most appropriate decision maker is an agent appointed for the purpose by the patient while of sound mind. Relatives then should be given the responsibility in order of degree of kinship.

6. The physician should never be placed in the position of deciding to stop or omit treatment.

7. In the rare cases where there is neither expression from the dying patient, agent for the patient, nor relatives, the courts should appoint a guardian whose sole responsibility shall be to serve the best interests of the patient.

8. No medical personnel should be required to participate in any course of action that would be morally objectionable to them.

9. All patients should be informed of their rights as patients including the right to refuse any medical treatment.

On the basis of these principles, I propose the following as model legislation for facilitating the decision to refuse treatment even when it leads to the death of the patient.

A Draft Bill to Permit Refusal of Medical Treatment

1. A physician shall not legally cease life-supporting treatment of a patient unless so authorized according to the provisions of the act.

2. An individual shall, while legally competent, (continue to) have the right to refuse any specific medical treatment on the grounds that his own dying process cannot morally be prolonged. Such refusal shall not in and of itself be taken as evidence of legal incompetency.

3. When an individual is determined to be legally incompetent for the purpose of making such a decision, the authority to refuse medical treatment on the grounds that the dying process cannot be morally prolonged shall rest:

   a) First, with an agent legally appointed for such purposes by the individual while legally competent.

   b) Second, with the spouse or person of first degree kinship, or

   in the event of two (2) persons of first-degree kinship, both such persons or

   in the event of three (3) or more persons of first-degree kinship, the majority of those persons.

   c) Third, if the person is legally incompetent and there be no next of kin, with a legal guardian appointed by the court to preserve the best interests of the patient.

4. In determining the authority of the patient's agent in cases of incompetency (including the authority of the agent of first-degree kinship), the court shall honor any document of the patient executed with the same formalities as required by law for the execution of a last will and testament, stating grounds for which he would want an agent disqualified. Such grounds may expressly include judgments about when life-prolonging treatment should be accepted.

5. Any patient entering an agreement for medical care must be informed of his right to be treated and to refuse treatment.

6. No medical personnel shall be legally guilty of any offense when acting in good faith without negligence in accordance with this bill.

7. No medical personnel shall be required to participate in any treatment or care of a patient in accord with the provisions of this bill which they find morally objectionable pro-

vided that they withdraw from the case and inform the patient and other available medical personnel of their withdrawal.

The bill as proposed is a modest one. It is based on the already existing right of the patient to refuse treatment, but will expand the legal acceptability of that act so that refusal of treatment for the dying patient would not in and of itself be taken as evidence of incompetency even for those patients who have dependents. The bill provides for actions on behalf of the incompetent patient which are most likely to conform to the patient's own moral judgments by placing responsibility first in someone appointed by the patient for the purpose and then in family who have traditionally borne a special obligation to protect the individual's welfare.

The bill will not in itself make legal the active hastening of death by direct action to end life even when requested by the patient, as is done in the Idaho bill. This introduces moral, practical, and political problems that would jeopardize the entire bill and remove safeguards built in against some actions to end the life of the living on less than moral grounds. Until it can be shown that there are a significant number of instances where active ending of life is morally preferable to withdrawal of treatment (as in a hypothetical case of intractable pain not treatable by high doses of narcotics), I feel there are greater moral risks in legalizing such positive action than in continuing the legal prohibition. The first authority for decision making on behalf of an incompetent patient would go to an agent appointed for that purpose by the individual while still legally competent. If our first priority is to protect the individual's interests and moral judgments, this will provide an important safeguard in those rare cases where an individual fears that the next of kin might act maliciously or foolishly or in cases where there are two relatives of equal degree of kinship and the individual prefers to designate one of them as the agent.

The fourth paragraph adds an anticipatory dimension to the draft bill. It is the only part of the bill, other than the provision for possible appointment of a legal agent, which is prospective. This provision would permit an individual to give specific instructions for the qualification of the patient's agent, whether a relative or court-appointed. This would be significant only in that rare case where an individual knows that relatives have serious disagreement over the refusal of treatment for the terminally ill patient and the individual wants to rule in or out certain perspectives. For instance, an elderly man might have several siblings whose survival is unpredictable. Since he would be unable to predict who would be in the first degree of kinship and what the majority opinion of the group might be, he might want to give instructions to refuse or continue treatment if he should ever be in an irreversible coma or be suffering from inoperable cancer.

The possibility of seemingly immoral actions by the patient's agent or next of kin still remains with the proposal. For this reason I have not included a provision to make it impossible for medical personnel or others with legal standing to go to court and have the patient's agent declared incompetent. At present parents sometimes refuse lifesaving treatment for their young children solely on religious grounds when, say, a transfusion would insure a normal lifespan for the child. The recourse is a court action declaring the parents unsuitable guardians for the purpose of refusing treatment. It seems to me that there is no safe way to remove this possibility for overriding the patient's agent. The bill should, however, recognize the moral and legal legitimacy of refusal of treatment for the dying patient. I feel that with such a policy clearly stated in law, the ordering of treatment by the courts can and would be limited to the truly exceptional case where treatment would not reasonably be seen as useless or burdensome for the patient.

Such a bill will not solve all of the moral dilemmas in the care of the dying, but I believe that it will minimize the moral risks and preserve in the best possible way the freedom, dignity, and humanness of the dying patient.

Of all the proposals which have been introduced into state legislatures thus far of which I am aware, the bill introduced in 1972 by Representative Holliday in West Virginia comes closest to my own policy conclusions. It is a bill that upholds the right to refuse treatment on the basis of patient ad hoc decision making, and in cases of incompetency the decision is made by those of the closest degree of kinship. The West Virginia bill differs from mine in several details, however.

First, refusable treatment is limited to "artificial, extraordinary, extreme or radical medical or surgical means or procedures." Since the legally competent adult patient without dependents already has the right to refuse any treatments whether extraordinary or not, the West Virginia bill may actually be restrictive for these patients. I have discussed the ambiguity of the term *extraordinary means* and suggest that it be dropped in favor of the already existing right to refuse any treatment.

Second, it does not include a provision for the appointment of a patient's agent in those cases where the individual places greater confidence in a relative of lesser degree of kinship, a clergyman, a lawyer, or a personal friend.

Third, it does not provide for anticipatory written instructions by the individual while competent to guide the selection of a guardian to act if the individual should become incompetent.

Fourth, while the bill provides for exemption from legal liability for actions taken in compliance with the refusal of treatment, it does not explicitly grant the right to withdraw from a case because of moral objection to the actions or omissions required.

Finally, there is no provision specifying that patients shall be informed of their right to refuse treatment.

6

She'll Be Happier if She Never Knows:
The Patient's Right and
Obligation to Have the Truth

It was the first hospitalization for the fifty-four-year-old patient. She was born in Puerto Rico and had lived in Spanish Harlem for the last ten years. She had come to the emergency room two weeks before with a severe pain and a mass in her right lower abdomen. The previous December she had had a severe attack in the same area. Her history revealed she was past menopause. She had worked in a nursing home and so was familiar with medical procedure. A third-year medical student obtained the pertinent material in her medical history and talked with her briefly. She told him that she was afraid that she had cancer. When the student assured her that she would have a complete work-up, she replied sadly, "If it was cancer you doctors wouldn't tell me." The student did not comment on the patient's statement, but said that the lab test and examinations would tell them much more about the possible causes of the pain and mass.

Two days later, after the patient had been examined by the medical students, the resident, the chief resident, and the attending physician, the diagnosis was made of a degenerating fibroid. This would explain the severe pain and the mass, although it was pointed out that after menopause the most common cause of a painful mass was cancer.

The patient went to surgery Wednesday morning. The medical student spoke to the resident the same day, who reported that she had stage IV cancer of the cervix. They had cleaned out all the tumor they could see, but since the tumor had spread to the pelvic wall, the only alternative was to try chemotherapy and radiation. The five-year survival rate of stage IV cancer is zero to twenty percent.

When the patient awoke from the surgery, the medical student's first reaction was to go to her and explain the findings. He felt he should speak frankly with her, attempt to share the grief, and be there to support her. However, since he had not had much experience with cancer and this was his first patient "who had been given a death notice," he decided to speak first to the chief resident about how best to approach telling this woman. The medical student explained that he wanted to tell the patient that she had cancer, and that he felt close enough to her to share some of the process. The chief resident's reaction was agitated. "Never use the word 'cancer' with a patient," he said, "because then they give up hope." He suggested using other words or medical jargon.

The student was in turmoil. He felt it was important to convey to the patient what he knew himself—according to their best medical understanding of her condition—she had a limited time to live. New biomedical technology and medical discoveries meant that there were several possible treatments, which would be tried. And new discoveries are continually being made. But he wanted to convey to her that the chances were that she would not live out her normal lifespan—in fact, she would not survive more than a few years.

The discussion got more heated. The resident angrily asked, "I'd like to know how you'll feel when the patient jumps out the window." The student's response was that he felt he had to evaluate the patient's desire to know and that this woman had given a clear message that she wished to know.

The resident told the young student a story about a distinguished internist, senior attending physician on their service, and internationally known as author of a major medical textbook, who while on grand rounds asked if there was anyone present who would tell the patient they had just seen that he had cancer. When one medical student raised his hand, the internist, who was the grand and awesome old patriarch of the medical school, said, "You march down to the Dean's office and tell him that I said you are to be kicked out of medical school." Since an authoritarian and often hostile relation between master and student is not unusual in the clinical teaching setting, the student took him very seriously and turned toward the door. At that point the internist said, "Now you know what it's like to be told you have cancer. Tell a patient that, and it will destroy the last years of his life."

The student left the meeting with the resident wondering what should be told to the patient and who should do the telling. He had a good idea what would be said by the senior attending, by the resident, and by himself.

THE UTILITARIAN CASE FOR WITHHOLDING THE TRUTH

Physicians are strongly committed, in the ideal at least, to protecting patients from potential harm, both physical and mental. According to one important study already mentioned, 88 percent of physicians responding reported that they follow a usual policy of not telling patients that they have cancer.[1] Some of these physicians may have decided not to tell for irresponsible reasons: to tell someone he is about to die is not a pleasant task and can be time-consuming. But physicians for the most part are morally dedicated to the principle of judiciously withholding information that they feel would do serious harm to the patient. To transmit it would violate their medico-moral responsibility to do what they consider to be in the best interests of their patient. The Hippocratic Oath has the physician pledge to follow that regimen which, "according to my ability and judgment, I consider for the benefit of my patients, and abstain from whatever is deleterious and mischievous." Bernard Meyer, a physician who has written on the ethics of what should be told to the terminal patient, says:

> Ours is a profession which traditionally has been guided by a precept that transcends the virtue of uttering truth for truth's sake; that is, "So far as possible, do not harm." [2]

1. Donald Oken, "What to Tell Cancer Patients: A Study of Medical Attitudes," *Journal of the American Medical Association* 175 (1961), pp. 1120–28.

2. Bernard C. Meyer, "Truth and the Physician," in *Ethical Issues in Medicine: The Role of the Physician in Today's Society,* ed. E. Fuller Torrey (Boston: Little, Brown, 1968), p. 176.

The medical student who wondered what to tell the woman who had carcinoma of the cervix faced the same argument.

This kind of moral argument is a particular type—well known to those familiar with ethical theory. We might call it situational, individualistic, utilitarianism.

First, the argument of the physician is utilitarian in that it looks to the consequences of the act of telling or not telling. The primary or sole concern is the potential benefit or harm in a course of action. The ethics of cost/benefit calculus is a subject of very long and confusing debate.[3] Utilitarians worth their salt will extend costs and benefits well beyond the economic to include physical factors of pain and suffering and even psychological factors such as happiness, anxiety, depression, and fear. In the ethical debate over whether to keep a terminal patient alive by using marginal or heroic means, the economic factor may have weight in a utilitarian argument, although many using this mode of reasoning would claim that the noneconomic factors so outweigh the economic ones as to make the monetary considerations practically irrelevant even in those cases. But in the case of what to tell the dying patient, a calculation of utility will focus on the factors of happiness, anxiety, and hope.

There is a special twist to the utilitarian ethics of the physician.[4] One summary of the physician's special moral duty is "Above all preserve life." One understanding of this principle is that life has such ultimate value and is to be so heavily weighted on the utilitarian calculus that other goods are trivial by comparison. The resident in the case under consideration is arguing that if the patient is told, she might commit suicide. This is an often made claim, but to my knowledge without documentation. Nevertheless, the resident may be saying that he thinks that if the patient is told, she will commit suicide, and that is the ultimate bad consequence—at least for those in

3. Richard B. Brandt, *Ethical Theory* (Englewood Cliffs, N. J.: Prentice-Hall, 1959); Michael D. Bayles, *Contemporary Utilitarianism* (Garden City, New York: Doubleday, 1968); Ernest Albee, *A History of English Utilitarianism* (New York: Collier Books, 1962); David Lyons, *Forms and Limits of Utilitarianism* (Oxford: Oxford University Press, 1965).

4. Of course, not all physicians share the dominant views outlined here.

the practice of medicine. If this is his argument, he is using a special utilitarianism in which the "goods" and "harms" are given a special weighting. The possibility of provoking suicide throws the scales completely off balance in favor of not telling.

Others using the utilitarian mode of ethical reasoning do not consider it the physician's primary duty to preserve life at all. Rather it is to prevent harm. For them the prevention of psychological harms—suffering, fear, and especially anxiety— are paramount. This is probably the dominant, normative, ethical theory operating in medicine. Yet it is not utilitarianism of the Mill-Moore school pure and simple. At least according to some physicians, there is a greater imperative to prevent harm than there is to produce good. This is often quite a conservative moral principle—one that would lead ultimately to never doing anything for any patient—but one that has played an extremely important role in medical ethics. W. D. Ross makes a similar sort of argument with similar antiinterventionist results.[5] He argues that to give special consideration to harms over benefits is to deviate from the simple utilitarianism of Mill and Moore. For him this deviation is morally required, because there is a special imperative to eliminate harms. There are serious problems with this kind of ethical weighting, but Ross is certainly correct in observing that it requires a deviation from simple utilitarianism. Thus the argument that the physicians presented to the medical student are utilitarian, but of a special sort.

Secondly, the physician's mode of ethical reasoning is situational to the extent that it focuses on the individual case as a unique moral entity. Any overarching rule such as "always tell the truth" or "truth for truth's sake" is unacceptable. This is certainly Meyer's position and probably that of the resident in our case although he says *never* use the word *cancer*. The attending physician seems to be less of a situationalist in saying, "Don't ever tell a patient if he has cancer. It will always destroy the last years of his life."

Finally, the physician's mode of ethical reasoning is individ-

5. W. Ross, *The Right and the Good* (Oxford: Oxford University Press, 1939).

ualistic. The Hippocratic Oath says that the physician's duty is to act for the benefit of the patient, not for the relatives, for patients as a whole, or for society. This then is still another modification of classical utilitarianism. For Mill [6] or Bentham [7] the morally required act is the one that produces the greatest total amount of good—"the greatest good for the greatest number." The physician, ideally, if not in practice, is committed to producing the greatest good for one individual—the patient. In the case of the dying patient, the physician believes the primary moral consideration should be to prevent anxiety, to stave off death (prevent suicide), or maintain the patient's hope. Under this kind of moral system, most physicians—or at least 88 percent of those in Oken's study—conclude that they should tend not to tell patients of a terminal cancer diagnosis when they find it.

The Formalist's Case for the Principle of Truth-Telling

The first and most obvious countervailing principle to the physicians' avoidance of harm by not telling the patient of a terminal diagnosis, is the common moral principle that there is a duty to tell the truth—at least under certain conditions. According to the upholders of this principle, even if withholding information from the dying patient would prevent harm (like suffering) or preserve life, one would still have to ask whether withholding or deceiving the patient is right.

Divorcing the rightness of withholding information from the good consequences produced (or the bad consequences prevented) is fundamental to the ethical instincts of many. Kant argues:

> An action done from duty has its moral worth, not in the purpose to be attained by it, but in the maxim in accordance with which it is decided upon; it depends, therefore, not on the realization of the object of the action, but

6. John Stuart Mill, *Utilitarianism.*
7. Jeremy Bentham, *An Introduction to the Principles of Morals and Legislation.*

solely on the principle of volition in accordance with which, irrespective of all objects of the faculty of desire, the action has been performed.[8]

Put bluntly by Kant, "The moral worth of an action does not depend on the result expected from it." Kant applies this to the defense of the inherent rightness of telling the truth in his essay "On the Supposed Right to Lie from Altruistic Motives" he claims:

> The duty of being truthful . . . is unconditional. . . . Although in telling a certain lie I do not actually do anyone a wrong, I formally but not materially violate the principle of right. . . . To be truthful (honest) in all declarations, therefore, is a sacred and absolutely commanding decree of reason, limited by no expediency.

> Thus the definition of a lie as merely an intentional untruthful declaration to another person does not require the additional condition that it must harm another. . . ."[9]

The inherent rightness of telling the patient the truth is a simple principle, one which may be retained or rejected by individuals according to their normative ethical position. While views on the subject appear never to have been tested empirically, it seems that physicians, being committed (theoretically) to the utilitarianian principle of working for the benefit of the patient, are particularly skeptical of the moral relevancy of the "truth for truth's sake" principle. On the other hand, many laymen are not so willing to discard it, especially on matters so fundamental as life and death. If patients and their physicians evaluate the validity of the truth-telling principle differently, it is only logical that they may differ on what a patient with a cancer diagnosis should be told.

Even those who would not want to discard the principle that

8. Immanuel Kant, *Groundwork of the Metaphysics of Morals,* trans. and analyzed by H. Paton (New York: Harper and Row, 1964), pp. 67–68.

9. Immanuel Kant, *On the Supposed Right to Lie from Altruistic Motives,* 1797. I shall discuss below the possible difference between the outright lie and merely withholding information.

truth-telling is justified on grounds of inherent obligation might not be willing to go so far as Kant. It may be that both inherent characteristics and consequences are relevant in determining rightness and wrongness. The technical name for this plausible resolution of the debate is "mixed deontologism." As seen in W. D. Ross and others it is simply the view that there are many factors determining moral rightness. Some characteristics are *prima facie* right-making such as justice in distribution, promise keeping, making restoration for previous wrongs done to another, and, most significant for our purposes, truth-telling. Yet also added to Ross's list of *prima facie* right-making characteristics is production of good (beneficence) and prevention of harm (nonmaleficence).[10] If we accept this position, we at least include the requirement to tell the truth as one of the relevant factors but we also examine the consequences. However, are there also some consequences leading to the conclusion that the patient should be told?

THE UTILITARIAN CASES FOR TRUTH-TELLING

Short-Range Personal Utility

In the earlier discussion of possible consequences from the action of telling the truth, we considered the harms (anxiety, suffering, and possible suicide) which might result. Both the utilitarian and the mixed deontologist, however, would be required to examine the possible bad consequences of not telling as well.

Most obvious is the general malaise that comes from not knowing one's condition. Lack of knowledge about whether the lump in the chest means death or means nothing can generate oppressive anxiety. Psychological variables like happiness and anxiety are hard, if not impossible, to measure. Most of the anecdotal reporting of the severe harm or great benefits of telling patients seems to be little more than evidence of bad scientific observation. Fitts and Ravdin, in a study of physi-

10. Ross, *The Right and the Good*, p. 21.

cians' views on what to tell cancer patients reported the comments of several. One declared:

> I feel strongly against letting the patient know he has cancer! To all people, intelligent or not, the word cancer means a death sentence, and, even if you meet an occasional patient who insists on knowing the worst and says that it will not affect him one way or another, he will be mentally affected by knowing the worst.[11]

But another seemed to have a different experience.

> I always tell the patient he has cancer. In forty years I have had only two instances where the full truth was not well received. . . . All patients can bravely face even death if they know the truth and trust the honesty of the one they have selected to aid. They condemn their physician or even their close family if they discover they have been deceived and will not even trust a favorable prognosis should such be possible. To deceive a patient or even evade a real fact of certain death, is to torture the intelligence of those who will know, even if it be at the very last, that they could trust no one.

Either these two physicians see very different patient populations or they are reading the psychological data very differently. The latter is more likely. To many patients at least, the anxiety from not knowing their diagnosis accurately must be at least as great as that from knowing the terrible truth—at least if the truth is revealed in a humane manner. In contrast to the anecdotal impressions of individual physicians, there are a few surveys of attitudes of larger groups. These surveys, which I shall discuss in detail later in this chapter, show a startling contrast between physicians, who are reluctant to disclose bad news, and patients, who claim to want the truth.

But the psychological factors of happiness and anxiety are not the only benefits and harms to consider. What of the physical? I have already suggested that the fear of provoking suicide may be exaggerated, often existing more in the mind

11. Williams T. Fitts, Jr., and I. S. Ravdin, "What Philadelphia Physicians Tell Patients with Cancer," *Journal of the American Medical Association* 153 (1953), p. 903.

of the death-fearing physician than in the patient. But if many potentially terminal illnesses are treatable so that perhaps several years of happy, productive life can be expected, it seems essential that patients know their real diagnosis and prognosis so that they will faithfully participate in their treatments. Patients whose denials are reinforced by the overly protective physician are denied the opportunity of knowing the seriousness of their conditions. This may, in some instances, lead to the lack of rigorous cooperation in treatment.

While the economic is not to be emphasized, there are cases where lack of knowledge can do serious economic harm to patients' interests. This is true not only in those cases where patients might refuse an expensive and protracted death-prolonging treatment and thus preserve their savings for their families, but in the more simple cases where economic decisions might be made differently if patients knew their real fates. If, for instance, patients are deciding whether to undertake speculative ventures for long-term gain, their decisions under the assumption that a lump is merely an innocent cyst may be totally different from what they would decide if they knew that their venture capital would be their families' sole means of support six months later. At least in some cases very bad decisions will be made when patients lack knowledge of their conditions.

Of course, not all decisions of the dying are of an economic nature. Practicing Roman Catholics, for example, have a duty, not merely a privilege, to prepare for death. Many choices ought to be made to fulfil what they consider their religious obligations. It is safe to say that many other people also believe that they should prepare for an imminent death. While this will not include last sacraments, it does mean preparing or reviewing wills, clarifying business arrangements, and perhaps making a final reconciliation with family members.

Finally, there is another noneconomic good—an ultimate value in many individuals' minds: freedom to control their own lives at least to the extent that it does not impinge on others' freedom. This is fundamental to human nature and applies no less to the dying. To deprive people of information is to deprive them of freedom to make a responsible choice.

This, according to some, is an ultimate harm—a moral outrage. And it is quite probably a violation of constitutionally protected liberties.

All of these consequences of telling and not telling must be added to the calculus of the utilitarian or mixed deontologist to determine the total balance of goods and harms. Even with the normative ethical theory of personalistic utilitarianism—of deciding what to do on the basis of what will benefit patients and protect them from harm—all of these factors must be weighed.

Long-Range Utility

The consequences of telling or withholding the terminal diagnosis do not stop here. The patient we have been discussing was reported to have said, "If it was cancer you doctors wouldn't tell me." Where did she develop this apprehension that she will be lied to? If it is true that 88 percent of physicians would tend not to tell a patient of such a diagnosis, it appears her fears are well founded. Each act of lying or withholding of potentially wanted information from the patient contributes to the general malaise of mistrust. To the physician, who is committed to benefiting only the individual isolated patient dying in the hospital bed at that moment, the significance of the long-range impact of an act is obscured. Nevertheless, any good utilitarian will be very much aware that there is indeed a cumulative, long-range impact from individual deceptions. That is commonsense to the ordinary man, who is concerned to protect his good word even if a little white lie would be quite harmless in the individual case. To many physicians however this long-range consequence is either imperceptible or irrelevant because it falls outside the scope of benefit to the present patient.

One patient, a woman near retirement age, became concerned over a lump in her breast and came to the tumor clinic with some fear. After extensive tests the chief physician called her in for a conference. "We have good news," he said. "The lump is nothing to worry about. You can expect a long and happy life." To this day she has been preparing for her funeral. "If it was cancer, you doctors wouldn't tell me." The medical profession, which has built its ethics on trust and confidence in the personal physician, is in danger of not only undermining confidence in medicine but destroying any workable relationship by perpetuating the image that patients can be lied to whenever it may benefit them. From the childhood innoculations ("This won't hurt a bit") to the published statements of world-famous kidney transplant surgeons that when they encounter potential donors whom they feel would have psychological difficulties, they tell them they have a "tissue incompatibility," the patient is learning, and usually learning correctly, that the medical professional cannot always be trusted.

Henry Sidgwick, one of the great philosophical ethicists of the turn of the century, was a strong defender of the physicians' principle that right and wrong are to be determined solely on the basis of consequence. But Sidgwick recognized that even where "benevolent deception" was thought to be beneficial to the individual patient, it still had to be weighed against the total impact of the individual act of deception. His argument is one which the medical profession has not dealt with adequately. It is summarized in his *Methods of Ethics:*

> The quality denoted by our term [veracity] is admittedly only praiseworthy in so far as it promotes individual or general welfare and becomes blameworthy—though remaining in other respects the same—when it operates adversely to these ends.

> It does not seem clearly agreed whether Veracity is an absolute and independent duty, or a special application of some higher principle. We find (e.g.) that Kant regards it as a duty owed to oneself to speak the truth, because "a lie is an abandonment or, as it were the annihilation of the dignity of man." And this seems to be the view in which lying is prohibited by the code of honour, except that it is not thought (by men of honour as such) that the dignity of man is impaired by *any* lying: but only that lying for selfish ends, especially under the influence of fear, is mean and base. . . .

Where deception is designed to benefit the person deceived, Common Sense seems to concede that it may sometimes be right: for example, most persons would not hesitate to speak falsely to an invalid, if this seemed the only way of concealing facts that might produce a dangerous shock. But if the lawfulness of benevolent deception in any case be admitted, I do not see how we can decide when and how far it is admissible, except by considerations of expediency; that is, by weighing the gain of any particular deception against the imperilment of mutual confidence involved in all violations of truth.[12]

Rule Utility

Even now, with the long-range implications of the individual act taken into account, we have not placed all of the weights on the scales. There is still another type of utility to consider. Over the last two decades there has been an extensive debate over the concept of "rule utilitarianism." [13] According to this view, it is not individual acts which are to be justified by appealing to their consequences, but general rules or practices.[14] To decide each individual act on the basis of a thorough examination of the benefits and the harms it may bring is likely to be impossible. It would require endless calculation, and is cumbersome at best. More than likely it would lead to confusion and lack of predictability in the actions of others because we could never know how they would calculate the benefits in each individual case. To avoid this chaos one opts instead for the general practices (rules) which will maximize the good.

How does the principle of rule utility apply to the decision about what to tell the dying patient? If it is true that physicians would tend not to tell, and 90 percent or more of patients say they want to be told, this suggests that if physicians use their

12. Henry Sidgwick, *The Methods of Ethics* (New York: Dover, 1966), pp. 312–19.

13. See Bayles, *Contemporary Utilitarianism,* and especially Lyons, *Forms and Limits of Utilitarianism.*

14. See John Rawls, "Two Concepts of Rules," *The Philosophical Review* 64 (1955), pp. 3–32.

own judgment about what is in the patient's interests, they may make many mistakes. Physicians, at least nonpsychiatrist physicians, are not trained in determining what is in the patient's interests. The calculation of what is in the patient's interests, the calculation of what is thought to produce the most benefit for the patient, may be wrong in many cases. Human beings are fallible creatures; they make mistakes. In the public realm men are subjected to the rule of law even in those cases where they think their own judgment is better. This is in part because there is value in order and predictability in life and in part because we know from experience that in many cases when individuals try to decide each case situationally they will make many mistakes.

Physicians are often individualists and inveterate situationalists. They pride themselves in their commitment to examine each case individually. Piatt, for instance, offers the classical if dangerous medical ethical platitude in response to his question "What shall the cancer patient be told?"—"Each case is an individual one and what is to be told the patient depends on the personal temperament of the individual." [15] Even Oken, who has provided some of the most dramatic data on the differences between physicians and patients on what should be told, offers the situationalist attenuator, "Intuitive understanding of what the patient experiences is a time proven and essential guide for the physician," although he does temper this with the warning, "instinctive judgments, however, can be terribly misleading." [16] Consequences might be better on the average if the general rule of truth-telling is followed than if fallible physicians try to decide each case individually by what they *think* will benefit the patient. This would be the case especially when patients say explicitly that they want information or even if they refrain from an explicit request that their diagnosis be withheld. The potential goods produced by following a rule which sets up a bias for truth-telling must also be added to the scales in the utilitarian weighing. Thus the short-range utility for the individual patient, the

15. Louis M. Piatt, "The Physician and the Cancer Patient," *Ohio State Medical Journal* 42 (1946), pp. 371–72.
16. Oken, "What to Tell Cancer Patients," p. 1127.

long-range impact on the patient-physician relationship, and the extra utility of following a rule even when it may not appear to be the benefit-maximizing solution all provide consequential reasons why the terminal patient should be told. These should be added to the formalist reasons discussed before.

THE CONTRACT THEORY CASES FOR AND AGAINST TRUTH-TELLING

There is still another moral dimension in the decision whether to reveal potentially meaningful information to the patient whose diagnosis is terminal. This is an inherent *prima facie* moral obligation arising from the relationship between medical professionals and laymen. There are several models for this relationship. Some see the physician as a priest. According to one establishment medical sociologist the doctor's office has "somewhat the aura of a sanctuary." He claims that "the patient must view his doctor in a manner far removed from the prosaic and the mundane." [17] Closely related to the priestly analogy is the view of the physician as parent. According to one senior physician presenting a case in which the medical team was trying to decide what to tell a dying middle-age woman, "Every patient is a dependent child who demands of his physician that he be a good parent." (For some reason the dying patient who is viewed as a child is very often female and the dominating physician's conclusion is, "She'll be happier if she never knows.") In the priestly or parental model of the patient-physician relationship, the physician assumes the role of moral and decision-making authority.

In rebound some offer a second model, a radical critique of the authoritarian pattern. They make the physician a plumber, an engineer plugging in tubes and cleaning out clogged pipes to meet the owner's specifications with no questions asked. This is a dangerous move, laying the groundwork for absolving the medical professional of any moral responsibility.

A third major model tries to equalize the status and author-

17. Robert N. Wilson, *The Sociology of Health: An Introduction* (New York: Random House, 1970), pp. 18, 20.

ity relationship by seeing the patient and physician as engaged in a common task—restoring or maintaining the patient's health. This model is pleasant but a bit utopian. Equality cannot be established by decree. The fact is that for the most part the patient and physician do not share a common status, knowledge, or social background to justify any assumption of a collegial relationship.

The fourth model is one which tries to maintain the shared authority and responsibility in the medical relationship, but without unwarranted assumptions of the collegial model. The patient and physician are seen as entering into something like a contract, often an implied contract, but the more explicit the better. The relationship between contracting parties is one where there will always be differences in abilities, resources, and needs. It is a limited relationship in which each party is committed to certain specific obligations and obtains in return certain goods or rights. Until the day when there can be a more natural sharing of perspectives, the more or less formal contract should be the model for specifying the relationship between patient and physician and protecting each party from potential abuses by the other.

The Contract Case for Withholding Information

It seems to me that the strongest case against telling dying patients their prognosis may be based on the limited rights and obligations of the contractual relationship between patient and physician. No matter what the purpose of the medical relationship, patients approach the professional with some idea of what they hope to gain. They do not turn to the physician for general wisdom on all areas of life. It may be argued that under certain circumstances the physician's advice is being sought about a particular limited condition. The physician has no business meddling in other, more general problems which the patient has not raised. If, for instance, a man came to a physician for the sole purpose of obtaining a physical examination for an insurance form, he might rightfully resent the physician's advice that he needs psychiatric counselling.

A forty-three-year-old woman came to a genetic counseling

center for the sole purpose of having an amniocentesis and prenatal diagnosis for Down's syndrome (mongolism). The chromosome examination that detects whether an extra chromosome is present that would be responsible for Down's syndrome also may discover other chromosomal abnormalities. In this case the genetic counselor did not find the extra chromosome responsible for Down's syndrome, but found an extra Y chromosome making the sex chromosome configuration XYY. There has been some recent and inconclusive speculation that this extra Y might correlate with antisocial aggressive behavior. No one is sure and some studies have failed to find the correlation. In this case there was a substantial debate in the center over what, if anything, the physician should tell the client. The benefits and harms of both telling and not telling were argued. There could be serious psychological damage if the mother was conditioned to look for antisocial behavior in her child. There would be anxiety in awaiting for behavior patterns to emerge. On the other hand, the woman could choose to abort if she had the information; her freedom of choice would be limited by withholding. Furthermore, if she were to gain the information from some other source, the trusting relationship between patient and physician would be destroyed. In short, consequentialist arguments were brought forth both for and against telling. Of course, the nonutilitarian formalist argument for the inherent value of truth-telling was also introduced.

In addition, however, it was argued that the woman came to the genetic counselor for one and only one reason. She wanted to know if her child was to be born with Down's syndrome. One genetic counselor argued that to go beyond this and meddle in another area (the XYY configuration) was well beyond the "contract." Even in this case, of course, one would have to establish that the woman really wanted only information about Down's syndrome and did not really want any other possibly meaningful and relevant genetic information the test would find. Counselors doing an amniocentesis and chromosomal analysis had better determine the exact scope of the agreement before making any such test—especially if they think they might be inclined not to reveal some findings.

With all of this in mind, the contractual limitation of the patient-physician relationship is too crucial to discount completely. If there is any reason for withholding information from a patient, this may be it.

Would this same contractual limitation ever apply to the case of patients with terminal diagnoses? It seems that in most cases the relationship between such patients and their physicians would be much more involved than the genetic counseling case. Physicians are dealing with the total disease process and only under very limited circumstances would the diagnosis and prognosis be outside the realm of the relevant. One such case, which we shall take up later in this chapter, might be where a patient specifically requests that he not be informed if the news is bad or even that he not be informed under any circumstances. A second more obvious case where the contractual relationship might justifiably limit the disclosure of known prognosis is that of a consultation. The physician who sees the patient casually for physical therapy or a neurology consultation or radiation therapy is probably limited by the "contract" from disclosing much that would be appropriate or even obligatory for the primary physician to disclose. If, however, the consulting physician feels that the primary physician is not fulfilling the obligation to discuss some condition with the patient, then the moral right and obligation to disclose may become much greater.

The Contract Case against Withholding Information

Of course, the same contract may require that the diagnosis and prognosis of a terminal illness be disclosed to the patient (with the obvious qualification that it be done in a sensitive and meaningful way). A contract is a set of mutual promises. A contractual relationship rests upon mutual trust and confidence that those promises will be fulfilled. If a patient approaches a medical professional with a problem and there is a finding which is in any way potentially useful and meaningful to the patient, it seems clear that there is an implied understanding in the contract that the patient will receive the information. In rare cases there may be a mutual agreement to

exclude certain factors from the discussion, but those com-
munications and agreements are special clauses in the contract
which raise special problems to be discussed below. Barring
such communication that an area is out of bounds, certainly
the physician must assume that, if the information is of any
potentially significant use or meaning to the patient, it should
be disclosed. Certainly a terminal prognosis must fall under
the category of potentially meaningful if not useful. To do
other than communicate with the patient is a violation of the
trust and confidence upon which the contract is based. According to this line of argument, the contract model of the
medical relationship provides a strong *prima facie* case against
withholding any potentially significant information.

THE BIG LIE

We have now examined a number of arguments both for
and against telling patients of their cancerous conditions and
prognoses. Obviously, there will be differences on the proper
conclusion in each case. The individual decision about what is
right and what is wrong will depend upon how one fills in the
data, the extent to which different moral factors are present or
absent in a given case, and one's implicit weighing and balanc-
ing of competing claims. One first has to decide how much
good and how much harm will be done by each alternative
and then how significant those goods and harms are for the
moral conclusion.

Before discussing the different ways physicians and laymen
carry out that process of evaluation, we need to give attention
to a serious problem, a kind of lying which far exceeds any
deception of the patient: the physician's own self-deception. I
call this the "big lie," a lie so big that it even fools the liar.

The big lie can take many forms. Five are discussed here.

The truthful lie.   The truthful lie seems to fool many physicians. One of the best ways to avoid the guilt of lying and at
the same time avoid the discomfort (to physician or patient) of
disclosing anything is simply to tell the truth, in fact, to tell it
in a very complete and scientific way. One physician discussing
what to tell a patient after abdominal surgery said he would

THE RIGHT AND OBLIGATION TO HAVE THE TRUTH

have no problem if the patient insisted on knowing. He would tell him he had a neoplasm with the characteristics of a leiomyosarcoma with possible secondary metastatic growth. Nothing could be more true and yet communicate less truth to the patient. To simply tell the patient he had a cancer in a kind and gentle way would be less precise but perhaps more honest. Unfortunately many physicians are able to fool even themselves into thinking that rapid spewing of jargon, preferably with words as polysyllabic as possible, fulfills their obligation to their patients and themselves. It seems far preferable to tell the bold-faced lie to the patient and at least know yourself what you are doing.

We'll never know for sure. A physician was discussing the case of a fourteen-year-old boy with leukemia. He introduced the case with the remark that there was not a chance that this boy would live another six months. He then commented that no one would think of telling him the horrible truth because the boy was still happy, was involved with his school work, and was planning to be a doctor—an ambition which must be seen very positively by the physician. When asked what he was telling the boy and why he felt that the prognosis should not be disclosed, he remarked rather defensively that it would be bad science and bad medicine to say that he had a 100 percent chance of dying soon. "After all, we have seen stretcher cases who we thought did not have a chance and they walked out of the hospital six months later. Miracles happen sometimes, you know."

Of course miracles happen, that is to say, our best scientific prognoses are sometimes still in error. It is wrong to tell a patient that there is 100 percent chance of dying soon if there is not. But that does not explain why the physician did not have the obligation to communicate the real picture to the patient in the best and most gentle way he could. It is indeed bad science and bad medicine to tell a patient he has no chance of surviving six months and it would take a miracle to save him. In fact one wonders about the initial comment of the physician who confidently said, "He doesn't have a chance." That we will never know precisely and without any doubt whatsoever is a solid reason for never telling a patient, "We know for sure; there is no doubt whatsoever." It does not justify, however, failure to convey in a sympathetic and meaningful way what the picture is to the best of the physician's knowledge with all of the proper qualifications including the possibility that a miracle will happen.

A more perverse form of this type of self-deception might be called the overoptimistic hope for the best. It at times becomes so clearly untruthful that it borders on a lie of the plain, ordinary type but, at least in some cases, the expression of hope in the face of a cancer diagnosis can be a "big lie," that particularly malicious form which seems to fool even the physician. Lund begins with a case of what we have called "the truthful lie." He parlays this into what is most probably overoptimistic hope for the best:

> Certainly at the start of the interview he should avoid the words carcinoma or cancer. He should use cyst, nodule, tumor, lesion, or some loosely descriptive word that has not so many frightening connotations. He should then suggest that the operation is indicated and give some rough idea of the extent of the operation. If the consent is given at this stage, this is enough. But he should inform the most interested relative that there is only a 50 per cent chance of a successul outcome. [If the patient fails to consent], however, no bridges have been crossed and many resources are still open to the doctor to secure consent for proper treatment. In one case the matter may be presented to the family and the family doctor who can take over at this point and who can frequently present the situation in such a light that the patient will consent. . . . It seems clear that the doctor can only fully meet his obligation to the patient if she makes her final decision after being put in possession of as close an approximation to the truth as can fairly be conveyed to her. One should, at least, state that the lesion is in imminent danger of becoming a cancer and that a good chance of cure still remains if action is immediate. If the patient asks directly, "Is this cancer?" the doctor is forced to answer, "Yes," but can always go on to explain in the same sentence, "but it prob-

ably is not as serious as you fear because you have a good chance of cure." [18]

This rather clever playing with the truth begins with a compulsive avoidance of language meaningful to the patient and a recognition of a 50 percent chance of survival, yet ends with an optimism that can hardly be called "as fair an approximation of the truth as can be conveyed." This kind of open and cavalier manipulation of the truth and of consent can only destroy what trust and confidence remains in the patient-physician relationship.

Meyer cites with apparent approval a case of planned overoptimism of a similar sort. He calls it "a carefully modulated formulation that neither overtaxes human credulity nor invites despair:

> A doctor's wife was found to have ovarian carcinoma with wide-spread metastases. Although the surgeon was convinced she would not survive for more than three or four months, he wished to try the effects of radiotherapy and chemotherapy. After some discussion of the problem with a psychiatrist, he addressed himself to the patient as follows: to his surprise, when examined under the microscope the tumor in her abdomen proved to be cancerous; he fully believed he had removed it entirely; to feel perfectly safe, however, he intended to give her radiation and chemical therapies over an indeterminate period of time. . . .[19]

While he may not have overtaxed the patient's credulity, he certainly has overstretched the truth in the case. The fact that his prognosis was unduly pessimistic and the patient lived longer than he had predicted does not seem to justify deceiving the patient and probably himself as well.

"You can't tell a patient everything."   The third way in which some physicians seem to deceive themselves is by arguing that the facts about a patient's case are literally infinite and futher-

---

18. Charles C. Lund, "The Doctor, the Patient and the Truth," *Annals of Internal Medicine* 24 (1946), pp. 957–58.

19. Meyer, "Truth and the Physician," p. 173.

more they are extremely complicated. The exact nature of the illness and prognosis would be impossible for a patient to understand and literally impossible for a physician to disclose. Of course this is true, but no one, or at least no one who has thought about the situation at all, ever claims that the physician's duty is to tell the patient "everything." The fact that the physician cannot tell everything does not, however, affect the obligation which may exist to tell that information which potentially may be meaningful and useful or of interest to the patient in his or her condition. The infinite range of possible facts about a patient's case will mean that the physician will have to do some selecting. There is no way around that, and some borderline pieces of information may be difficult to evaluate, but certainly the impending death of the patient can never be confused with such trivia. To claim that some information must be classified as too trivial to tell the patient in no way justifies withholding everything from the patient, including that which is rather obviously potentially meaningful or useful.

Lying and withholding information. In discussing the decision to end the prolongation of dying, we examined the difference between the direct action which brings about the hastening of death and the mere omission or withdrawal of treatment which, provided there is an inherent terminal morbidity, leads to the same result. This difference between an action and an omission is sensed even more readily on the verbal level. Physicians discussing the disclosure of information to the dying patient will, upon occasion, say they could never lie to the patient, but they sometimes fail to tell all that they know. Sachs for instance states, "Do not tell the patient all you know or all you think you know." [20] He says he even refuses to tell patients whether their blood pressure is five or ten points higher or lower for fear of alarming them.

In our discussion of actions and omissions I concluded that actions assign responsibility for the result invariably to the actor, while omissions may or may not, depending upon the relationship of the actor to the recipient of the action. The

20. B. Sachs, "Be An Optimist," *Journal of Mount Sinai Hospital* 8 (1942), pp. 323–25.

same applies in the direct telling of the lie and the mere withholding of information. Physicians who tell the outright lie
normally seem to feel that they have done something that is
prima facie morally wrong. They very well may justify it on the
grounds that the greater good is done to the patient, but they
will probably try to avoid such actions if they can. Withholding
information is treated quite differently, however. Instead of
using one of the earlier forms of the big lie (fancy language,
the claim that miracles might happen, or the claim that you
can't possibly tell all) they may simply refuse to communicate a
piece of information significant to the patient. The omission
is felt to be not nearly as offensive as the outright direct lie.

While there is some validity in this distinction, just as there
is in the distinction between killing a patient and omitting or
withdrawing treatment, it may be greatly overplayed. The responsibility for an omission is dependent upon the relationship of actors. If the patient is in contact with the physician for diagnosis, prognosis, and treatment of an illness the
physician believes to be terminal, a contractual relation is established. It is hard to see how the physician could argue it did
not include the responsibility for disclosing potentially meaningful or useful information. In this sense withholding meaningful information differs significantly from withholding
treatment a patient has refused. While withholding information is an omission for which one is responsible—because the
patient has a right to expect such information to be transmitted, withholding a treatment refused by the patient can hardly
be a culpable act. In fact there seems to be an affirmative duty
not to treat if consent is lacking. The relationship of physician
to patient in the case of transmitting information is one where
omissions may produce culpability on a par with direct action.
The physician may want to argue that the deception is justified—to save the patient's life, to preserve hope, or to promote some treatment program—but the act-omission distinction cannot be used to soften the moral act of deception.
Physicians are lying to themselves if they think they have
avoided moral culpability simply because they have engaged in
an omission instead of a positive lie.

Indirect Communication.   Once a physician recognizes some moral obligation to tell the truth, the second line of defense is a claim that a communication is "indirect." This is a platitude which may or may not be justified. Information is sometimes communicated more effectively in a less blunt and more indirect manner. Lund, for instance, says, "This must always be done gently, and perhaps, indirectly." [21] William May has suggested that there are at least four types of discourse available: (1) direct, immediate, blunt talk; (2) circumlocution or double-talk; (3) silence (which he points out can be a mode of sharing, but often is a way of evading); and (4) discourse that proceeds by way of indirection.[22] He claims that we often assume that "direct, immediate, blunt talk is the only alternative to evasive silence and circumlocution." He gives as an example the perceptive recognition that the questions, "Should I marry or buy a house?" may really be an indirect search for a clue from patients about their diagnosis. A simple "No" he claims would make discussion impossible, but saying that one recognized the importance of the question leads to further discussion of uncertainties, anxieties, and fears. The language of indirection, he says, is appropriate because death is a sacred event, one which requires a special language.

Yet when does the language of indirection become the language of avoidance and self-deception? Often one hears the excuse that the patient seems to know anyway as a justification for avoiding the difficult subject. But the language of indirection is a dangerous language to speak, perhaps more dangerous than simple, direct communication. It is not an adequate substitute for the real alternative, which is not "direct, immediate, blunt talk," but direct talk that is gentle, considerate, and open. Even this is no guarantee that the patient has received the truth, but it at least provides some assurance that the physican is not self-deceived in feeling justified in failing to communicate.

While it may be justifiable to lie to a patient or withhold the truth in some cases, the big lie, the lie in which physicians fool themselves as much or more than their patients, cannot be jus-

21. Lund, "The Doctor, the Patient and the Truth," p. 958.
22. William F. May, "The Sacral Power of Death in Contemporary Culture," *Social Research* 39 (1972), pp. 484–85, 463–88.

tified under any circumstances. These are cases where self-deception is an element—in the truthful lie, in claims that miracles do happen, claims that the whole truth is impossible, claims that give excessive weight to the act-omission distinction, and claims that one has communicated indirectly. Before taking up those rare cases where deception may be justified, we first need to examine the apparent gap between professional and lay perceptions of the moral justification of lying or withholding information from the dying patient.

WHY PATIENTS AND PHYSICIANS DIFFER

Physicians and patients tend to differ dramatically on what they say should be told a terminal patient, yet it seems that there has been no study of the views of both groups, in the same setting, using exactly the same questions. The data from those studies which are available are so remarkable, however, that subtle differences, questionnaires, and samples would probably not change the overall pattern that emerges.

There have been two major studies of physicians' attitudes about what the dying patient should be told. Fitts and Ravdin asked 444 Philadelphia physicians, 89 percent of whom responded.[23] They found that 3 percent "always tell" their patients and 28 percent usually do, while 57 percent "usually do not tell" and 12 percent "never do." A serious shortcoming of the study is the undersampling of nonspecialists, who were less likely than average to tell patients, and the oversampling of dermatologists, who were most likely to tell. Thus the percent of physicians telling may actually be even lower.

The second study shows even fewer physicians willing to disclose information. Oken asked 219 physicians affiliated with a major hospital in Chicago to indicate their "usual" policy and the frequency of exceptions to this policy.[24] From the table below, it is clear that only 12 percent usually tell their cancer patients of the diagnosis.

Yet despite these reported opinions of physicians, several

23. Fitts, and Ravdin, "What Philadelphia Physicians Tell Patients with Cancer," pp. 901–04.
24. Oken, "What to Tell Cancer Patients," pp. 1120–28.

TABLE 2 Surveys of Attitudes about Disclosing Cancer Diagnoses

Physicians

Study group	% that tell	% that do not tell
208 Physicians [a]		
"What is your usual policy?"	12	88
"How often do you make exceptions to your rule?"		
Exceptions made:		
"Often"	4	3
"Occasionally"	5	29
"Very rarely"	3	47
"Never"	0	9
Internists	10	90
Surgeons	12	87
Generalists	22	78
364 Physicians [b]	30	70
Dermatology	94	6
Psych-Neurology	60	40
Surgery	41	59
General Practice	30	70
Nonspecialty	25	75
Internists	21	79
Ob/Gyn	19	81
Radiology	12	88

Patients and Other Lay People

Study group	% that tell	% that do not tell	% indefinite
100 Cancer patients [c]	89	6	5
100 Noncancer patients	82	14	4
740 Patients at cancer detection center	98.5	0.9	0.5
105 Patients [d]			
51 Cancer patients	76	24	
54 Noncancer patients	88	12	
560 People [e]	81	11	
183 People aged 50–86 [f]	80	—	

a. Oken, "What to Tell Cancer Patients," pp. 1120–28.
b. Fitts and Ravdin, "What Philadelphia Physicians Tell Patients with Cancer," pp. 901–04.
c. Kelly and Friesen, "Do Cancer Patients Want to Be Told?", pp. 822–26.
d. Branch, "Psychiatric Aspects of Malignant Disease," pp. 102–04.
e. Samp and Curreri, "A Questionnaire Survey on Public Cancer Education Obtained from Cancer Patients and their Families," pp. 382–84.
f. "Over 65," Medical World News (December 11, 1970), p. 32G.

other studies have found patients consistently reporting that they would like to be told. Samp and Curreri asked patients and visitors in a waiting room of a tumor clinic: "If a patient has cancer, should he or she be told this fact?" Of 517 responding to the question with a yes or no answer, 451, or 87 percent, said yes.[25] Branch found that 48 of 54 cancer-free patients (88 percent) reported that they would prefer to be told about their condition.[26]

Kelly and Friesen studied two groups of 100 outpatients, the first, known cancer patients, and the second, patients without known cancer. In the first group, 89 indicated they preferred knowing that they had cancer, 6 said they would rather not, and the remaining 5 were indefinite. In the second group, 82 said they would want to be told, 14 said they would not, and 4 were indefinite.

In another study, when the researchers asked the same question of a group of 760 patients being examined at the cancer detection center of a university hospital, 729 or 98.5 percent wanted to be told, 7 (0.9%) did not, and 4 (0.5%) were indefinite.[27] While it is difficult to ascertain whether patients are expressing their real desires, the data are very strong and consistent. What can account for these dramatic differences? There seem to be three possible answers, all of which may be relevant.

Differing Data

One critical difference between the medical professional and the lay person may be that they are using different data in their decision making. The surveys ask patients and other laymen to report what they want or would want; while the responses are probably reasonably honest, normal subjects who are not facing an immediate prospect of a terminal illness may

25. Robert J. Samp and Anthony R. Curreri, "A Questionnaire Survey on Public Cancer Education Obtained from Cancer Patients and their Families," *Cancer* 10 (1957), pp. 382–84.

26. C. H. Branch, "Psychiatric Aspects of Malignant Disease," *CA: Bulletin of Cancer Progress* 6 (1956), pp. 102–04.

27. William D. Kelly and Stanley R. Friesen, "Do Cancer Patients Want to Be Told?" *Surgery* 27 (June 1950), pp. 822–26.

not really know what they would want in that distant and threatening moment. On the other hand those patients who already know they have a fatal illness might feel compelled to say that they are happier knowing. In surveys asking parents if their children were "wanted," ex post facto reports of what was desired at a previous time are not particularly reliable. To report that a dying man would be happier not knowing the truth would at least be a blow to his ego. But Kelly and Friesen also questioned the patients being examined in a cancer detection center, finding that a dramatic 98.5% said they wanted to be told. It is hard to account for this result by the explanations given for the other groups of lay people.

It may be more plausible, however, to claim that the data may be inaccurate because skewed by a widespread and significant psychological factor operating at the unconsciscious level—patient denial. By its very nature denial is not a type of datum available to the lay people responding to the survey. Yet most physicians consider patient denial of illness and death to be an extremely important phenomenon. It is safe to say that it is an important element in leading typical physicians to judge that they should not tell the usual patient of a terminal diagnosis.

W. A. Crammond, a professor of mental health, in an article, "Psychotheraphy of the Dying Patient," warns that "common defensive manoeuvres are denial, withdrawal, and counterphobia." [28] Freud goes as far as to say, "At bottom, nobody believes in his own death," and his influence on modern psychiatry has been considerable. Meyer warns:

> There is the naive notion, for example, that when the patient asserts that what he is seeking is the plain truth he means just that. But as more than one observer has noted, this is sometimes the last thing the patient really wants.[29]

Aldrich claims that the appropriate way to handle denial is to provide patients with an opportunity to select either acceptance or denial of the truth." [30]

---

28. W. A. Crammond, "Psychotherapy of the Dying Patient," *British Medical Journal* (August 17, 1970), pp. 389–93.
29. Meyer, "Truth and the Physician," p. 169.
30. See ibid., p. 174.

Meyer exemplifies the physician's resistance to generalization about truth-telling in general and fascination with the uniqueness of the individual case we saw earlier when considering the rule-utilitarian basis for truth-telling:

> From the foregoing it should be self-evident that what is imparted to a patient about his illness should be planned with the same care and executed with the same skill that are demanded by any potentially therapeutic measure. Like the transfusion of blood, the dispensing of certain information must be distinctly indicated, the amount given consonant with the needs of the recipient, and the type chosen with the view of avoiding untoward reactions.[31]

This extreme situationalism can be both dangerous and insulting for the patient. In the first place the physician is frequently conditioned to look for subconscious cues from the patient. Yet the reliability of the reading of those data is open to serious question.

A psychiatrist in the United States who has gained much attention for her warm and sensitive dealing with the terminal patient is Elisabeth Kübler-Ross. Dr. Kübler-Ross recognizes denial of death as the first major stage in the psychology of dying.[32] She certainly gives denial a much more significant place than most medical lay people would. She reports one case where a twenty-eight-year-old Roman Catholic woman dying of a terminal liver disease, confronted with her diagnosis before hospitalization, "fell apart" until a neighbor assured her that there was always hope. Dr. Kübler-Ross claimed that in this case the patient "made it quite clear from the very beginning that denial was essential in order for her to remain sane."[33]

Yet, even with her extensive discussion of the need for denial in some patients at a certain stage of their illness, Dr. Kübler-Ross still raises serious problems about the ability of physicians to read denial in their patients:

31. Ibid., p. 172.
32. Elisabeth Kübler-Ross, *On Death and Dying* (New York: Macmillan, 1969), pp. 34–43.
33. Ibid., pp. 38–41.

I am convinced from the many patients with whom I have spoken about this matter, that those doctors who need denial themselves will find it in their patients and that those who can talk about the terminal illness will find their patients better able to face and acknowledge it. The need of denial is in direct proportion with the doctor's need for denial.[34]

This differential perception of denial based on differential need for denial may cause many physicians to conclude that the truth should not be told to the patient. If they are using different data, they may well reach different conclusions.

Different Weighting of Different Kinds of Good

Recognizing that physicians may include denial in the moral calculus raises the more general question of the different kinds of goods considered in deciding the course that will be most likely to benefit the patient. Lay people and physicians seem to differ on what goods they give the most weight. Surgeons and other nonpsychiatric physicians seem to place a unique emphasis on physical health and sheer survival. Perhaps they would not have become physicians if they did not.

There are other goods, however, and a lay person may be more willing to balance health and even survival itself against some of them. Cigarettes, sweets, and excess weight may be definitively demonstrated to be harmful to your health, but many knowing this still prefer the psychological or other benefits and are willing to trade health off for them. It is reasonable to compromise ideal medical care for a kind of care which costs less. A surgeon may justify a deception in order to get the patient to consent to a procedure, saying "We have all seen miracles." Yet the patient might give relatively little weight to that one-in-a-thousand chance of survival and prefer to save his rapidly dwindling estate for his children. Psychiatrists join other physicians in placing great emphasis on mental suffering, depression, and anxiety as crucial factors in deciding whether to withhold the truth from a patient. To argue that

34. Ibid., pp. 28–29.

the patient will suffer, be depressed, or more anxious is often considered a definitive argument against revealing bad news. But in order for that argument to work, at least three things must be true.

First, anxiety and other psychological harm must be weighted heavily in calculating the benefits and harms to be done by telling or not telling. Physicians and especially psychiatrists might give that uniquely heavy weighting to psychological harms, but there is little data comparing the opinions of medical professionals and lay people on this point.

Second, there must be a belief that in fact a great deal of psychological harm is done by telling the patient the terminal diagnosis. Here we do have more evidence although it is not as clear as we would like. In a brief but provocative study by Herman Feifel and his colleagues,[35] physicians' fear of death was measured in depth using a forty-item questionnaire with open-end questions such as "What does death mean to you personally?" The answers were coded independently by two of the investigators, all of whom hold diplomas in clinical psychology and psychiatry. A group of eighty-one physicians was compared with a group of seriously ill and terminally ill patients and another group of ninety-five normally healthy individuals. The physicians were significantly more afraid of death then either the healthy or sick lay people. This was the case even though sixty-three percent of the physicians said they were less afraid of death now than they had been heretofore.

Speculating on the origin of this difference, the authors note that physicians report that they first became afraid of death at a significantly earlier age than the lay people. The major reasons for this were personal accident, threat of death, or personal illness. They speculate that this above-average fear of death may be a factor in physicians' selection of medicine as a career. However, they also compared their findings from physicians with those from a group of medical students and found that the students were more fearful of death than the lay people, but less so than the experienced physicians. This seems to suggest that despite the physicians' reports, part of

35. Herman Feifel et al. "Physicians Consider Death," Proceedings of the American Psychological Association, (1967), pp. 201–02.

the abnormally high fear may be learned through years of daily contact with death and their inability to conquer it.

If physicians do have an unusually high fear of death, as Feifel and his colleagues suggest, and psychological harm, anxiety, and depression are critical factors in their deciding whether the patient would benefit from knowing a terminal diagnosis, it is obvious why physicians as a group would be peculiarly reluctant to tell: the two groups are simply making different estimates of the potential harms in comparison with the benefits. It is not surprising then that this study, like the others, found that the physicians were significantly less willing than the patients to inform others of incurable disease.

Data on the psychological condition of patients who have been given a terminal diagnosis are harder to come by. The fact that 89 percent in the group with known cancer said they preferred knowing implies they had adjusted to the knowledge. This is so too in the findings of a British study by Aitken-Swan and Easson.[36] They found that only 7 percent of 231 patients could be classified as disapproving of the disclosure. Another 19 percent denied having been told, which might be taken as evidence of some patient denial, but it is not clear from the published study whether some of this is attributable to faulty, incomplete, or "indirect" communication by the physicians.

A psychiatrist, Arthur Peck, investigating the emotional reactions of fifty outpatients having cancer found that twenty-seven were also diagnosed as having a psychiatric disorder, but in all but one case the psychiatric disorder antedated the cancer.[37] As would be expected, he did find what he termed emotional stress in the patients. All but one (a devout Jehovah's Witness) showed anxiety. For twenty-two it was labelled severe. Thirty-seven patients were said to have depressed affect, of which five were judged severe. There were also eighteen instances of guilt, with patients feeling that their own ac-

36. Jean Aitken-Swan and E. C. Easson, "Reactions of Cancer Patients on Being Told Their Diagnosis," *British Medical Journal* (March 21, 1959), pp. 779–83.

37. Arthur Peck, "Emotional Reactions to Having Cancer," *CA—A Cancer Journal for Physicians* 22 (September–October 1972), pp. 284–91.

tions had caused them to develop the cancer, and twenty-two instances of overt anger.

The physician discussing the case of the Puerto Rican woman at the beginning of this chapter expressed the well-rumored fear that the patient would jump out the window if told. Stories of suicide following disclosure run rampant in medical school corridors, but when the perpetrators are pressed for documentation the evidence turns out to be remote hearsay. A director of a major suicide prevention center has said that there is no evidence of abnormally high suicide rate after revelation of cancer or other terminal diagnosis, and I have been able to find no such evidence. Peck found that no patient in his group of fifty admitted an attempted suicide and only four had suicidal thoughts, ranging from one patient with firm suicidal intent to others who placed such thoughts completely in the past. For patients in such condition, that rate of suicidal thinking seems remarkably low.

Data measuring patient anxiety and suicidal risk are difficult to interpret. Physicians are quick to point out that patients may not report accurately their true feelings on emotionally charged subjects such as death. They are more reluctant to recognize that the same is true for them. All studies are filtered through the values and psychological biases of the researchers. This gives rise to the startling possibility that the finding that psychiatrists are less willing to tell about terminal diagnoses than laymen may mean exactly the opposite of what it first suggests. Since the critical variables under consideration are psychological—anxiety, depression, guilt and anger—we would hope and expect that psychiatrists would have the most expertise in evaluating the risk of these kinds of harms.

Fitts and Ravdin found that only 60 percent of the Philadelphia psychiatrists and neurologists in their study preferred telling in contrast to the 90 percent of lay people who would want to be told. This suggests that professional judgment about psychological harms inclines experts to be less willing than laymen to reveal terminal diagnoses. Yet the low percentage of psychiatrist-neurologists who prefer telling may have a more subtle explanation. Psychiatrists' views may be seen as being made up of at least two components: professional judgment about psychological risks and general psychosociological characteristics of physicians. If we were to eliminate the general psychosociological characteristics of physicians, there would remain some factor which makes psychiatrists much more willing to tell than others in the class of physicians. This may well be the professional judgment of psychological risk.

Of course there may be other factors. Psychiatrists are known to score low compared with other physicians on the F-scale, which measures authoritarianism, for instance. But this is simply to argue that the views of psychiatrists are based on other extraneous psychosociological characteristics irrelevant to professional judgment of psychological harms. Thus either psychiatrists' views are based predominantly on special values and psychological biases, in which case they should be ignored, or they may indeed be influenced by professional expert judgment about psychological risk. This factor when isolated from the extraneous influences may well point toward telling patients the truth about their condition.

The discussion of suicidal risk and prevention of anxiety presupposes a heavy weighting of physical and psychological harm in the utilitarian calculus in contrast with the other social, cultural, religious, and economic goods and harms that would be given relatively greater weight by others. Different weighting of the significance of anxiety, as well as different levels of fear of death which gives rise to that anxiety, will certainly lead to different moral conclusions about what information should be transmitted and when.

Differing Normative Ethical Principles

All of this discussion assumes that the proper way to make a moral judgment about what should be done is to estimate as accurately as possible the benefits and harms and choose the course most likely to benefit the patient. This personalistic utilitarianism is deeply entrenched in the medical profession: it is seen in the Hippocratic principle that the physician's duty is to do what he thinks will benefit the patient. A third basis for the difference between lay people and physicians over whether patients should be told the truth may be a difference in the overriding moral principles.

For the physician, whether the patient will benefit— physically or psychologically—may well be taken as the definitive factor for telling or not telling the patient. Patients, however, may with all rationality respond that the physician may think they would be "happier" if not told, but still they want (or feel an obligation) to be told. Such patients are simply rejecting the normative ethical principle that the proper course is to be determined by the physician according to what the physician thinks will benefit the patient. The patient may not trust the judgment of the physician, fearing that he is using different data or weighting anxiety too heavily, but even bracketing the paternalism problem, the patient may reject the principle that the physician should do what will indeed make the patient happiest.

Patients may plausibly hold that they have a right or even a duty to know their medical condition even if they will be less happy in knowing. They may feel a duty to their wives or children to make proper arrangements. They may feel a religious obligation to set things in order. They may simply feel a right and duty to knowledgeably exercise self-determination in consenting to their medical treatment in a responsible manner. Even if physicians and patients were to agree on the data used in the utilitarian calculus and also agree on the proper weighting of the different kinds of good incorporated into that calculus, they might still disagree if they were basing their judgments on different moral principles. All three of these factors seem to account for gaping differences between physician and lay judgments in this matter. If one holds that the decision is to be made on the basis of what the physician thinks will benefit the patient and is willing to let the physician use his or her own selection of data (including his or her readings of patient denial whether or not it is actually present) and his or her own weighting of the amount of psychological harm to be done by telling the patient, then the decision to withhold critical information about fatal illness may be justified. If the patient is to be respected, however, we will have to abandon the paternalism of the Hippocratic ethic and recognize the right of patients to have the information necessary for them to make crucial decisions about their own care even if, in some cases, there is some risk of increasing their level of anxiety or driving them into deeper depression. If there is also risk of anxiety and despair from *not* telling patients their conditions there may not be a great deal to lose. But even if there is some risk, disclosure may be required by the need to respect the patient and the individual's right to determine his or her own medical treatment, combined with the inherent duty to tell the truth, the contractual obligations of the professional, and the utilitarian considerations that require disclosure of potentially meaningful and useful information.

THE "EXCEPTIONAL CASES"

To conclude our discussion of the serious gap in general views on truth-telling, we must mention three particularly difficult special cases. The reluctance to telling the truth normally grows out of the paternalism of the physician doing what he thinks is for the benefit of the patient. This stand may be overridden by the benefits which can come from telling, the duty to tell the truth and fulfill contractual obligations, and the right of the patient to self-determination. There may still be some cases, however, where withholding information from the patient may be justified.

When the Family Requests Withholding

A somewhat senile gentleman with a history of cardiac disease has exploratory surgery for a mass thought to be a cyst. After laboratory analysis of the mass it is found to be cancerous. Surrounded by wife, children, in-laws, and grandchildren of various ages, he has received much loving attention. After leaving the patient, the surgeon turns to the spouse and children and asks for advice about what to tell him. There is concern about the patient's health, fear that the shock might trigger another coronary, and perhaps a general aversion to having to discuss death. The wife asks the physician, "Doctor, what do you think is best?" Together they agree with the concurrence of the children that it would be better to let the gentleman continue to believe that the "cyst" was removed so that he can spend his last days in peace.

This scenario is so common that it would not be worth discussing if it did not happen to violate both the most fundamental principles of medical ethics and the laws of many jurisdictions. No one ever seems to ask on what basis the family members are told about a diagnosis of which the patient himself is still ignorant. The World Medical Association's Code of Medical Ethics is blunt in its condemnation of unauthorized disclosure of information: "The doctor owes to his patient absolute secrecy on all which has been confided to him or which he knows because of the confidence entrusted in him." How then can a physician acting in accord with this principle have given the relatives enough information for them to make an informed decision about whether to tell the gentleman of his cancer?

The Hippocratic Oath is, of course, the traditional moral guide of physicians. It squirms so evasively on the question of confidentiality that it offers no help on any difficult question such as whether to tell the patient's family first. It simply says, "Whatever, in connection with my professional practice, or not in connection with it, I see or hear, in the life of men, which ought not to be spoken abroad, I will not divulge, as reckoning that all such be kept secret." So, that which should not be disclosed should not be, and presumably that which should be should be. All of this taken in the context of the overarching Hippocratic benefit-the-patient principle, may be taken to justify violating patient confidentiality by disclosing to relatives first. The Declaration of Geneva, however, which is an updating of the Hippocratic Oath for modern times, is much more blunt. It has the physician pledge: "I will hold in confidence all that my patient confides in me."

American physicians have more loopholes. The Principles of Medical Ethics of the American Medical Association make three specific exclusions to the requirement of confidentiality:

> A physician may not reveal the confidence entrusted to
> him in the course of medical attendance, or the deficien-
> cies he may observe in the character of his patients, unless
> he is required to do so by law or unless it becomes neces-
> sary in order to protect the welfare of the individual or of
> the society.

Here the Hippocratic patient-benefiting principle is made
explicit. If physicians think that patients will benefit, according
to the A.M.A. they apparently have the right to violate their
patients' confidence. The British used to have a similarly
worded clause, but after the famous case where a Dr. Brown
decided it was in the best interests of a sixteen-year-old patient
to disclose to her parents that she was taking birth control
pills, the British Medical Association amended its confidentiality principles to read:

> If, in the opinion of the doctor, disclosure of confidential
> information to a third party seems to be in the best medi-
> cal interest of the patient, it is the doctor's duty to make
> every effort to allow the information to be given to the
> third party, but where the patient refuses, that refusal
> must be respected.

Of course, in deciding whether to tell a patient a terminal
diagnosis, it is impossible in principle to obtain the permission
to disclose to the relatives.

It is apparent that the medical profession is very confused
about its principle of confidentiality where it conflicts with
physicians' perceived duty to do what they think is in their patients' interest. One may legitimately ask why the lay person is
interested in this little publicized and little recognized dispute
within the medical profession. The personal moral opinions of
private citizens—even when those views represent the consensus of a group of professionals—are not in any way binding on other individuals who are not members of that profession. This is less true, however, if the members of that
profession act upon those opinions in their relations with the
lay person often without the lay person's consent or knowledge.

The violation of patient confidentiality may not only infringe the principles of professional medical ethics (at least, unless the A.M.A. exceptions are invoked); independent of that it may violate more universally held moral principles. Also important, in some jurisdictions it may be illegal. The laws on patient-physician confidentiality are extremely complex. In common law the right to privileged communication existed between husband and wife, priest and penitent, and attorney and client, but not between physician and patient. In 1828 New York State enacted the first statute to forbid a physician to disclose any information acquired while attending a patient. Now two-thirds of the states in the United States have such laws. That they are called within the medical profession laws of "privilege" indicates their primary objective: protecting physicians from disclosing against their will information about their patients in a legal proceeding. The legal statutes and case law make clear, however, that if privacy is a privilege, that privilege is the patient's. Only the patient can waive it. Just recently the Supreme Court has adopted in a new set of rules of evidence this regulation:

> A patient has a privilege to refuse to disclose and to prevent any other person from disclosing confidential communications, made for the purposes of diagnosis or treatment of his mental or emotional condition. . . .

These federal rules are now being debated and may be modified over the next few years. In any event, it is an open question whether these and similar state statutes on confidentiality apply to the disclosure of a diagnosis to relatives when the physician feels that the patient's mental condition would not permit the handling of bad news. The laws have not generally been applied to disclosures outside a courtroom although in some cases pretrial disclosures have been interpreted as being illegal. Whether or not such disclosures to relatives are illegal, they may well be in violation of the moral rights and duty of the patient.

Patients have both a right and a duty to consent to their medical treatment based upon reasonable knowledge of their medical conditions. This right and duty cannot be waived on behalf of a mentally competent patient by a spouse, children, or relatives. This, of course, would not apply to the legally incompetent patient—the child, the patient declared incompetent by the court, or the unconscious patient who may receive emergency treatment according to law. But in the case of the legally competent—even one who happens to be a bit senile or mentally unstable—paternalism even by one's spouse or children is still paternalism. When requirements of patient consent for surgery or other medical treatment are waived by relatives, it may be illegal as well as immoral.

When the Patient Requests Withholding

The principle of patient self-determination must be confronted in a more challenging way when the patient is the one who personally says "Doctor, if it's cancer I don't want to know." Based on the surveys, even among patients in a cancer detection center perhaps 1.5 percent say they would rather not know if the news is bad. While that is a small percentage it represents a large number of patients. Physicians hear (or think they hear) such requests frequently.

In the hospital truth-telling debate, the defender of the Kantian imperative to tell the patient the diagnosis will usually make the proviso, "Of course, if the patient says he does not want to know that is different." But does even the patient's own request justify withholding information?

In the first place it is not clear whether patients are always saying they do not want to be told in all cases where physicians feel they hear that message. If it is true that physicians find denial when they need to or want to, then arguments by physicians against truth-telling based on receiving "indirect communication" or nonverbal cues from the patient must be taken as very suspect. If, however, we limit consideration only to those cases where the patient has made a blunt request to the physician saying, "Doctor, you do what you think is best and don't bother me with the details," there still may be problems.

Here the principle of self-determination that has led us to reject the paternalistic withholding of information by physician or family cuts in exactly the opposite direction. Most would accept that it is reasonable at some point to say that further information is not worth it. While consent for further treatment under these conditions may not be informed, it will be free, and it can be informed to the extent that one knows that there is relevant information that one chooses not to have. This can hardly violate the principle of self-determination.

This may end the debate if we are concerned only about the duty of physicians to tell patients their diagnoses. Virtually no physician would want to tell a patient a diagnosis when the patient is actively requesting not to be told. The fallibility of the physician in knowing what is in the patient's interest as well as the overriding importance of patient freedom both would create strong barriers against the physician imposing the truth upon the patient. But that is not the end of the matter. We still must face the question: is it morally acceptable for the patient to make such a request in the first place?

There are two kinds of countervailing claims. First consider the case of the thirty-eight-year-old married man with three children, aged seven through thirteen. He owns a real estate firm and speculates in housing development projects and similar ventures. He has just initiated negotiations for a large shopping development when he goes to the local physician for his first checkup in nine years. He has had persistent cold symptoms and skin rashes for some time, but is unconcerned. He is a busy man with little time for health matters. As he begins his physical exam he tells the physician that he is sure he is in good health. The physician will not find anything significant, and he does not want to hear any sermons about watching his diet and getting plenty of exercise. He also adds firmly that if the physician really does find something, he doesn't want to be troubled by being told. The physician should do what he thinks best.

After discovery of nodular lesions in the respiratory tract and repeated examinations, the physician's eventual diagnosis of Wegener's granulomatosis leads to his moral dilemma. The disease involves the breakdown of normal immune mechanisms and is usually relentlessly progressive. It is normally fatal in six to eight months although occasionally the condition does not become acute for years. Very little treatment is possible although steroid injections are recommended. The physician feels there is little he can do. Faced with the patient's plea to be left alone, what is the morally appropriate response?

In avoiding the burden of a fatal diagnosis, the patient has jeopardized the welfare of his family, since he is considering risking his savings in a speculative shopping center which may pay off but not for many years. The physician, committed to narrow patient-centered concern, may not be moved by the potential harm to the family, but fortunately the moral obligations of the layman are not so constraining. Most would grant that in this case when the welfare of others is at stake, there is a moral obligation not to avoid the trouble of getting the medical facts. When others stand to be harmed, especially those in a relationship of special obligation, there is a duty to have information that is potentially meaningful and useful.

Suppose, however, that this same thirty-eight-year-old man was a bachelor without dependents. If the welfare of others is not at issue, is there any obligation to have potentially meaningful information about one's condition? The case is finally forced to the most difficult extreme. There seem to be virtually no utilitarian reasons for the disclosure. Presumably the patient, who has instructed that he not be given the details, is as good a judge of his own desires as any one else involved in the case. There is virtually no treatment to which the patient could be motivated by knowing his condition. Others will not benefit in any measurable way from his knowing. Aside from the rule-utilitarian concern with maintaining a trustworthy image for the profession, there would seem to be no harmful consequences from withholding the information. If the physician could act on the rule, "Always tell the truth except in those cases where the patient has clearly requested not to know and where others would not suffer from the withholding," there would be little risk even to the image of the profession.

The case against the patient's position, if there is one, must rest on the most fundamental moral obligations growing out of the nature of man's interaction with man. It is possible to grant that the principle of patient freedom would be sufficient to restrain a physician from imposing unwanted bad news upon such a patient and yet hold that human dignity requires responsible decision making by individuals especially about matters of such ultimate significance as life and death. A desire to avoid the extreme psychological stress of dealing with a diagnosis of dying can certainly be understood and perhaps even excused, but that is not to say it is a responsible way of dealing with one's life. Even in this extreme case, where the patient has freely chosen to avoid knowledge of his condition and no one else will suffer directly from his refusal, there may still be a moral duty to know one's self and one's fate.

Overwhelmingly Negative Consequences

If there are moral arguments in favor of a patient knowing his condition when his family requests that information be withheld and even when he requests that information be withheld, is there a case for a hard and fast rule upholding truth-telling in all circumstances? The argument has been made against the dangers of situationalism—that mistakes made in violating moral rules in the name of the good can be serious. But in the end ethical decision making is a trade off of a number of competing norms and values. The principles of truth-telling and contract-keeping may not always lead to the same moral conclusions as the principles of benefiting and not harming.

There are extreme cases when the truth-telling principle must be compromised. Should a captured soldier tell the truth to the enemy if doing so will expose the position of and risk the lives of comrades? Of course not, at least if the consequences of the dishonesty are serious enough compared with the consequences of the lie. Are there similar conditions in the care of the dying patient where overwhelmingly bad consequences of telling the patient would justify withholding potentially meaningful information? There may be, but simply arguing that there will be some bad consequences in the eyes of someone such as the physician is not sufficient cause for breaking a rule designed to promote the general good and protect the dignity of the responsible patient as well as to maintain minimal conditions for human interaction.

Upon occasion the prospect of overwhelmingly negative consequences may justify, not total withholding of information, but moderating what is told for the time being—for example, in the case of a patient known to have a history of infrequent, brief, intermittent suicidal depressions who was in such a period of crisis when a terminal diagnosis was made, complete information might be withheld until the crisis period had passed and psychiatric help could be arranged. Postponement of disclosure to a patient whose malignancy was discovered during a physical examination in conjunction with a commitment proceeding might well be justified until competency had been determined by a court in order to determine whether the decision to disclose should be placed in the hands of a guardian.

Withholding information rightfully the patient's, like positive killing of the terminally ill suffering patient, may best be handled under the rubric of civil disobedience. The term may be more metaphorical here, although treatment of the patient without consent would certainly violate the law. Rather I mean violating the normal moral law, a suspension of the normal requirements of man's relationship with man, justified by the conviction that in some cases the consequences of disclosing some information to a patient would be so bad that it is morally necessary "to take the law into one's own hands."

This might lead to abuses. Physicians, prone to take civil and moral law into their own hands under the paternalistic Hippocratic patient-benefiting principle, could use this license to excuse antinomial situationalism. We would then have to retrench into the legalism of a flat rule mandating truth-telling. Perhaps in the end society must stand by this rule. Only in extremely rare instances of overwhelmingly negative consequences can withholding be tolerated. Only in extremely rare exceptional cases—whose gravity extends well beyond the ordinary sort where the physician feels that harm would justify withholding the bad news—can withholding information potentially useful or meaningful to the patient be condoned.

7

The Newly Dead:
Mortal Remains or Organ Bank

Urgently wanted—Kidney. Will pay $3,000 to next of kin for a kidney which is an appropriate match and suitable for transplant.

So read a want ad in the *Dover Daily Advocate*. Carl Sala-mensky, at thirty-seven, had spent the last two years without kidneys of his own. They had been so diseased that they had to be removed. Now he spent five hours every two days at-tached to machinery which removed toxic substances from his blood. Life on the hemodialysis machine can be difficult.[1] Sal-amensky said he would give himself two or three months more. "It sounds like an impossible thing to say, I know— unless you've lived on the machine. After two years on the machine, I've decided I'd rather be dead." He was prepared to decide that continued living under those conditions was intol-erable and to walk away from his job as director of a college placement office—to walk away from life itself—if a kidney could not be found.

THE REMARKABLE NEWLY DEAD

The great moral debate among the medical staff over the appropriate care of the heroin overdose victim probably

---

1. F. Patrick McKegney and Paul Lange, "The Decision to No Longer Live on Chronic Hemodialysis," *American Journal of Psychiatry* 128 (September 1971), pp. 267–73; Renée C. Fox, "A Sociological Perspective on Organ Transplantation and Hemodialysis," *New Dimensions in Legal and Ethical Concepts for Human Research* (Annals of the New York Academy of Sciences) 169, no. 2 (January 1970), pp. 406–28; Rich-ard C. W. Hall, "Psychiatric Complications of Chronic Renal Hemodialysis and Renal Transplantation," *The New Physician* (April 1971), pp. 255–58; and Chad H. Calland, "Iatrogenic Problems in End-Stage Renal Failure," *New England Journal of Medicine* 287, (1973), pp. 334–36.

would never have taken place had there not been an interest in his kidneys. Uses of the newly dead body are so remarkable that the biological revolution may really be said to have begun with the age of transplantation. When Dr. Christian Barnard, in December 1967, cut out Louis Washkansky's heart with the faith that he could put a new one its place, the biological revolution had its symbol. Here was the first decisive campaign of an all-out war on the mortal flaws of the human body. There had been preliminary skirmishes: the seventeenth-century ventures in blood transfusion, the great debates about dissection of the corpse, the discovery of penicillin, the first transplant in 1954 of a kidney to a patient whose kidneys had been destroyed.[2] But these were really only border forays into the new territory. The vision of the surgeon purposefully cutting the heart from the human breast has symbolized the new era of the biological revolution as much as Sputnik has that of the physical sciences.

At the beginning of 1976, 23,919 people had had their lives extended with kidneys from other human beings.[3] In 1974, 3,620 transplants were performed, and in 1975, 2,756.[4] Approximately 10,850 of the recipients are living today, the longest-living surviving more than nineteen years.[5] Half of these kidneys have come from cadavers (70.4% in 1973) and the use of cadaveric organs is increasing.[6] Although the survival rate when kidneys come from a corpse is still somewhat lower (65.6½ compared with 81.8% from living parents and 86.8% from siblings after two years),[7] the potential for transplants from cadavers is much greater. While there is a better chance of tissue compatibility from a related living donor willing to donate one of the body's two vital kidneys, the more

2. See George W. Miller, *Moral and Ethical Implications of Human Organ Transplants* (Springfield, Illinois: Charles C. Thomas, 1971), p. 4, for some of the complexities of that history.

3. ACS/NIH Organ Transplant Registry, winter newsletter, 1975–1976.

4. Ibid.

5. Ibid.

6. Advisory Committee to the Renal Transplant Registry, "The 12th Report of the Human Renal Transplant Registry," *Journal of the American Medical Association* 233 (1975), p. 787.

7. Ibid., p. 790.

readily available cadaver organ seems quite acceptable in cases where there is no suitable relative. It is tragic that, in the United States alone, perhaps 8,000 of the more than 50,000 who die of kidney failure each year, could be helped with a transplant. We have the way but seem to lack the will to save the lives of thousands of human beings each year either with transplants or hemodialysis.

By contrast, the heart transplant, the flashy standard of the revolution, has much less tactical significance. As 1976 began, 296 had received hearts, 52 of whom were still alive. The longest survival has been over seven years.[8] In looking at the lifesaving potential, however, in the United States alone of the million who die annually of heart disease, between 12,000 and 32,000 are potential candidates for heart replacement.[9] Furthermore, since living donors are obviously not available and the artificial heart is not yet as available as the artificial kidney, the main potential lifesaving device is the heart transplant from corpses.[10]

There are remaining technical problems. Rejection by the body's own immunological system is a well-known problem with transplants—especially with hearts from unrelated donors. Transplanted hearts are now known to develop something akin to atherosclerosis. But if these technical problems were solved would there be enough organs to meet the demand? Estimates even for the United States are very difficult to come by, but there may be from 10,000 to 15,000 kidneys annually available coming primarily from persons suffering subarachnoid hemorrhage and violent or accidental brain injury.[11] That would probably supply more than enough kidneys to meet the demand, but hearts as well as lungs and other

8. ACS / NIH Organ Transplant Registry, winter newsletter, 1975–1976.

9. *Cardiac Replacement: Medical, Ethical, Psychological, and Economic Considerations,* A Report by the Ad Hoc Task Force on Cardiac Replacement, National Heart Institute, 1969, p. 15.

10. *The Totally Implantable Artificial Heart,* A Report by the Artificial Heart Assessment Panel, National Heart and Lung Institute, June 1973, pp. II–27.

11. N. P. Couch, "Supply and Demand in Kidney and Liver Transplantation," *Transplantation* 4, no. 5 (September 1966), pp. 587–95; and Joseph Fletcher, "Our Shameful Waste of Human Tissue," in *Updating Life and Death,* ed. Donald R. Cutler (Boston: Beacon Press, 1969), p. 3.

organs may be in short supply. Assuming that kidney sources would also be able to supply a heart, there would appear to be only a half to a sixth of the needed organs. Even so, it is clear that potentially thousands of lives could be extended by heart transplantation if the technical difficulties were solved.

Hearts and kidneys are not the only transplantable organs. As many as twenty-five different kinds of organs and tissues have now been transplanted in humans beings with varying degrees of success, including livers, lungs, pancreas, spleen, bone marrow, and skin, as well as eye corneas, bone, cartilage, fascia, and teeth.[12] Recently an ovary transplant was reported. Lung transplants have been uniformly unsuccessful. In thirty-seven attempts, no patients have survived for more than ten months. Forty-six pancreas transplants have resulted in only one surviving patient living at last report for $3\frac{1}{2}$ years. Liver transplants are clearly still experimental, but more than 242 attempts have produced 28 survivals, with the longest living 6 years.

When signing a donor card according to the Uniform Anatomical Gift Act (which we shall look at in more detail below), one does not simply agree to make body parts available for needed transplants. Unless the donation is restricted, then it is "for the purposes of transplantation, therapy, medical research or education." The new corpse is amazing not only for its transplantable parts but also for its other uses for the living. The use in the anatomy laboratory comes readily to mind, but other medical uses are not so apparent. Medical research can use body tissues and organs for physiological and biochemical tests. The placenta is now used routinely, often without the new mother's permission.

Tissues from a fresh corpse are a major new source of human tissue for research. Dangerous new drugs could be tested on some fresh cadavers, as could experimental surgical and other procedures. The thought of therapeutic uses of the corpse other than transplant is rather bizarre, but certainly the blood might be used; in fact a transfusion is really a tissue transplant. But what of a "respiring cadaver"—a human body

12. Irving Ladimer, *The Challenge of Transplantation*, Public Affairs Pamphlet no. 451, 1970, p. 5.

pronounced dead according to brain-oriented criteria of death for which respirator and other maintenance systems have not been stopped? Suppose that respiring corpse is producing a rare blood factor, enzyme, or other therapeutically valued substance. If it were "worth it," it might be possible to maintain such a cadaver for a long period in order to obtain the valued substance. It has been proposed that new cadavers be used for educational purposes not only in anatomy labs, but also for practicing surgical and difficult diagnostic procedures including pelvic exams. The dead body has unlimited use for the imaginative living.[13] These valuable contributions of the dead to the living are not, however, the only or even the most significant reasons that the new corpse is so remarkable. We have already discussed the danger of revising the meaning of death as a way to obtain more body parts for transplantation. Although it is only responsible to clarify our meaning of death when lives may be saved by doing so, it is unacceptable to change the definition of death for this purpose. The discussion of the meaning of death, however, does shed light on the significance of the body. In discussing the concept of death that sees man's ultimate significance in human consciousness, in human experientiality, in the human ability to interact socially, we finally face the science fiction possibility of transferring the experiential information of the brain onto magnetic tape and hooking it up to some rudimentary inputs and outputs. Could such a human data machine be confused with a human being? The thought may be repulsive, at least in Western, Judeo-Christian culture, where the body is essential to our concept of man.

Occasionally a distinction will be made between the *body* and the *self*, suggesting a gnostic view of man where the personal essence is set apart from the body which is its temporary captor. But even the Platonic view of man separates not the *self* but the *soul* from the body, suggesting that the *self* is essentially more than either of these components taken alone. In the Judeo-Christian tradition, however, man is inseparable

13. I am indebted to Hans Jonas for many of these suggestions. See also Willard Gaylin, "Harvesting the Dead: The Potential for Recycling Human Bodies," *Harper's Magazine* 249 (September 1974), pp. 23ff.

from the body. William May, one of the few who has specifically addressed our attitudes toward the newly dead, puts it
more forcefully: "A man not only *has* a body, he *is* his
body. . . ." [14]

Paul's great exhortation to the Romans begins, "I appeal to
you therefore, brethren . . . to present your bodies a
living sacrifice." [15] Some knowledgeable interpreters say this is
a conscious maneuver on Paul's part to shock the Roman spiri-
tualizers and confront those who would find repulsive the
thought of a body being a spiritual sacrifice worthy of being
called "holy and acceptable."

But Judeo-Christianity is the religion of the resurrection of
the body. For those who interpret this doctrine literally the
significance of the corpse is obvious. Another example of respect for the body is seen in Orthodox Judaism's grave reservations about autopsy, generally forbidding it unless the living
will benefit (for example, an accused murderer might be acquitted if the cause of death were determined). [16] Even then
there is great concern that all organs be returned for burial.

The point is not that resurrection would have to
depend upon the intact corpse. Should victims of fire, explo-
sions and other violent accidents be deprived of eternal life by
the sovereign God? Even those who demythologize the doctrine still place great emphasis on the body. The tradition goes
back at least to Augustine, who dealt with the problem by arguing:

> But as for burying the body, whatever is bestowed on that
> is no aid to salvation, but an office of humanity, according
> to that affection by which, "No man hateth his own flesh."
> [Eph.5:29] Then it is fitting that he take what care he is
> able for the flesh of his neighbor, when he is gone that
> bare it. [17]

14. William May, "Attitudes toward the Newly Dead," *Hastings Center Studies* 1, no.
1 (1973) p. 3.

15. Romans 12 : 1.

16. Immanuel Jakobovits, *Jewish Medical Ethics* (New York: Block Publishing, 1959),
pp. 134–52; Fred Rosner, *Modern Medicine and Jewish Law* (New York: Yeshiva University Press, 1972), pp. 132–54.

17. Augustine, "De Cura Pro Mortius," *Nicene and Post-Nicene Fathers*, 1st series, vol.
3, ed. Philip Schaff, trans. H. Browne (Grand Rapids: William B. Eerdmans, 1956),
cited in May, "Attitudes toward the Newly Dead," p. 12.

At least for the newly dead intact corpse there is still an aura of sacredness felt by even the most secular of us. The medical student's experience of the anatomy lab is one of highly charged emotion, in fact a training ground for the physician in dealing with death.[18] The careful control of lab access, the draping of the corpse, and the gallows humor are all ways of coping with the trespass of the sacred that is anatomical dissection. I personally recall the great impact of the intact cadaver, especially in the autopsy room but in the anatomy lab as well. Preserved specimens of internal organs in glass jars can be displayed for the uninitiated in hospital corridors; even isolated external body parts which are available in the anatomy lab for students to study do not inspire the same quality of awe. But the intact body, recognizable as the "mortal remains" of a human individual—not simply the shell in which the individual was once encased—still retains a quality of the sacred which gives it special significance.

If the philosophical concern of modern man with death is uniquely focused on this world, the experiences of the living before death, rather than on the more traditional interest in life after death, this intra-worldliness does not mean that modern man's concern stops at the moment of death. This intra-worldliness still generates great ethical and policy issues after the moment of death. It is to these that we now turn.

Responsible Treatment of the Newly Dead

A discussion of the ethical issues in the care of the newly dead is not the same as a survey of the ethics of transplantation. This is a volume on the ethical and policy questions related to death and dying. There are crucial and medical ethical issues outside the scope of this discussion: kidney donation by a child to an identical twin, rejection on psychological grounds of donors who are given the excuse of "tissue incompatibility," the gift of an organ by a nonrelated living donor,

18. Harold I. Lief and Renée C. Fox, "Training for 'Detached Concern' in Medical Students," in *Psychological Basis of Medical Practice,* ed. Harold I. Lief, Victor F. Lief, and Nina R. Lief (New York: Harper and Row, 1963), pp. 12–35; William F. May, "The Sacral Power of Death in Contemporary Experience," *Social Research* 39, no. 4 (winter 1972), pp. 463–88.

and the morality of an allograft (transplant from an animal). These are dealt with in many discussions of transplantation.[19] We shall limit our attention very narrowly to questions of the treatment of the newly dead.

An Ethic of Responsibility

The great significance of the newly dead body both to the living who may benefit from it and simply as the mortal remains of a once living human being suggests serious ethical issues. The first concerns the rights and responsibilities of the survivors vis-à-vis the newly dead.

THE DANGEROUS NOTION OF PROPERTY RIGHTS

The relationship of the living to the newly dead has had a confusing history. Originally in English common law, there was no clear guidance because the ecclesiastical courts had jurisdiction over matters involving dead bodies.[20] When the common law began to take jurisdiction in the seventeenth century, no "property rights" to the dead body existed for the survivors. From the advertisement offering $3,000 for a kidney, we can see the potential dangers. Presumably the courts feared undesirable commercialization of the care of the corpse. Nevertheless the courts began to recognize that the kin should have some role in determining the mode of burial. The unfortunate notion of a "quasi-property right" emerged, implying some authority to dispose of the remains.

19. F. E. W. Wolstenholme, ed., *Ethics in Medical Progress: With Special Reference to Transplantation* (Boston: Little, Brown, 1966); Miller, *Moral and Ethical Implications of Human Organ Transplants;* Catherine Lyons, *Organ Transplants: The Moral Issues* (Philadelphia: Westminster Press, 1970); Johannes Grundel, "Ethics of Organ Transplantation" in *Organ Transplantation Today*, ed. N. A. Mitchison, J. M. Greep, and J. C. M. Hattinga Verschure (Baltimore: Williams and Wilkins, 1969), pp. 333–44; J. Russell Elkinton, "Ethical and Moral Problems in the Use of Artificial and Transplanted Organs," in *To Live and To Die: When, Why, and How,* ed. Robert H. Williams (New York: Springer-Verlag, 1973), pp. 123–33; James B. Nelson, "Organ Transplants: Their Human Dimensions," in *Human Medicine: Ethical Perspectives and New Medical Issues* (Minneapolis: Augsburg, 1973), pp. 149–70; Gerald Leach, "Transplants," in *The Biocrats* (New York: McGraw-Hill, 1970), pp. 245–81.

20. David W. Meyers, *The Human Body and the Law* (Chicago: Aldine, 1970), p. 101; and Alfred M. Sadler and Blair L. Sadler, "Transplantation and the Law: The Need for Organized Sensitivity," *Georgetown Law Journal* 57, no. 1 (October 1968), pp. 9–13, provide the basis for this summary.

From the beginning society has been uncomfortable with this concept of a "quasi-property right." Even the opinion in *Pierce* v. *Swan Point Cemetery,* which was important in the development of the concept, seethes with ambiguity:

> That there is no property right in a dead body, using the word in the ordinary sense, may well be admitted. Yet, the burial of the dead is a subject which interests the feelings of mankind to a much greater degree than many matters of actual property. There is a duty imposed by the universal feelings of mankind to be discharged by someone towards the dead; a duty, and we may also say a right, to protect from violation; and a duty on the parts of others to abstain from violation; it may therefore be considered a sort of quasi-property.

This is really not so much a specification of a quasi right as a set of duties—or at minimum a set of rights derivative from a set of duties. The "rights" of the survivors are those of treating the newly dead body properly: obtaining proper burial, bringing damages for harm done to the corpse, and otherwise fulfilling responsibilities. It is strange that these ethical relations should become labeled *rights.*

FAMILY RESPONSIBILITY FOR THE NEWLY DEAD

We would maintain that the critical ethical relation is really one of duties and obligations—of responsibility—rather than one of rights. It makes no sense to talk of the kin having a right to protect the corpse from violation. To do so implies that such protection would be offered merely at the survivor's discretion. Clearly the so-called right to bury a corpse is in fact a duty. The liability for costs for interment is placed upon a surviving spouse.[21]

Throughout this volume we have discovered that the ethics of death and dying is not simply an ethics of rights. It is also one of duties, obligations, or responsibilities. To confuse a corpse maintained in irreversible coma with the living human who was once that body is not simply a wasteful luxury, it may be an ethical affront. The decision by the patient or the

---

21. Meyers, *The Human Body and the Law,* p. 102.

patient's agent to stop a particular no longer appropriate medical treatment is not simply a right to be enjoyed; it may, at the appropriate time and place, be affirmed as the morally more acceptable course. Dying patients have not only the right to knowledge of their condition, but a duty to have the information necessary to make decisions about their care. Of course there may be circumstances modifying the duty to act responsibly, but in all of these ethical dilemmas generated by the biological revolution, we are first and foremost dealing with an ethic of human responsibility.

One might be puzzled how there can be a duty to the deceased. There might be a duty to their memory, some would argue, or to the living who retain a respect for the deceased, but can there be a duty to nonliving creatures? The complementary relationship between rights and duties has often been noted. Yet where rights often imply specific reciprocal duties for other individuals (the right of patients to reasonably meaningful knowledge of their condition implies a duty of those primarily responsible for the patients' care to disclose that knowledge), it is not clear that all duties have their source directly in other individuals.

Antigone contested Creon's claim that her brother's body was at the disposal of the state. When ordered to leave the rebel's body exposed, she claimed no simple right to bury it. To do so would have been a weak and hollow appeal. Rather she appealed to a duty decreed in the "unwritten laws, eternal in the heavens." That Polynices was now dead in no way affected the obligation to care appropriately for him. At least according to many theories of moral authority, obligation has its origins in universal sources beyond the claims of another person. This is a perspective we are learning once again from those who remind us of our duty to the environment. That man has dominion over nature is not the same as man being the origin of all value and obligation.[22]

22. Respected readers of early drafts of this chapter challenged me to abandon these paragraphs. How, they ask, can one have a duty toward nonliving things? A duty to a corpse or a duty to the environment might, they argued, be formulated more carefully as a duty to the living in relationship to that corpse or environment, that is, as a duty to the community. As an example one critic suggested there is a duty to the community not to cause disease by putrefaction. After careful reflection I still

If we stand with Antigone in recognizing that duties vis-à-vis the dead take precedence over any rights of the survivors, then who has the obligation to act responsibly to the newly dead? Antigone seemed to claim the duty because it was her brother who died. William May also argues for the centrality of the familial unit. "The corpse, the deceased, and the family belong, as it were, to a continuum which should enjoy a certain sanctuary against the larger society and the state." [23] I would have to go even further to hold that the family is and should be the central unit of responsibility. The question is similar to that of who should be the incompetent patient's agent to make decisions about appropriate medical treatment or who should ensure that the patient will have information which could reasonably be expected to be meaningful or useful. There are other options, of course: the physician, the hospital staff, a clergyman, or the state. Their commitment cannot compare, however, with the strength of the familial bond, with its loyalty and responsibility.

If the responsible treatment of the corpse by the family is not simply a right but a responsibility, what is the content of that responsibility? It must include at least the following obligations:

1. To honor the wishes of the deceased. Instructions by the deceased about how the body is to be treated after death

affirm as starkly as possible: a duty to the corpse as well as to the environment.

This is not the place to expound a metaethical theory (see my "The Metaethical Foundation for an Ethic of the Life Sciences: Does Ethics Have an Empirical Basis?" *Hastings Center Studies* 1, no. 1 [1973], pp. 50–65), but let me concede that it would be possible to construct a theory of obligation to carry out certain behavior toward corpses—or trees—derived from our duties to other living humans who enjoy the trees and want to avoid diseases which the unattended corpse might produce. While all that may be true and sufficient to explain our felt sense of obligation, it is not what I am saying. A certain branch of secular philosophical thought seems for some reason to posit that duties have their origins in human desire or will or commitment. While they might, I see no convincing reason why this ought to be the case. If duties are simply human in origin, why are they given such weight? On grounds of prudence? Yet ethical obligation must be separated from personal prudence. Stoic and more modern natural law thinkers, the Judeo-Christian tradition, as well as any other theistic and many secular thought systems have no difficulty finding extrahuman sources of obligation. The hypothesis that they originate from conventions among human beings strikes me as implausible, beyond demonstration, and the height of hubris.

23. May, "Attitudes Toward the Newly Dead," p. 7.

have a strong claim on the family. This is partially a matter
of protecting the common good; the living would lead uncomfortable lives if they feared that their wishes would not
be respected following death. But the obligation goes
beyond that, and is based on respect for the newly dead
one.
2. To fulfill commitments to the deceased. The duty of keeping promises, of fulfilling the covenantal relationship, is
   particularly important.
3. To protect the integrity of the corpse. This is already clear
   in the legal and moral tradition. The family has not only
   the right, but the duty to insist that the corpse not be muti-
   lated or exposed to injury or assault without good justification.
4. To provide a fitting removal of the body from society. This
   is also clearly established within the law. Whether the removal be burial, cremation, or other means, it is both rit-
   ualistically and practically important that the separation of
   the dead from the living be carried out properly.
5. To offer reasonable and responsible service to the living.

   Here a new obligation is added to those traditionally recognized. It is not simply that for its own satisfaction the family has the right to help out others. That can hardly be an
   adequate justification for the familial donation of a body or
   body parts for the benefit of the living. The exact nature of
   what would be a reasonable and responsible service to the
   living will depend greatly on the system of beliefs and values held by the family and by the deceased. But certainly
   the contribution of the body or body parts must be recognized as significant within many family relationships.

The Jewish tradition holds that conducting an autopsy is a
most serious action but can be justified for the service of the
living. At least some interpreters of that tradition believe that
if an autopsy can realistically benefit the living, it is not only
permitted but required. Immanuel Jakobovits, Great Britain's
chief rabbi, is reported to have said autopsy in the case of sav-

ing a life "is not only a matter of permission but of obligation and *mitzah*." [24]

It would be irresponsible for the family to refuse to aid the living for no reason at all. The obligation is more universal than simple loyalty to the living, and is one we should reasonably be able to assume the deceased also would have assented to—or there is no obligation at all. This is emphatically not to say that the family always has an obligation to provide the body or body organs of the deceased whenever they would be useful. There is certainly no such obligation when it is known that the deceased would have objected, and there may well be other valid reasons. I say simply that there is a *prima facie* obligation of the family to consider service to the living, an obligation which may be negated by many good reasons. At least when the family believes that donation of the body or body parts is consistent with its beliefs and values and particularly with those formerly held by the deceased, the responsibility to serve the living should not be set aside for no reason at all. It is this ethic of responsibility which must be the moral basis for using the newly dead body for the service of the living.

The Ethics of the Heart Transplant Moratorium

If there is an ethic of responsibility in the donation of the body and body parts of the newly dead for the sake of the living, there is also an ethic of responsibility in the use of those bodies and body parts. The decision to participate in an organ transplant is essentially a value choice. This is true not only for the physician but also for the potential recipient of the organ. Although it is not yet generally recognized, these decisions take place in a framework of ethical and other values. Superimposed on these choices, however, is a complex social structure which also has a substantial effect on these decisions.

We are particularly interested in the decision to participate

24. David Hendin, *Death as a Fact of Life* (New York: Norton, 1973), p. 57, Cf. Jakobovits, *Jewish Medical Ethics*, pp. 126–52. I am unable to locate the original quotation.

in heart transplantation, first because cardiac transplant always involves the use of a heart from a newly dead body, and second, because we are now in the midst of what has been identified as a clinical moratorium in heart transplants.[25] The moratorium, in this case a prolonged slowdown in clinical use, reflects the collective judgment of the society and especially the medical professionals involved that, all things considered, it is better to postpone use of the procedure. The period of assessment can be used to review the clinical results of transplants that have taken place, to conduct further animal and laboratory studies, and to resolve specific problems which have emerged in the early trials. The moratorium followed rather poor results from the early transplants and a growing awareness that immunological problems needed to be conquered before transplants could be really successful.

In the six months after Louis Washkansky's pioneering acceptance of the first heart transplant in December 1967, there were nineteen further attempts. The next six months there were seventy-seven, and in following six-month periods thirty-eight, fifteen, nine, nine, and six. But unlike the earlier total suspension of mitral valve surgery (lasting from 1928 to 1945), heart transplants, at least until this writing, have continued at the rate of one or two a month.

What accounts for this decision to decrease the use of the dead to help the living? Clearly the poor results are partly responsible. In January 1976, of the 296 original recipients, 52 were alive with functioning grafts, 35 more than one year after surgery, five for more than six years. With more successful transplant teams such as Norman Shumway's at Stanford University, however, 30 to 35 percent are surviving two years or more. Since patients have to be in imminent danger of death before they are accepted, this more fortunate group have added years to their lives and had relieved the constant physical and mental distress they suffered.

The decrease in transplants is not normally attributed to a lack of volunteers. Both theoretical and practical discussions

25. Judith P. Swazey and Renée C. Fox, "The Clinical Moratorium: A Case Study of Mitral Valve Surgery," in *Experimentation with Human Subjects*, ed. Paul A. Freund (New York: George Braziller, 1970), pp. 315–57.

of the moratorium make clear that the primary reason is that surgeons and their physician colleagues are shunning the procedure. Only Shumway's Stanford group now transplants hearts regularly. And he is now reportedly much more selective in those he accepts, refusing both those whom he considers not sick enough and those whose chance of survival is not great—including all over the age of fifty. Christiaan Barnard reportedly is unhappy that his fellow South African physicians are refusing to send him patients.

A clinical moratorium is a complex social phenomenon within the medical profession, and it has a significant normative component. On one hand, there is moral and psychological pressure on a research physician to pioneer and persevere in lifesaving work. But gradually moral pressures build to stop the experimenting. The physician who does not conform to peer pressure, whether to stop prescribing amphetamines or to stop transplanting hearts, is subject to the formal and informal disciplinary pressures of the profession.

This is a classical clinical decision-making dilemma. It is what I would call the "condition of doubt." All would agree that there is not enough information to go on, that more immunological research and animal trials would be of great value. But in the clinical setting these arguments from scientific uncertainty are not valid. It is striking that all the arguments for the moratorium discussed thus far do not consider the patient perspective. The demand for further research may make sense for the scientist, but is not helpful at all for the patient who meets the criteria for transplantation—including the imminent danger of death. The need for a time to assess progress before taking up transplantation again will not meet the particular patient's needs. While peer pressure to observe the moratorium may originate in part in what the peers think is the hypothetical patient's "interests," certainly it is not based upon specific knowledge of a particular patient's interest.

The choice in the "condition of doubt" is fundamentally based on a highly generalized value orientation. When there is not enough information to know with certainty what the outcome will be, what is the better course of action? Those affirming a faith in nature may well say "he who hesitates is lost," but another value orientation is more conservative, with less confidence that the unknown experimental procedure will be successful. The value question is, "All things considered is the risk worth it?" or better, "Is the choice a responsible one?" The answer will depend on the value system of the individual patient.

That the physician may not share that fundamental value orientation is once again an example of the value conflict problem encountered so often in our discussion of the individual in relation to the technical experts. It is certainly reasonable for a patient to decide against a heart transplant, considering it an unacceptable or "extraordinary" treatment even if it would increase chances of survival. But I am not prepared to say that it is irresponsible for a patient to conclude that a transplant is reasonable treatment, from the perspective of her or his own interests.

Responsible Transplants and Social Justice

While a transplant decision may be responsible from the standpoint of the patient's own interests, that is not the only perspective. There are effects beyond those on the chests of the donor and the recipient. The Ad Hoc Task Force on Cardiac Replacement of the National Heart Institute reports that in 36 transplants studied at 6 American institutions, the costs ranged from $3,300 to $44,205. The average was $18,694 with over $15,000 in postoperative costs.[26] They also estimate that if immunological problems are solved there could be at least 12,000 transplants annually at an average cost of $5,000 to $10,000 for a total cost between $60 million and $120 million.

The cost-accounting method of determining what is morally responsible leaves a great deal to be desired.[27] The literature

26. *Cardiac Replacement,* p. 51.

27. See Laurence H. Tribe, "Technology Assessment and the Fourth Discontinuity: The Limits of Instrumental Rationality," *Southern California Law Review* 46 (1973), pp. 617–60 (especially pp. 625–41); Rashi Fein, "On Measuring Economic Benefits of Health Programmes," in *Medical History and Medical Care,* ed. Gordon McLachlan and

is filled with suggestions that abortions of genetically abnormal fetuses might save the state millions, yet surely there is more to ethical judgment than saving the state money. The same argument might apply to decisions about prolonging life by a cardiac transplant.

It makes a great deal of difference whether it is the potential recipient who is making a judgment or some impersonal and bureaucratic decision maker. The patient personally could hardly be faulted for taking into account the economic, social, and psychological factors and deciding that the resulting small chance of a significant increase in lifespan is not worth it. On the other hand, from the perspective of others involved, the justice question may be more complicated. If the transplant decision involved only substantial sums of money, a good argument could be made that even the $120 million a year required for American transplants would be well within the national budget's capacity. Inclusion of transplants in governmental catastrophic illness insurance coverage might not only be possible but morally required.

But more is at stake than the economics of American heart transplants. People the world over have heart attacks and if an argument from justice can be made for covering all Americans, a similar case can be made for the rest of humanity. And if a case can be made for providing heart transplants, would not justice also require provision of medical services for other major expensive treatments including hemodialysis, hemophilia prophylaxis, and the implantation of the artificial heart? Even if there were a radical reordering of the economy in the direction of health concerns—which there should be along with fundamental commitments to other aspects of social justice—the requirements for fully meeting the need might be beyond the society's capabilities, certainly involving billions and billions of dollar equivalents a year.

More important, not only money is needed. Heart trans-

Thomas McKeown (Oxford: Oxford University Press, 1971), pp. 181–217 and reprinted in *Ethics and Health Policy,* ed. Robert M. Veatch and Roy Branson (Cambridge, Massachusetts: Ballinger Press, forthcoming); and Charles Fried, *Medical Experimentation: Personal Integrity and Social Policy* (New York: American Elsevier, 1974), pp. 79–90.

plants and other needed major medical services consume the valuable scarce medical resource of trained personnel. A cardiac transplant team, according to estimates made by the institutions involved, must include between fifteen and eighteen physicians (at least six surgeons, anesthesiologists, cardiologists, pathologists, microbiologists, immunologists, radiologists, and psychiatrists), between fourteen and twenty nurses, as well as technicians, social workers, engineers, therapists, dieticians, and consultants. Even assuming that justice requires a reordering of our national and international priorities to provide more trained medical professionals, requirements of this level of personnel for major and experimental surgical procedures with limited chances of success must raise serious questions. When making a responsible decision, potential recipients can hardly be faulted for deciding a transplant is unreasonable in their cases. But society faces a moral crisis in allocating scarce medical resources among those who decide that treatment is reasonable in their case. While such allocations cannot be based on rationalizations of the recipient's worth, yet, de facto, that is what we find ourselves doing when our policies are not consciously developed.[28]

A Policy for Obtaining Newly Dead Bodies and Body Organs

While at the moment our policy for allocating scarce resources related to uses of the newly dead body amounts to little more than responsible self-selection, we do have a substantially clearer policy on how such bodies and body parts shall be obtained. In fact of all the policy questions dealt with

28. A full exploration of the allocation of scarce resources is beyond the scope of this volume. See Paul Ramsey, "Choosing How to Choose: Patients and Sparse Medical Resources," in *The Patient as Person* (New Haven: Yale University Press, 1973), pp. 239–75; "Scarce Medical Resources," *Columbia Law Review* 69, no. 4 (April 1969), pp. 620–92; James Childress, "Who Shall Live When Not All Can Live?" *Soundings* 53 (winter 1970) pp. 339–62; Nicholas Rescher, "Allocating of Exotic Medical Lifesaving Therapy," *Ethics* 79 (April 1969), pp. 173–86; "Scarce Medical Resources," *Columbia Law Review* 69 (April 1969), pp. 620–92; and the essays in Veatch and Branson, eds., in *Ethics and Health Policy*.

in this volume, this is the one where there has been enough public debate that a consensus is beginning to emerge. As early as 1968—soon after the first heart transplant—seven out of ten Americans approved the donation of their organs to science.[29] Yet it is a tragedy of our depersonalized world that organs, particularly hearts, are in short supply because only a tiny fraction (one author suggests 200,000) of those approving of organ transplants have taken the necessary steps to make their own available should they become suitable donors.

Several major policy alternatives have been suggested to increase that supply. Theoretically, at least, organs could be sold on the open market—as the newspaper advertisement contemplated. Proposals have also been made for a crediting system where a family account of donations might be kept, anticipating future need for an organ much as is done with blood banks. Two major alternatives have emerged among those who are generally in favor of some kind of transplantation.

Routine Salvaging of Cadaver Organs

In 1968 lawyer Jesse Dukeminier and physician David Sanders proposed the routine salvaging of cadaver organs for purposes of transplantation.[30] Declaring, "The need for cadaver organs to save human life is so great that the law should be changed to satisfy this need," they proposed four principles as a basis for organ salvaging:

1. Making removal of useful cadaver organs routine.

2. Removing organs in a way which does not burden the bereaved.

3. Honoring objections by the "donor" made during his lifetime but also honoring his express wishes even if next of kin objects.

29. *New York Times,* January 17, 1968, p. 18.
30. Jesse Dukeminier and David Sanders, "Organ Transplantation: A Proposal for Routine Salvaging of Cadaver Organs," *New England Journal of Medicine* 279 (1968), pp. 413–19.

4. If donor neither objects nor expressly assents, honoring kin's objection to organ removal.

Dukeminier and Sanders defined their proposal as a way of
saving life, a goal they call "the first and most important principle of medical ethics." Once this is accepted as the most important principle it is hard to deny that routine salvaging
might be a logical outcome, but we have seen there is reason
to doubt that preserving life is always the totally dominant
concern in medical ethics even among physicians, let alone lay
people.

Another of their controversial arguments for routine salvaging is that it will "minimize the traumatic effect of the practice
upon bereaved relatives." [31] They argue that "to someone
whose relative is about to die, asking for the kidneys may seem
a ghoulish request." This argument can be challenged on two
grounds. First, empirically, it is not immediately clear that
routine organ salvaging without informing relatives would
always minimize the trauma. What would be the response of a
relative who independently approached the medical staff to
volunteer a donation of organs only to discover that the vital
"gifts" were already on their way to several primed recipients?

The Giving of Cadaver Organs

The strongest objection to proposals for routine salvaging is
really one of human values. Do we want a society which conceives of body parts as essentially property of the state to be
taken by eminent domain or is that a dangerous misordering
of moral priorities? If the state can assume that human bodies
are its for the taking (unless contested by the individuals or
the relatives as in the Dukeminier and Sanders proposal),
what will be the implication for less ultimate, less sacred pos-
sessions? If the body is essential to the individual's identity, in
a society which values personal integrity and freedom, it must
be the individual's first of all to control, not only over a lifetime, but within reasonable limits after that life is gone as well.
If the body is to be made available to others for personal or

31. Ibid., p. 416.

societal research, it must be a gift. This has given rise to proposals for the giving rather than the taking of bodies and body parts.[32]

When the need for organs became dramatically apparent in the late 1960s, many states began passing laws permitting individuals before their deaths to donate all or part of their bodies for medical, scientific, or therapeutic purposes.[33] A committee under the chairmanship of E. Blythe Stason approved a model Uniform Anatomical Gift Act designed to bring order to the confusion of differing state policies. In contrast with Israel, France, and Sweden where routine salvaging proposals have been adopted, all fifty states have now adopted the provisions of the act making the giving of organs the standard for the United States. The model act is reprinted in full at the end of this chapter. Its basic provisions are:

1. Any individual over eighteen may give all or part of his body for educational, research, therapeutic, or transplantation purposes.

2. If the individual has not made a donation before his death his next of kin can make it unless there was a known objection by the deceased.

3. If the individual has made such a gift it cannot be revoked by the relatives.

4. If there is more than one person of the same degree of kinship the gift from relatives shall not be accepted if there is known objection by one of them.

5. The gift can be authorized by a card carried by the individual or by written or recorded verbal communication from a relative.

32. The terms are Paul Ramsey's from his important chapter "Giving or Taking Cadaver Organs for Transplant," in *The Patient as Person*, pp. 198–215.

33. Sadler and Sadler, "Transplantation and the Law," pp. 19–20. Also see by the same authors, *Organ Transplantation: Current Medical and Medical-Legal Status: The Problems of an Opportunity* (Washington, D. C.: U. S. Government Printing Office, 1970); "Recent Developments in the Legal Aspects of Transplantation in the United States," *Transplantation Proceedings* 3 (March 1971), pp. 293–97; and "Transplantation and the Law: Progress Toward Uniformity," *New England Journal of Medicine* 282 (1970), pp. 717–23.

6. The gift can be amended or revoked at any time before the death of the donor.

7. The time of death must be determined by a physician
who is not involved in any transplantation.

The procedure is made simple by providing that the donation can be made by a card, signed before witnesses and suitable for carrying on the person. The National Kidney Foundation has designed this "Uniform Donor Card" (see next
page).

Problems with Giving Organs

Although there has been widespread acceptance of the Uniform Anatomical Gift Act in the medical and legal community,
there are still problems. The first is pragmatic. There simply
are not enough people who know about the program and take
the initiative to sign the card. While more than 70 percent of
the public may approve in principle, only a tiny fraction of the
approvers have actually signed up to be organ donors. Since
only the very rare death provides organs suitable for donation, there is a desperate need for a massive pool of potential
donors. There have recently been renewed pleas for routine
salvaging or some other mechanism to make organs available.

There are also some ethical problems remaining in the Uniform Anatomical Gift Act. For one, although individuals can
object to particular or even any uses of their bodies, they must
make their objections known by an actual notice of contrary
indications. If few willing donors know about the law making
donation possible, it may also be that many with reservations
(for instance, to the use of their bodies for practice surgery or
prolonged medical experiments) may not be fully aware that
their bodies may be subjected to such use after their death by
a blanket permission from the next of kin.

Furthermore, the act provides that if no relatives are available at the time of death, the decision to donate may be made
by "any other person authorized or under obligation to dispose of the body." We have already on record the case of the
accident victim in Virginia whose heart was removed by authorization of the medical examiner without notifying the rela-

UNIFORM DONOR CARD

OF _____

In the hope that I may help others, I hereby make this anatomical gift, if medically acceptable, to take effect upon my death. The words and marks below indicate my desires.

I give: (a) _____ any needed organs or parts

(b) _____ only the following organs or parts

_____
Specify the organ(s) or part(s)

for the purposes of transplantation, therapy, medical research or education;

(c) _____ my body for anatomical study if needed.

Limitations or
special wishes, if any :_____

Signed by the donor and the following two witnesses in the presence of each other:

_____   _____
Signature of Donor   Date of Birth of Donor

_____   _____
Date Signed   City & State

_____   _____
Witness   Witness

This is a legal document under the Uniform Anatomical Gift Act or similar laws.

For further information consult your physician or

National Kidney Foundation
116 East 27th Street, New York, N.Y. 10016

tives. When there is more than one relative equally close to the deceased, any one of them who is available at the time of death may donate the organs. When the closest relations are not available, someone less close may authorize the organ removal.

All of these provisions leave loopholes where the personal wishes of the individual or the next of kin might not be honored, either because in the rush to get authorization the wishes are not discovered or there is an attempt to hide those wishes. It would clearly be preferable if actual donation were on the basis of a responsible personal judgment of the individual. It is the individual's last chance to make a responsible ethical choice, and that freedom and responsibility should be honored if at all possible.

One solution might be a routine and organized solicitation of the donation. Creation of a central information depot might either exacerbate or ameliorate problems created by our new biomedical technological capabilities. Whether the potential for error in centralized, presumably computerized data storage is judged greater than the moral offense of culpable indifference in the present method of donation, will in part depend upon one's faith in the technological revolution which created this dilemma in the first place. I would favor such a system as one where the risk is not great, given the continued protective responsibilities of family members who would have the authority and the obligation to intervene should a computer printout schedule your body for organ donation when it is clearly against your wishes.

There are other ingenious proposals. Several jurisdictions including New York, Ohio, the District of Columbia, and Ontario now connect the donation of organs to the driver's license. In Ontario, for instance, a detachable card was added to the driver's license beginning in 1975. The driver has the option of conveniently completing the card or simply detaching and discarding it. The risk of moral error as well as dehumanizing subordination of the individual to the state is much less than in the routine salvaging proposals. If there is not only a moral right, but also a responsibility to let the newly

dead serve the still living, such regular opportunity for donation may be our best alternative.[34]

UNIFORM ANATOMICAL GIFT ACT

(*Copy of final draft as approved on July 30, 1968, by the National Conference of
Commissioners on Uniform State Laws*)

An act authorizing the gift of all or part of a human body after death for
specified purposes.

SECTION 1. (*Definitions*)

(a) "Bank or storage facility" means a facility licensed, accredited or approved under the laws of any state for storage of human bodies or parts
thereof.

(b) "Decedent" means a deceased individual and includes a stillborn infant or fetus.

(c) "Donor" means an individual who makes a gift of all or part of his
body.

(d) "Hospital" means a hospital licensed, accredited or approved under
the laws of any state and includes a hospital operated by the United States
government, a state or a subdivision thereof, although not required to be
licensed under state laws.

(e) "Part" includes organs, tissues, eyes, bones, arteries, blood, other
fluids and other portions of a human body, and "part" includes "parts."

(f) "Person" means an individual, corporation, government or governmental subdivision or agency, business trust, estate, trust, partnership or association or any other legal entity.

(g) "Physician" or "surgeon" means a physician or surgeon licensed or authorized to practice under the laws of any state.

(h) "State" includes any state, district, commonwealth, territory, insular
possession, and any other area subject to the legislative authority of the
United States of America.

SECTION 2. (*Persons Who May Execute an Anatomical Gift*)

(a) Any individual of sound mind and 18 years of age or more may give
all or any part of his body for any purposes specified in section 3, the gift to
take effect upon death.

(b) Any of the following persons, in order of priority stated, when persons in prior classes are not available at the time of death, and in the absence
of actual notice of contrary indications by the decedent, or actual notice of

34. A surgeon in Birmingham, England, was strongly criticized by members of a
family for removing the kidneys from one of his patients who had just died. He had
failed in his attempts to contact the family members for permission. Not wanting to
lose the kidneys he made the decision to go ahead without permission—"Kidney
Donor Cards," *British Medical Journal* (July 28, 1973), p. 189.

opposition by a member of the same or a prior class, may give all or any part
of the decedent's body for any purposes specified in section 3.

(1) the spouse,

(2) an adult son or daughter,

(3) either parent,

(4) an adult brother or sister,

(5) a guardian of the person of the decedent at the time of his death,

(6) any other person authorized or under obligation to dispose of the
body.

(c) If the donee has actual notice of contrary indications by the decedent,
or that a gift by a member of a class is opposed by a member of the same or
a prior class, the donee shall not accept the gift. The persons authorized by
subsection (b) may make the gift after death or immediately before death.

(d) A gift of all or part of a body authorizes any examination necessary to
assure medical acceptability of the gift for the purposes intended.

(e) The rights of the donee created by the gift are paramount to the
rights of others except as provided by section 7(d).

SECTION 3. (*Persons Who May Become Donees, and Purposes for Which Anatomical Gifts May Be Made*) The following persons may become donees of gifts of
bodies or parts thereof for the purposes stated:

(1) any hospital, surgeon, or physician, for medical or dental education,
research, advancement of medical or dental science, therapy or transplantation; or

(2) any accredited medical or dental school, college or university for education, research, advancement of medical or dental science or therapy;
or

(3) any bank or storage facility for medical or dental education, research, advancement of medical or dental science, therapy or transplantation; or

(4) any specified individual for therapy or transplantation needed by
him.

SECTION 4. (*Manner of Executing Anatomical Gifts*)

(a) A gift of all or part of the body under section 2(a) may be made by
will. The gift becomes effective upon the death of the testator without waiting for probate. If the will is not probated, or if it is declared invalid for tes-
tamentary purposes, the gift, to the extent that it has been acted upon in
good faith, is nevertheless valid and effective.

(b) A gift of all or part of the body under section 2(a) may also be made
by document other than a will. The gift becomes effective upon the death of
the donor. The document, which may be a card designed to be carried on
the person, must be signed by the donor, in the presence of 2 witnesses who
must sign the document in his presence. If the donor cannot sign, the document may be signed for him at his direction and in his presence, and in the
presence of 2 witnesses who must sign the document in his presence. Deliv-

ery of the document of gift during the donor's lifetime is not necessary to make the gift valid.

(c) The gift may be made to a specified donee or without specifying a donee. If the latter, the gift may be accepted by the attending physician as donee upon or following death. If the gift is made to a specified donee who is not available at the time and place of death, the attending physician upon or following death, in the absence of any expressed indication that the donor desired otherwise, may accept the gift as donee. The physician who becomes a donee under this subsection shall not participate in the procedures for removing or transplanting a part.

(d) Notwithstanding section 7(b), the donor may designate in his will, card or other document of gift the surgeon or physician to carry out the appropriate procedures. In the absence of a designation, or if the designee is not available, the donee or other person authorized to accept the gift may employ or authorize any surgeon or physician for the purpose.

(e) Any gift by a person designated in section 2(b) shall be made by a document signed by him, or made by his telegraphic, recorded telephonic or other recorded message.

SECTION 5. (*Delivery of Document of Gift*) If the gift is made by the donor to a specified donee, the will, card, or other document, or an executed copy thereof, may be delivered to the donee to expedite the appropriate procedures immediately after death, but delivery is not necessary to the validity of the gift. The will, card or other document, or an executed copy thereof, may be deposited in any hospital, bank or storage facility or registry office that accepts them for safekeeping or for facilitation of procedures after death. On request of any interested party upon or after the donor's death, the person in possession shall produce the document for examination.

SECTION 6. (*Amendment or Revocation of the Gift*)

(a) If the will, card or other document or executed copy thereof has been delivered to a specified donee, the donor may amend or revoke the gift by:

(1) the execution and delivery to the donee of a signed statement, or

(2) an oral statement made in the presence of 2 persons and communicated to the donee, or

(3) a statement during a terminal illness or injury addressed to an attending physician and communicated to the donee, or

(4) a signed card or document found on his person or in his effects.

(b) Any document of gift which has not been delivered to the donee may be revoked by the donor in the manner set out in subsection (a) or by destruction, cancellation, or mutilation of the document and all executed copies thereof.

(c) Any gift made by a will may also be amended or revoked in the manner provided for amendment or revocation of wills, or as provided in subsection (a).

SECTION 7. (*Rights and Duties at Death*)

(a) The donee may accept or reject the gift. If the donee accepts a gift of the entire body, he may, subject to the terms of the gift, authorize embalming and the use of the body in funeral services. If the gift is of a part of the body, the donee, upon the death of the donor and prior to embalming, shall cause the part to be removed without unnecessary mutilation. After removal of the part, custody of the remainder of the body vests in the surviving spouse, next of kin or other persons under obligation to dispose of the body.

(b) The time of death shall be determined by a physician who attends the donor at his death, or, if none, the physician who certifies the death. This physician shall not participate in the procedures for removing or transplanting a part.

(c) A person who acts in good faith in accordance with the terms of this Act, or under the anatomical gift laws of another state (or a foreign country) is not liable for damages in any civil action or subject to prosecution in any criminal proceeding for his act.

(d) The provisions of this Act are subject to the laws of this state prescribing powers and duties with respect to autopsies.

SECTION 8. (*Uniformity of Interpretation*) This Act shall be so construed as to effectuate its general purpose to make uniform the law of those states which enact it.

SECTION 9. (Short Title) This Act may be cited as the Uniform Anatomical Gift Act.

8

Natural Death and Public Policy

Thou shalt not kill; but need'st not strive
Officiously to keep alive.
—Arthur Hugh Clough

We have come a long way in exploring what it means for individuals and groups to be responsible in making decisions regarding death and dying in the day of the biological revolution. There is much more openness in discussing the tragic decisions which sometimes must be made if individuals are to be responsible for their own life histories. In fact "death with dignity" has become something of a movement; the "right to die" has become an almost faddish slogan. Although this book is in some sense part of that movement, I have avoided the notions of death with dignity and the right to die. For one thing it is not clear what the legal status of the right to die is. Robert M. Byrn, in a recent article convincingly challenges the idea that there is any such legal right at all.[1] The right to refuse medical treatment, which in certain circumstances will also lead to the eventual death of the individual refuser, rests on much firmer legal and ethical ground. It is the principle I have emphasized as integral to a theory of responsible medical decision making by individual patients or guardians as well as by society.

There is a more basic reason for avoiding the slogans. Although it is clear to me that there may be more or less undignified ways of doing one's dying, I remain uncomfortable with the thought that the death of a person can really be called something of "dignity." One of the remaining philosophical challenges is to reconcile our new willingness to face death and dying responsibly with the more traditional Judeo-Chris-

1. See "Compulsory Lifesaving Treatment for the Competent Adult," *Fordham Law Review* 44 (1975), pp. 1–36.

tian notion that death is an evil, a punishment for sinfulness which has cost man immortality. Along with many others,[2] I have been forced to face the implications for our health care policy of this more open acceptance of death.

Strange world this. That a serious argument must be made that death is an evil to be conquered. That now when for the first time in human history we have the power to conquer at least some deaths we should begin to romanticize the beauty, the grace, the "right" of a natural death. That when Arthur Hugh Clough tried with bitter sarcasm to chide us for our indifference to the plight of the dying in the "Latest Decalogue" his couplet should be taken a century later as the slogan of a death with dignity movement.[3]

The concept of "natural death" has crept up on us. We are not sure what it means for death to be natural and yet are quite certain it is a good thing. The concept has public policy implications—dangerous implications it seems to me. If death is not only natural, but good somehow because it is natural, then as a matter of public policy we ought not combat it. Perhaps the time has come for a full-blown exploration of the impact of this seductively alluring concept. We may find that the temptress is not without her dangers. Those who dance at Death's festival may find that she has lured them with false promises; the morning after—if there be one—may be filled with lurid memories of the night before.

Dylan Thomas has become the straw man of the death with dignity movement when he urges to "Rage, rage against the dying of the light." We poke fun at his pathological resistence to that which is clearly natural and inevitable. Certainly, in the

2. See Peter Steinfels and Robert M. Veatch, eds., *Death Inside Out* (New York: Harper and Row, 1975), especially the essay by Paul Ramsey entitled "The Indignity of 'Death with Dignity,'" pp. 81–96, and the responses by Robert S. Morison and Leon Kass.

3. That he was indeed poking fun at the philosophical gamesmanship which distinguishes between killing and letting people die, there can be no doubt from the other lines of his updating of God's message to Moses:

> Thou shalt not steal; an empty feat,
> When it's so lucrative to cheat.

> Thou shalt not covet; but tradition
> Approves all forms of competition.

case of the Welsh poet, the struggle was not terribly fruitful. He died at thirty-nine. Yet it may be that in this strange world where the artificial has become the natural, the heroic the expected, and the eternal punishment for Adam's sin a glory to be praised that a time has come to make a case for the goodness of, life, even for the ideal of immortality. In this chapter I hope to make that case, or at least to make it *prima facie*. In the end I shall argue that the concept of natural death is at least dreadfully ambiguous and dangerous and possibly romantically elitist. If prolonging of physical life even to the point of immortality is an ideal long cherished by the common man and consistent with the most profound image of the human and the human community, we should prepare for profound policy dilemmas. Realistically the ideal will never be achieved and other policy goals are also crucial for the image of the human individual and of the human community. This means that the case for immortality in the end is only a modest one, and a task of complex research in economics and philosophy confronts us.

First, I want to examine some of the public policy issues at stake, presenting two scenarios to dramatize the working out of the concept. Once some of the issues are presented, it will be necessary to clarify some terms and make some basic analytical distinctions. Then I will give two arguments for supporting research designed to prevent certain deaths and ideally even death itself. Once the arguments have been made, I want to examine some of the cases for death and against immortality. Finally, I want to discuss why the case for ever extending life can only be a *prima facie* one and why two qualifications are necessary in a public policy designed to prolong healthy physical life without limit.

NATURAL DEATH: ITS PUBLIC POLICY IMPACT

At this point in history much more rides on the outcome of the debate over whether death is a good or an evil than it did in the day of Socrates. When the traditional arguments were made against the physical immortality of the body, little more rested on the outcome than the mental satisfaction of an elite of Athens. Philosophers have always tried to resolve one of life's great philosophical dilemmas: Why it is that man must die?

Even if the struggle over the meaning of death once was rather esoteric, as soon as death was seen as a "natural" phenomenon, it acquired political policy implications—or at least that is Ivan Illich's thesis.[4] He claims that from the first signs in the fifteenth century of the shift in man's understanding of death as a supernatural messenger from God to a natural force, the impact was to keep the doctor away from the deathbed of the peasant. By the eighteenth century humans had become unequal in death as in life. Death in active old age had become the ideal for elites. The leisure class could live longer because their lives had become less wearing. They refused to retire because an expanding bureaucracy favored the ageless who had been around for a long time. By the nineteenth century, according to Illich, health had become a privilege of living long enough to have a natural death. Industrial workers began demanding the right to medical and retirement insurance. Finally with the union movement, demands for equality in death produced a proletarian form of natural death. Workers were redefined as health care consumers, a move which first had revolutionary potential, but soon became a means of social control. Man now feels obliged to die a natural death. The right to die a natural death has become a duty. The physician now gives the patient "permission to die."[5] Biomedical intervention—a condition for a natural death—becomes compulsory, unless special dispensation is received.

It is clear that making complex biomedical technologies necessary for a natural death was a blatant contradiction which could not survive long. Nor could the radical egalitarianism of the proletarian form of natural death. It is natural that someone would seize upon the ambiguities in the term *natural*, that a death with dignity movement would recognize that the artifacts of biomedical technology need not be called natural. Those who no longer need worry about life's necessities—

4. Ivan Illich, "The Political Uses of Natural Death," *Hastings Center Studies* 2, no. 1 (January 1974), pp. 3–20.

5. Eric J. Cassell, "Permission to Die," *BioScience* 23 (August 1973), pp. 475–78.

food, shelter, and especially medical care—now seem to have discovered the right to die the new natural death.

If that is the case then Illich's clever analysis may be open to reinterpretation. He sees the proletariat enslaved by a medical elite and demanding what as "health consumers" they have been taught is the natural death of the intensive care unit. But it could also be that the elite is outflanking the masses, preparing the ground for a new stage in the combat—a stage where a basically healthy group can undermine the newly won right to life-extending medical interventions. The new natural death is the new gnosis, accepted willingly by the enlightened and enforced upon the masses.

Whether Illich's interpretation and this reinterpretation of the modern history of natural death are correct, today the question whether death is a good or an evil is argued for much higher stakes. Budgets of the National Institute of Health depend upon whether conquering arteriosclerosis in old age ought to get more or less priority than death in infancy from rare genetic disease. They depend on whether it is more important to extend the life span of those already living or to overcome the infertility affecting as many as 10 percent of the married couples of the society. They depend upon whether natural death or natural weather disasters producing very unnatural deaths ought to get the greater share of the national resources.

An estimated $49,643,000,000 was spent in fiscal 1973 by the federal government alone on problems related to aging. Most of this was in support and social services for the elderly. Of that a comparatively tiny $12,300,000 was spent on medical research on the aging process, this by the National Institute of Child Health and Human Development. Excluded, however, are the $426 million for cancer research and $247 million for research on heart disease, the two diseases with public images of being enemies of natural death. The recent debates about the bill establishing the National Institute of Aging will provide a focus for research on the aging process and probably generate additional funding.

Drugs as diverse as procaine, vitamin E, and butylated hydroxytolvene (BHT), which may significantly extend the life span, are now in various stages of research and clinical trial in the United States.[6] A set of plausible theories accounting for a general aging process now focuses on genetic programing of the cell's DNA, protein and enzyme theories (such as synthetase function), the buildup of free chemical radicals, surplus monoamineoxidase, cross-linkage formation, and autoimmune damage which may or may not be related to errors in cell replication.[7] Extending the life span by twenty or forty years would not produce immortality, but it would extend life well beyond what is now thought "natural," and it would produce a radical social, political, and psychological change in society.

If a natural death is a good to which all are entitled, then this research is malicious. If we still live after the fall when man is entitled to three score years and ten and no more, then pharmacologists are trying to bite the fruit of the tree of life, the tree from which Adam and Eve were barred when they were forced from the garden. Adam's most recent descendants have gained that knowledge of good and evil which was the fruit of that first fruit. Now they must decide whether Gerovital being tested in Nathan Kline's hospital ward for its life-extending properties is an antidote for that apple or merely a synthetic and more flavorful modernization of that first temptation. The Food and Drug Administration, however, must make a choice. Unlike Plato's inquisitive colleagues in speculation, the FDA must have an answer. Should they decide that tasting this new fruit is as evil as biting the first, then they must decide how they will regulate it under the present requirements of safety and effectiveness—their mandates since the Kefauver amendment.

In order to present the policy implications of the concept of natural death most starkly, let me sketch two scenarios for the future of the concept over the next decade or two.

6. D. Harmon, "Free Radical Theory of Aging," *Triangle* 12, no. 4 (1973), p. 155; Harold M. Schmeck, "Disputed Drug Is Restudied for Use in Geriatrics," *New York Times*, March 18, 1973, p. 57.

7. See Leonard Hayflick, "The Biology of Human Aging," *The American Journal of the Medical Sciences* 265, no. 6 (June 1973), pp. 432–45; A. Comfort, "Biological Theories of Aging," *Human Development* 13 (1970) pp. 127–39; and Samuel Goldstein, "The Biology of Aging," *New England Journal of Medicine* 285 (1971), pp. 1120–29.

Natural Death: Two Scenarios

THE DIGNIFIED DEATH SCENARIO,
OR, DEATH OUGHT TO BE NATURAL

The world of the dignified death is the world of Marya Mannes,[8] the signers of the *Humanist's* "Plea for Beneficent Euthanasia," [9] and sometimes the Euthanasia Educational Council. Over the next decade fiefdoms for a dignified death will emerge. Walter Sackett will convince the representatives in the Florida house to pass his legislation for death with dignity just as in the past year he has convinced his fellow senators. Gradually other states will catch on. Oregon, West Virginia, Massachusetts, Idaho, Montana—all of whom have already considered legislation—will make clear that patients and patients' agents have the right to refuse medical treatments. Living wills will be discussed in Protestant churches from Darien to Palo Alto. The recently developed Catholic Hospital Association version will spread among Roman Catholics.

Since the Living Will is not a legally binding instrument (because it says it is not), Sidney Rosoff, legal counsel for the Euthanasia Educational Council, and the American Civil Liberties Union will be brought into a law suit. Eighty-seven-year-old Clarence Connolly will have signed a Living Will and lapsed into coma. His daughter, Hortence, serving as guardian, will ask to have the respirator turned off and will end up in court. Mrs. Martinez's case in Miami will be used as a precedent. As we saw, seventy-two-year-old Mrs. Martinez screamed her protests against continual cutdowns on veins in her legs until she convinced her physician to go to court. Mrs. Martinez was ruled incompetent to make such a crucial judgment for herself so her daughter was appointed her agent. She affirmed her mother's refusal and Judge Popper let the guardian's refusal stand—the only case I know of other than Karen

8. Marya Mannes, *Last Rights: A Plea for the Good Death* (New York: William Morrow, 1974).
9. "A Plea for Beneficent Euthanasia," *The Humanist* (July-August 1974), pp. 4–5.

Quinlan's where a court condoned a guardian's refusal of death-prolonging medical treatments. But this was only a circuit court decision. Hortence Connolly will have to win her case on its merits.

Medical ethics courses will complement clinical instruction in medical schools so that physicians will gradually if reluctantly abandon what Francis Bacon called the third and new duty of the physician: the prolongation of life. The grounds will be that in medicine physicians have always believed that every case is so unique that no general rules can apply. Decisions will have to be made about continuing treatment on a case by case basis.

Meanwhile the country will still be in the latest stages of its third major depression. Pressures will surface for cutting the national budget as an act of compassion to curb inflation. Since national defense cannot be compromised, sacrifices will have to be made in the domestic sphere. The National Institutes of Well-Being (NIW) and its parent Department of Health (formerly Health, Education, and Welfare) will have to make a 20 percent budget cut.

At this point someone will realize that the Department of Health is spending billions of dollars annually to prevent our distinguished senior citizens from exercising the well earned right to die with dignity. It is bizarre indeed for a government, which by then will have as its sole task the protection of the health of its citizens, to be engaged in such unhealthy behavior as combating nature's own way of giving meaning to life. Hortence Connolly and Judge Popper will have not simply a right, but a duty to promote a natural death.

THE DEATH IS EVIL SCENARIO, OR, NO DEATH IS NATURAL

Natural death may have a rather different future over the next decade or two. We may discover that "natural death" was nothing more than a temporary accident in human history, arriving in the fifteenth century as man began to discard the accretions of supernaturalism and departing in about 1984 when we realized that no death is a natural death. In this scenario the pathologist is prophet. For the pathologist today as for the rest of us tomorrow, something always causes death.

It never just happens. If this view dominates we may be at a transition point in history where some deaths are thought caused by specific disease processes or acts of man, but others are just the natural wearing out of the machinery. At the present time the nonpathologists among us still are able to think of deaths caused by specific diseases and voluntary acts of man as controllable, as potentially conquerable if we are aggressive enough in applying Western ingenuity and modern biomedical technologies. The goal is to let everyone spend eighty or ninety years wandering the face of the earth so that death may come the way nature intended it.

Research on aging may change that. The work of Hayflick, Strehler, Goldstein, Comfort, and others begins to suggest that that "natural" limit may be subject to human control. In the No-Death-Is-Natural future, every death will be seen as caused by events potentially subject to human control. Deaths will be of three types, each someone's responsibility.

One large group of deaths will be caused by the deceased's own behavior. Heart attacks are already believed caused in part by bad diet, poor exercise, smoking, and other controllable behaviors. The first critical development for this view was the germ theory of disease and the recognition that there were things we could do to keep microorganisms out of our bodies. Deaths resulting from failure to take medicines or have proper immunizations before foreign travel would now be thought to be culpable. Cervical cancer in the woman who has failed to have a pap smear and automobile accident injury for one not wearing seat belts are now inevitably on their way to being seen as voluntarily induced medical conditions.

Second, there will be those diseases that are the responsibility of one's parents. If Tay-Sachs disease is evil and is predictable, can acceptance of the risk of the disease be anything but voluntary and culpable behavior? Parental culpability is clearly a growth category.

Finally, there will be those deaths for which the NIW is responsible. To be convinced that a particular death is the result of potentially controllable processes and not make the societal effort to understand and control those processes is a voluntary political choice. It may well come to be seen as a culpable choice, especially if those afflicted are senile, or children, or otherwise incapable of making a rational claim to be happy in their condition. In any event, the notion that there is no responsibility for getting a disease—a concept which has been the core of the medical model—will be short-lived. If no death is natural, death will be seen as even more evil than it is now. Individual deaths will be the responsibility of someone or some group.

While both scenarios are caricatures with unpalatable elements, I think a case can be made that the second view—that death is combatable and ought to be combatted—is the more human course. Much depends on the meaning of the term *natural* and on some distinctions that must be made if we are to be clear in formulating a policy about death. It also depends on our conception of *human*.

DISTINCTIONS NEEDING TO BE MADE

The Meaning of Natural

"Natural death" is not the only place where the term *natural* is encountered in doing ethics and the life sciences. We have a frustratingly rich tradition of natural contraception, natural foods, natural drugs, natural sexual preferences, and natural instincts. Equally frustrating is the closely related concept of *normal,* as in normal behavior, normal intelligence, normal life span, and normal temperature. Standing behind some uses of both terms is an ethical-legal tradition of natural law.

The concept of the natural is one of the most used, misused, and abused in the field. It is central to both the fields of ethics and the life sciences. Before examining the policy implications of the concept of natural death, a brief linguistic analysis of the term *natural* will be helpful. There are at least five distinct conceptions of the natural:

The statistical. The natural is the "usual," that which is the modal or near the mean. It is "natural" for a couple to prefer that their first child be a male. It is natural for man to die, so natural that the class of those who do not may be a null class.

Certainly it is limited to those humans who have been born in the past 100 or 150 years with possibly very few exceptions who are thought god-like for their unique properties. The opposite of *natural* in this sense is *unusual*. It is clearly impossible to draw any policy conclusions about what we *ought* to do from this empirical description of the natural without an additional evaluative premise. To be ordinary is not necessarily to be right.

The biological. The natural is that which occurs "among the animals" or "among the higher animals" or "according to man's biological nature." It is natural for humans to desire food and sexual activity, to avoid pain, and to die. Most if not all forms of contraception are unnatural in that the animal species do not practice them. Those who seek the normative from man's biological nature—an Epicurus, a Nietzsche, a Spencer, or a Darwin—are very interested in this sense of the natural. It should be clear, though, that from this biological descriptive use as with the statistical use of the term, another premise is needed to reach policy conclusions. The needed premise, that what occurs in animals is good or right, and good or right for man, seems most implausible.

The anthropological. The natural is that which occurs in nature, that which is not man-made or processed. Detergents are artificial; soap is natural. Dannon yogurt is one hundred percent natural; it contains no artificial ingredients. It all comes straight from the cow and the culture without any man-made chemicals added. The opposite of *natural* in this sense is *cultural, artificial,* or *artifactual.* The distinction between the natural and the man-made seems to be a very primitive one. Levi-Strauss in *The Raw and the Cooked* analyzes myth systems for their symbolic differentiation of the world into natural and the cultural.[10] Talcott Parsons distinguishes between those deaths which American society conceives to be natural and those caused by disease or accident which he calls "adventitious."[11] A death by murder or by automobile accident is not

---

10. Claude Levi-Strauss, *The Raw and the Cooked* (New York: Harper and Row, 1969).

11. Talcott Parsons and Victor Lidz, "Death in American Society," in *Essays in Self-Destruction,* ed. Edwin S. Shneidman (New York: Science House, 1967).

natural in the sense that it is caused by man's intervention into the natural. In the "back to nature movement" we affirm that if it is natural (not man-made) it is good. Once again the evaluative premise is needed. Stated in its boldest form—that all that is man-made is evil, and all that comes raw from the state of nature is good—it is certainly wrong. Some of man's interventions must be evil on balance. That is the judgment of those who are repulsed by the tubes and tracheostomy and technicians that keep the corpse respiring in the modern intensive care unit. But by this same notion disease caused by the natural invasion of the body by pathological microorganisms would have to be thought of as good, while the antibiotics (or at least synthetic ones) which save the child from pneumonia, an evil. Artificiality, by itself, cannot be sufficient to declare an innovation to be an evil.

The religious. The natural is that which is part of the creation as opposed to the "supernatural," that is, the events and forces which result from direct divine activity. There is a parallel dualism between the nature-supernatural dichotomy and the nature-artifact dichotomy. Levi-Strauss's Hegelian dualism is also at home with the natural-supernatural distinction of the Greeks, Thomas, and Eastern conceptions of nature. Illich has claimed that the notion that death is a natural rather than a supernatural event is a uniquely modern phenomenon.

The moral. The reason the natural and natural death cause us so much trouble at the policy level is that *natural* can also mean *moral*. The natural is that which is in accord with the nature of man and the nature of the universe. Murdering innocent children is unnatural for man. Lying, war-making, and hatred can be unnatural even if they are ubiquitous. Classical natural law tradition—Ulpian's trichotomous theory of law, the Stoics, Thomas, Troeltsch, and modern Roman Catholic moral theologians—all understand the moral to be natural. So does the contemporary naturalist tradition in metaethics.[12]

12. G. E. Moore, *Principia Ethica* (Cambridge: Cambridge: University Press, 1903); W. K. Frankena, "The Naturalistic Fallacy," in *Readings in Ethical Theory* (New York: Appleton-Century-Crofts, 1952), pp. 103–14; Roderick Firth, "Ethical Absolutism and the Ideal Observer," *Philosophy and Phenomenological Research* 12 (1952), pp. 317–45; Robert M. Veatch, "Does Ethics Have an Empirical Basis?" *Hastings Center Studies* 1, no. 1 (1973), pp. 50–65.

Problems arise when the conception of the natural is applied in two or more senses simultaneously. This may happen in three ways: (1) A particular object or event may fit more than one conception: "It is natural (statistical and biological) for grass to be green." (2) It may also happen when certain schools of thought hold that one conception of the natural provides the content for another conception: "To determine what is natural (moral) for man, see what is in accord with his (biological) nature. This is Ulpian's *ius naturale* formulation. (3) Finally, the multiple conceptions of the natural may occur as fallacious arguments: "I have demonstrated that homosexuality is unnatural (statistical and maybe biological). Therefore, since it is unnatural (moral), it should not be practiced." "Death is a natural event (statistical, biological, nonsupernatural); therefore, the scientifically trained expert should determine when natural (morally significant) life ceases." Making these leaps is what G. E. Moore called the naturalistic fallacy. Frankena persuasively refutes Moore's argument, though, by claiming that what really must be attacked is defining something into moral categories by demonstrating that it fits empirically into a certain nonmoral category without defending the claim that such a definition is justified.[13]

The problem with the concept of the natural death is that while death is clearly statistically and biologically natural, and presumably natural in the sense of not being caused by divine spirits, it is not clear whether natural deaths are always to be preferred to man-made ones. Presumably all agree that adventitious deaths by gunshot or rampaging automobiles are not desirable, but there is utter chaos in deciding whether deaths prolonged by technological interventions are better or worse than those brought about in nature's uninterrupted course. The critical problem for public policy is whether such deaths are to be evaluated as good or as evil. Are they moral because they are natural or should they be conquered if possible through the use of man's rational capacity for technological intervention?

13. Frankena, "The Naturalistic Fallacy."

Specific and Systemic Causes of Death

The received tradition gives natural death two types of enemies: specific and systemic. Parsons, astute as he is in observing culture, seems to accept that adventitious deaths can be clearly distinguished from the category of "the inevitable 'natural' deaths of all individuals." [14] Specific causes of death are normally thought to thwart natural death by making death premature. But the death with dignity movement has made us aware that the biomedical assault on these specific death causes can also make us view arteriosclerosis as natural and the struggle against it as artificial and evil. Thus specific diseases can interfere with natural death both by hastening it and by creating a situation where death is unnaturally prolonged. Even Parsons holds to the notion that there is a natural, inevitable death which will occur if we only leave the body alone and give it a chance.

The field of gerontology is rapidly emerging as a new science with a rather old set of conceptual tools. Even the leaders in research on aging accept the view that the systemic aging process, "the biological clock," is fundamentally different from specific diseases. Leonard Hayflick speaks of the death of cells and the destruction of tissues and organs to be a "normal part of morphogenic or developmental sequences." [15] Harman views the human being as having a "natural human maximum life span." The basic aging processes have diseased states "superimposed and intertwined." [16]

This commonly received view may not stand scrutiny. The generalization often made that conquering specific diseases such as heart disease and cancer would add little to the life span appears to rest on a model of total system collapse after a "natural" life span. This in turn requires two assumptions. One, that other disease systems (respiratory or neurological) will not in turn be mastered leading to further extensions of life expectancy and, two, that the aging process is not itself a

14. Parsons and Lidz, "Death in American Society," p. 138.
15. Hayflick, "The Biology of Human Aging," p. 442.
16. Harman, "Free Radical Theory of Aging," p. 154.

"disease" or set of diseases subject to medical control. Most of the theories of aging, though, appear to lend themselves to medical intervention. Antioxidants may bind free radicals. Autoimmune reactions may be controlled with the emerging techniques of immunology. Genes programmed for aging may be controlled with genetic engineering. Monoamineoxidase inhibitors or appropriate analogues may correct enzyme defects. The view that aging is somehow different from disease may be wrong. The famous graphs showing life expectancy at birth approaching asymptotically to one hundred years and capable of modification with age span or biological clock modifiers may simply be a product of a false dichotomy between natural life span and disease-induced shortening of that span. That arteriosclerosis or phenylketonuria are considered diseases but free radical accumulation or synthetase malfunction are considered natural aging may be a temporary accident of history. If distinguishing the natural and the abnormal has policy implications—as it apparently does in the minds of many—then clarifying such distinctions will be crucial for priorities in research and clinical health care.

Socioeconomic and Philosophical Problems of Immortality

The fifty billion dollars spent yearly on aging, primarily for services to the elderly, makes clear the enormous social and economic problems in modifying the life span. Several authors have pointed out the phenomenal impact that would be made on our social institutions if we tamper successfully with the aging process. If the years of retirement are significantly changed the social security system will require radical reorganization. The labor force, housing market, family structure, political alliances, and to some extent the population size will change. To calculate just the economic impact of extending life expectancy by ten years would be an incredibly large task.

As critical and complex as these social and economic problems would be, there is a separate set of issues which really should be dealt with first. These are the philosophical-ethical considerations of whether such life-extending innovations are good, independent of the social and economic costs. A strong case has been made in the history of philosophy for the goodness of death. If death's defenders are correct and influence policy accordingly, then the social and economic problems will be avoided. This chapter concerns itself only with these latter problems—whether death is essentially an evil to be conquered.

Extended Mortal Life and Immortality

If it is concluded that life is indeed a good and death is an evil, then two alternatives are conceivable: extended mortal life and immortality. It is possible to find either alternative good in theory while judging the other unacceptable. One might conclude, for instance, that immortality would be ideal, but that extended mortal life (which is all that we can realistically hope for) is no better than our present finite existence. If it all must end, than what does it matter when? On the other hand, some might find the prospect of immortality unbearable, but the option of an additional twenty to forty years quite attractive.

Since extended mortal life is accessible to human endeavor as immortality is not, the most difficult problem is presented by the individual for whom immortality is an ideal utopia but mere extension of mortal life has no value. The Stoics distinguished two natural laws: one, more absolute, was the law of the utopia. The other was the relative natural law for the real world. Pacifism might be an absolute law of nature, while just-war theory might be appropriate for the real and sinful world. I have always found one of the most perplexing dilemmas in philosophy to be whether one ought to pursue an ideal which probably can never be achieved or whether one ought to accommodate to the real world and pursue the relative ideal which is the best course once one concedes that the ideal cannot be achieved. Building the perfect jail is conceding that crimes will be committed. Establishing peer review committees is conceding that individual researchers will not always make the wisest, most detached judgments.

The idealist holds that one should not deviate from the telos, that approaching the real goal is better than achieving the substitute.[17] We in fact do not abandon the ideals of love, peace, justice simply because we know they cannot be achieved, but realists do modify their behavior because they cannot be perfectly achieved. For idealists the prospect that the quest for immortality will only lead to extended mortal life would not dissuade them even if they think that extended mortal life would be no gain. Realists, on the other hand, may have to be convinced that extended mortal life is a good in itself. This desire for extended mortal life appears to be in accord with the normal behavior of most humans and may be a sufficient justification for policy commitment to life extension even in the face of the reality of failure to achieve the eschaton. Commitment to life-prolonging efforts, then, may have two independent justifications: the idealist's quest for immortality or the realist's desire for extended mortal life. At the policy level it may not be necessary to distinguish the justifications if identical policies result.

THE CASES FOR LIFE

It seems strange to make a case for life. Like happiness, truth, freedom, or justice, life seems to be an intrinsic good. Yet philosophers have been remarkably ingenious in putting forth arguments why the ending of life is not necessarily an evil. In fact I believe life is not an intrinsic good in the same way that happiness, truth, freedom, or justice are. On the other hand it is not simply an instrumental value either. If we are forced to make arguments against death and for life, presumably they must have more substance than the gut level affirmation of the pro-life movement. When pressed, two arguments seem cogent.

The Rationalist Case for Life

The first argument is that of the rationalist. Life should be affirmed as good and death as evil if doing so is consistent

17. I am, of course, using the terms *idealist* and *realist* not in their technical philosophical meanings, but rather to contrast one who is guided by ideals and one who is influenced by more practical considerations.

with promotion of the prudent, personal self-interest of the rational person. This argument is really history's response to Epicurus' frustratingly coherent argument that we should not fear death: "So long as we exist death is not with us; but when death comes, then we do not exist." [18] Epicurus may be comforting about what follows death, but even if he is right about that, he does not convince me that I should not fear the process of dying. More significantly, he does not convince me that I should not anticipate with regret the nonexistence of my self. Since the fear of dying is uniquely horrifying because of the anticipatory regret of nonexistence, it is really the latter which leads to the proposition that my death is an evil for me.

But why this anticipatory regret? There are many future states which I desire. Some have nothing to do with me; they will occur or fail to occur quite independent of my existence. Others involve me in some way or another. Some of those involving me I desire only on the condition that I am alive. An example is my desire to have my pension.[19] The desired future state in that case in no way makes me desire to continue to live. A second group of future states I desire involve me because I think I am able to promote those states better if I am alive. My desire to see my children receive a college education is an example. Finally, some of the future states I desire involve me because I must be present. My desire to see my research on my favorite project completed or my desire to see my children graduate from college requires that I be around. These desires differ from my pension in that for the pension I desire that it exist only if I am around, but for the research and the commencement I desire to be around in order to have those experiences. For anyone who has desires about future states requiring his own existence, it is rational that he regret the anticipation of his nonexistence.

That I may desire my existence, of course, does not demonstrate that it is desirable that I continue to exist, much less that

18. Epicurus, "Epicurus to Monoeceus," in *Ethical Theories,* ed., A. I. Melden (Englewood Cliffs, N.J.: Prentice-Hall, 1967), p. 144.

19. I am indebted to Bernard Williams for much of the argument presented in this paragraph. See his essay "The Makropulos Case: Reflections on the Tedium of Immortality," in *Problems of the Self* (Cambridge: Cambridge University Press, 1973), pp. 82–100.

the state has a reason to undertake efforts to see that I continue to exist. The common desire of many people for future
states which require their existence does, however, create a
common interest. To the degree, however, that the state has a
legitimate interest in promoting the general welfare, and particularly promoting it when the individual efforts of individual
citizens taken separately would not be effective, the state may
prudently adopt a policy of supporting research and medical
services which will tend to promote the general welfare. Prudent individuals form a contract to achieve together what they
cannot achieve separately.

While this may provide an argument that the state can legitimately support death-averting programs, I do not think it is
the strongest argument. First, it may confuse the desired and
the desirable. That I desire future states requiring my existence does not make my future existence a good and my death
an evil. That the vast majority of citizens desire their future
existence does not mean it is right that the state should promote their future existence. Second, and I believe more devas-
tating, the case for life and against death based on the prudence of the rational individual contracting with other
individuals is, in the end, both too egocentric and too individualistic. A stronger argument for life and against death, I
believe, rests in what, for lack of a better label, I will call the
social-eschatological case.

The Social-Eschatological Case for Life

To argue the evilness of death is to argue man's place in the
cosmos. Man must come to grips with death through understanding of his nature and his vision of his place in the telos—
the ideal world toward which we strive. Western man is inces-
santly teleological. He dreams of a Kingdom of God which is a
social, political reality—*kingdom* is a very political metaphor.
He dreams of life immortal (if influenced by the Greeks) or of
resurrection of the body (if taught by the Christian vision). In
combining the two strands of our heritage, the body has won a
place for itself from which we need never again feel we must
escape. Common to all the significant Western eschatologies is

a vision of perpetuation. While the pre-Christian Jewish tradition devoted relatively little attention to the problem of death, it transmitted the belief that death is the wages of sin. At least by the period of the Maccabees, it also had a vision of a messiah who would atone for that sin and create a perpetual Kingdom.

Modern Western man is deeply rooted in this social eschatology. Anticipated in the Johannine realized eschatology, it becomes much more this worldly in the modern era. Man prays, "Thy kingdom come on earth," and means it. He is an activist who sees it as part of his task to bring into reality that vision of the new world, the world where evil is no more. And one of the evils that he has dreamed about conquering is the evil of death. His social vision is one that he himself must play a part in constructing—and one in which life can be prolonged through the use of human ingenuity to master diseases one by one. Life shall be a struggle. But in the end the goodness of life is to be affirmed. Man shall have dominion over the earth and subdue it. Life shall prevail and death shall be no more.

If this social eschatology is made the basis for a commitment to a governmental policy of prolongation of life, we need not be confined to the individualism of the rationalist. Overcoming death—my own and my fellow man's—is the final step in overcoming evil and building human community.

> Any man's death diminishes me, because I am involved in Mankind; And therefore never send to know for whom the bell tolls; It tolls for thee.

THE CASES FOR DEATH AND AGAINST IMMORTALITY

Against this vision stands a long line of argument from Plato and Aristotle through Darwin to Hartshorne, Morison, and Kass. I have identified five arguments as potent counters thrust against the goal of extended mortal life or the ideal of immortality. Let us examine each in turn.

Death as Relief from Suffering

Perhaps the most common case to be made for death is that it is the great liberator. The poet cloys with death's sweetness:

Come lovely and soothing death,
Undulate round the world, serenely, arriving, arriving,
In the day, in the night, to all, to each
Sooner or later, delicate death.
Prais'd be the fathomless universe,
For life and joy, and for objects and knowledge curious,
And for love, sweet love—But praise! praise! praise!
For the sure-enwinding arms of cool-enfolding death.[20]

That death can be the great liberator was clear to Socrates. Plato has Socrates say in the *Crito,* "When man has reached my age, he ought not to be repining at the approach of death." While in Plato's account escaping the miseries of old age plays a secondary role for Socrates, in Xenophon it becomes the main reason for Socrates' uncompromising position before his judges:

Do you not know that I would refuse to concede that any man has lived a better life than I have up to now? . . . But now, if my years are prolonged, I know that the frailties of old age will inevitably be realized. . . . Perhaps God in his kindness is taking my part and securing me the opportunity of ending my life not only in season but also in the way that is easiest.[21]

In speaking of ending his life "in season" Socrates is the original advocate of the naturalness of death. Xenophon has Socrates say, "Have you not known all along from the moment of my birth nature has condemned me to death?" But in our day, that condemnation by nature to a natural death is being challenged. The choice need not be as with Socrates between "the frailties of old age" and death, but between death and medical treatments which may prolong the prime of life and conquer at least some of the debilitating diseases from which death was a humane release.

20. Walt Whitman, "When Lilacs Last in the Dooryard Bloom'd," *Leaves of Grass.*
21. See Jacques Choron, *Death and Western Thought* (New York: Macmillan, 1963), p. 45.

Death as Relief from Boredom

A related case for death and against immortality is made by those who fear the unbearable tedium of an endless life. To be condemned to eternal life is seen as a Sartre-esque torture of enormous proportion. Here the distinction between extended mortal life and immortality may be crucial. Those who believe they fear immortality more than death may be quite delighted with a few score more years for completion of their earthly projects. The case for death as a relief from the boredom of immortality does not create a problem for those who advocate only a public policy of support for research to extend the life span. If, however, immortality would be boring, it does present a formidable challenge to the other principle upon which support for such research is based, that ever-extended life is the ideal toward which we strive.

Does this argument against the ideal work? I think not. I find in it a hollow, sour-grapes quality which might be satisfying to some, but would be rather unconvincing to a broader public. There is a play by Karel Capek in which a woman named Elina Makropulos was given an elixir of life by her father, a sixteenth-century emperor. At the time of the play she is 342 and lives, apparently physically healthy, but in a state of boredom, indifference, and coldness. Bernard Williams has examined this situation. His argument, as I understand it, is that it is not an accident of her particular life that she is bored, but that it is essential to human nature that an endless life would be a meaningless one. Elina Makropulos's problem, according to Williams, is that "everything that could happen and make sense to one particular human being . . . had already happened." He then maintains that the fact that life ceased to have meaning for her, that she "froze up," is essential to human nature and not dependent on her particular contingent character or on the failure of others around her to share her immortal capacities.[22]

In developing his arguments he considers several alterna-

22. See Williams, "The Makropulos Case," pp. 89–90.

tives: one continuous life, a series of lives connected by a common memory, and theories of an afterlife. The core of the argument, though, focuses on the primary case of one continuous life. Williams argues that two conditions would have to be met for the prospect of living forever to be attractive: (1) it should clearly be *me* who lives forever and (2) "the state in which I survive should be one which, to me looking forward, will be adequately related, in the life it presents, to those aims which I now have in wanting to survive at all." [23]

I readily concede the first condition. It poses no problem for the kind of ideal relevant to public policy for research on aging. It *would* be me who lives forever. The second condition is more difficult. It includes two component arguments: (1) it is irrational to pursue a future desire if it is clearly impossible to achieve it, and (2) it is impossible to have an infinite agenda of categorical desires (desires requiring my presence for their fulfillment).

Williams does not explicitly deal with either of these assumptions. I think both can be challenged. We have already discussed the first. I find the position implausible, especially when holding that ideal would reasonably lead us toward that ideal even though it cannot realistically be achieved and when approaches to the ideal are considered progressively better in and of themselves. The second forces us to deal with the claim that human nature is such that boredom will eventually result from living forever, that Elina Makropulos's plight was not an accident of her personality, but integral to the human condition.

This position requires the presumption that man necessarily has finite categorical desires or at least a finite capacity to develop new ways of fulfilling all of those desires. If my more eschatological understanding of man as a community builder is correct, I see no reason why this must be the case. If man's hopes are infinite, it is possible to have hope of continually fulfilling some categorial desires while at the same time not fulfilling all of them. If the vision is utopian, the possibility of new and fulfilling experiences is infinite. Furthermore some

23. Ibid., p. 91.

realistic categorical desires, some of the most important ones, do not depend on the newness of experiences. The desire to live in a loving and happy relationship with one's family does not necessarily require continual novelty for its fulfillment. In fact such a relationship conceivably might be quite stable without inevitably leading to boredom. While the prospect of death might enrich some such experiences by giving them a timely quality, it certainly also introduces great tragedy.

Finally, Williams appears to argue that for immortality to be attractive boredom must be unthinkable.[24] It could be that he is simply not a gambler and is not willing to take a chance. If, however, continual nonboring existence is really an ideal, it should not be necessary to rule out failure as unthinkable in order to be willing to give it a try. It might not be worth the gamble if the boring immortality were compulsory, but Elina Makropulos's was not. She stopped taking the elixar and died. Certainly any realistic public policy effort to combat death should hold out the same escape. Compulsory immortality is not among the conceivable treatments. As long as continual fulfillment of categorial desires is possible, it would seem both that there is hope that total boredom might be avoided and that it is worth the risk—especially since failures can be aborted. On the contrary, it would seem that the burden of proof is on those who would hold that boredom is inevitable. I do not see that as either plausible or provable.

Death as a Source of Meaning

Teleologists may make their case for as well as against death. Death, it may be argued, gives life a sense of timeliness and purpose. This is the argument explored by Paul Ramsey, that death gives us reason to "number our days." [25] Were we to believe that we had forever to complete our projects, the sense of urgency and excitement in life would be lost. This is probably one of the most convincing cases for death faced by Judeo-Christian man, whose world view is temporally orien-

24. Ibid., p. 95.
25. Paul Ramsey, "The Indignity of 'Death with Dignity,' " *Hastings Center Studies* 2, no 2 (May 1974), pp. 47–62.

ted. Were immortality to come at the price of giving up a sense of time and timeliness, the price would be high indeed. But would that in fact be the result? Certainly not unless the eschatological ideal is achieved, but even then it is not clear why perpetual life would be a timeless life. The test of this objection to immortality as with the previous one rests with the human—the wise and the many. Would indeed humans who are not part of Illich's elite seriously consider abandoning the possibility of extending physical life for fear of endless boredom and loss of a sense of time? I think not.

Death as a Force for Progress

For this particularly modern argument for death I cite the poet Morison:

> Every human death is ultimately for the good of the group. . . .
> To rage against death is to rage at the very process which
> made one a human in the first place.[26]

That evolution has depended upon the death of the weak so that the more fit may thrive is the first law of Darwin. Until now, it has seemed irrefutable. But need the evolutionist's position remain valid? To be sure, were immortality to be achieved, reproduction would have to cease if population were to remain stable. But if mortal life is extended the reproductive process would at the most merely be slowed. Even if biological evolution ceased completely it is not clear to me that at this point in history this would necessarily be an evil. For one who believes as firmly in progress as I, that may be heresy, but I wonder whether, for instance, continual evolution in intelligence so that more and more people have the intellectual capacities to build world-destroying weapon systems is an adaptive development. If evolution was once only biological it may now be cultural as well. If continued adaptation is necessary for survival in an ever-changing universe, possibly cultural adaption may be sufficient or even preferable.

26. Robert S. Morison, "The Last Poem: The Dignity of the Inevitable and Necessary," *Hastings Center Studies* 2, no. 2 (May 1974), p. 66.

Natural Death as a Comforting Fiction

We are left with one last-ditch line of defense by the advocates of death. Natural death, they may concede, is a fiction. Indeed deaths all do have a cause and that cause is potentially susceptible to description and control. But the fiction is a comforting one. It is agonizing to realize that every death, and the suffering which accompanies it, is the result of some human choice. Some human individual or group is responsible. Perpetuating the fiction of natural death at least relieves the common man of the burden of responsibility.

Relieve us it does, but at the expense of continuing the suffering of death striking out in random and unregulated viciousness. It is the death of the animal species, but in being so it is subhuman. If our vision of man is correct, if man is a responsible agent charged with the task of creating and sustaining his life and his environment, then such fictions are escapist. Such fictions may give freedom, but the result is a tyranny. To escape from responsibility to the imagined comforts of natural death cannot be a sustainable defense.

QUALIFICATIONS ON A PUBLIC POLICY OF PROLONGING LIFE

If prolonging life and combating "natural" death are goods that are part of man's responsibility in building human community, problems still remain, problems hinted at in the arguments in favor of death. Socrates' choice of death over the frailties of old age anticipates the first.

Death as a Relative rather than an Absolute Evil

To maintain that death is fundamentally incompatible with the ideal human community is not to say that death must always be fought. It is possible to maintain that immortality is a desirable goal and still hold that some deaths may be preferred to a painful and dehumanizing struggle to that goal. If death is an evil there still may be lives that are worse evils.

Both the evil of death and the acceptability of individual deaths may be affirmed. To hold death to be an evil and still feel that individual deaths are acceptable may be a tragic view of death; it may mean that "accidental" deaths and deaths from the culpable choices of individuals or governments may be seen as much more traumatic. The ideal, however, is not incompatible with living wills, legal documents to facilitate refusal of intolerable death prolonging medical treatments, or even legislation to clarify the right of individuals and their guardians to make such refusals. As an active participant in the movement for the right of the dying to refuse treatment, I write this present chapter really as a footnote to correct any mistaken implication that affirming the evil of death and the relative acceptability of particular deaths is incompatible. Until the day of the eschaton, such tragic choices will still have to be made.

The Priorities Problem

If (and only if) life is worth prolonging and death is worth combating, then the social and economic problems of policy choices become central. To make a case for immortality or extended mortal life is not to say conquering death has the highest priority on the human agenda. This is an allocation of resources question. The answer will depend on both economic and social data and on philosophical-ethical choices. If the total amount of good to come in a life is roughly proportionate to the quality of life yet to be lived, and if one opts for the utilitarian distributional principle of maximizing the total good, then research on aging and on overcoming causes of death late in life will receive very low priority. Even if the quantity of life can be extended without lowering the quality, research on diseases of infants and children surely will take priority. If, however, the good of a life is unrelated to quantity yet to be lived and the distributional principle is not the utilitarian one, then the priorities may be very different. If, for instance, the distributional principle is that medical resources should go first to those least well off—a plausible general principle of justice in health care delivery which I have supported elsewhere [27]—then the aging may have a much stronger claim to our health care dollars. If the aging constitute a minority group of the medically (and socially) disadvantaged, then perhaps a case can be made that justice demands special funding priority for their special concerns.

That all of us who are fortunate will one day count ourselves among the aged can only make the policy determination more complex. To give extending life less than highest priority is radically different from holding that "natural" death is a good, a right, or a duty. It may be that we will conclude that giving everyone a reasonable chance to have a relatively normal life span free from pain and suffering has a higher priority than extending life. If so, let the implications fall where they may—let the dollars flow from the cancer and heart institutes to the pediatrics projects. But we should not in the process imply that our task will be complete if ever that goal should be achieved. If indeed life is a good, then short of achieving immortality, the struggle will continue. To hold otherwise is to concede that there are things we could do to extend life with high quality that we choose not to do. Our care of the elderly and dying demands more.

Euripides said, "When death approaches old age is no burden." Modern man's revision might appropriately be, "The less one has to fear that death is approaching, the less will be the burden of old age."

When God created the human being—so the Judeo-Christian heritage tells us—it was in God's own image. Human beings are creatures to be sure, but they are responsible creatures. They are to have dominion over the earth and subdue it. There are two ways they may have dominion to lessen that fear of death. In some cases it will mean ingeniously using their scientific and technological skills to responsibly challenge particularly evil deaths. In other cases it will mean ingeniously using their intellectual and humanistic skills to responsibly decide that death should no longer be challenged.

The primary purpose of this book has been to explore this

27. Robert M. Veatch, "What is a 'Just' Health Care Delivery?" in *Ethics and Health Policy* (forthcoming).

second alternative. The human can and must decide what death means, when we may appropriately treat individuals as if they were dead; when, if ever, it is acceptable for patients or their agents to refuse medical treatment; when, it ever, patients should not be given potentially meaningful and useful information about their condition; and when it is reasonable to make use of the mortal remains for the newly dead so that others may live longer or better. The purpose of this last chapter has been rather different: to affirm that deciding in individual cases that the struggle against death need not continue is not incompatible with a more general social commitment to a public policy that sees at least some deaths as evil, that promotes research to overcome them. Affirming simultaneously that death is an evil and that certain deaths ought to be accepted is a difficult task. Individual and social decisions in response to these questions are required. Making such decisions is part of our quest for responsibility in the era of the biological revolution.

Bibliography

Annas, George J. "Rights of the Terminally Ill Patient." *Journal of Nursing Administration* 4 (March/April 1974), 40–44.

Ariès, Philippe. *Western Attitudes toward Death: From the Middle Ages to the Present*. Translated by Patricia M. Ranum. Baltimore: Johns Hopkins University Press, 1974.

Becker, Ernest. *The Denial of Death*. New York: Free Press, 1973.

Boase, T. S. R. *Death in the Middle Ages: Mortality, Judgment and Remembrance*. New York: McGraw-Hill, 1972.

Book of the Dead. Translated by E. A. Wallis Budge. New Hyde Park, New York: University Books, 1960.

Brim, Orville G., Jr., et al., eds. *The Dying Patient*. New York: Russell Sage Foundation, 1970.

Cartwright, Ann, et al. *Life Before Death*. London: Routledge & Kegan Paul, 1973.

Choron, Jacques. *Death and Western Thought*. New York: Macmillan, 1963.

Feifel, Herman, et al. "Physicians Consider Death." *Proceedings of the American Psychological Association*, 1967, pp. 201–02.

Gatch, Milton McC. *Death: Meaning and Mortality in Christian Thought and Contemporary Culture*. New York: Seabury Press, 1969.

Goldberg, Ivan K.; Malitz, Sidney; and Kutscher, Austin H., eds. *Psychopharmacologic Agents for the Terminally Ill and Bereaved*. New York: Columbia University Press, 1973.

Gorer, Geoffrey. *Death, Grief and Mourning*. New York: Doubleday, 1965.

Hendin, David. *Death as a Fact of Life*. New York: Norton, 1973.

Holck, Frederick, ed. *Death and Eastern Thought*. Nashville: Abingdon, 1974.

Kastenbaum, Robert, and Aisenberg, Ruth. *The Psychology of Death*. New York: Springer, 1972.

Kübler-Ross, Elisabeth. *On Death and Dying*. New York: Macmillan, 1969.

Mack, Arien, ed. *Death in the American Experience*. New York: Schocken Books, 1973.

May, William F. "On Not Facing Death Alone." *Hastings Center Report* 1 (June 1971), 8–9.

Montange, Charles H. "Informed Consent and the Dying Patient."
Yale Law Journal 83 (July 1974), 1632–64.

Morison, Robert S. "Dying." *Scientific American* 229 (September
1973), 55–62.

Neale, Robert E. "Between the Nipple and the Everlasting Arms."
Archives of the Foundation of Thanatology 3 (Spring 1971), 21–30.
(Reprinted in part in *Hastings Center Report* 2 (June 1972), 12–14.)

Parsons, Talcott; Fox, Renée C.; and Lidz, Victor M. "The 'Gift of
Life' and Its Reciprocation." *Social Research* 39 (1972), 367–415.

Parsons, Talcott, and Lidz, Victor. "Death in American Society." In
Essays in Self-Destruction. Edited by Edwin S. Schneidman. New
York: Science House, 1967.

Ramsey, Paul. *The Patient as Person*. New Haven: Yale University
Press, 1970. (See especially chapter 2, "On Updating Procedures
for Stating That a Man Has Died" and chapter 3, "On (Only) Caring for the Dying.")

Riemer, Jack, ed. *Jewish Reflections on Death*. New York: Schocken
Books, 1975.

Solzhenitsyn, A. *Cancer Ward*. New York: Bantam Books, 1969.

Sudnow, David. *Passing On: The Social Organization of Dying*. Englewood Cliffs, N.J.: Prentice-Hall, 1960.

The Tibetan Book of the Dead. Translated by W. Y. Evans-Wentz. New
York: Causeway Books, 1973.

Tolstoy, Leo. *Death of Ivan Illyich*. New York: Signet Books (New
American Library), 1960.

Toynbee, Arnold, et al. *Man's Concern with Death*. New York: Mc-
Graw-Hill, 1968.

DEFINING DEATH

Becker, Laurence C. "Human Being: The Boundaries of the Concept." *Philosophy and Public Affairs* 4 (Summer 1975), 334–59.

Biorck, G. "On the Definitions of Death." *World Medical Journal* 14
(September–October 1967), 137–39.

Bleich, J. David. "Establishing Criteria of Death." *Tradition* 13
(Winter 1973).

Brierley, J. B., et al. "Neocortical Death after Cardiac Arrest." *Lancet*, September 11, 1971, pp. 560–65.

Capron, Alexander M. "Determining Death: Do We Need a Statute?" *Hastings Center Report* 3 (February 1973), 6–7.

———, and Kass, Leon R. "A Statutory Definition of the Standards
for Determining Human Death: An Appraisal and a Proposal."

University of Pennsylvania Law Review 121 (November 1972), 87–118.

Committee on Evolving Trends in Society Affecting Life. *Death and Dying: Determining and Defining Death—A Compilation of Definitions, Selected Readings and Bibliography.* San Francisco: California Medical Association, 1975.

Curran, W. J. "Legal and Medical Death: Kansas Takes the First Step." *New England Journal of Medicine* 284 (1971), 260–61.

Dworkin, Roger B. "Death in Context." Capron, Alexander M. "The Purpose of Death: A Reply to Professor Dworkin." *Indiana Law Journal* 48 (Summer 1973), 623–48.

Halley, M. M., and Harvey, W. F. "Medical vs. Legal Definitions of Death." *Journal of the American Medical Association* 204 (1968), 423–25.

————, et al. "Definition of Death." *New England Journal of Medicine* 279 (1968), 834.

Harvard Medical School, Ad Hoc Committee of the Harvard Medical School to Examine the Definition of Brain Death. "A Definition of Irreversible Coma." *Journal of the American Medical Association* 205 (1968), 337–40.

Institute of Society, Ethics and the Life Sciences, Task Force on Death and Dying. "Refinements in Criteria for the Determination of Death." *Journal of the American Medical Association* 221 (1972), 48–53.

Jonas, Hans. "Against the Stream." *Philosophical Essays: From Ancient Creed to Technological Man.* Englewood Cliffs, N.J.: Prentice-Hall, 1974.

Kennedy, Ian McColl. "The Kansas Statute on Death—An Appraisal." *New England Journal of Medicine* 285 (1971), 946–50.

Korein, Julius. "On Cerebral, Brain, and Systemic Death." *Current Concepts of Cerebrovascular Disease: Stroke* 8 (May/June 1973), 9–14.

————, and Maccario, Micheline. "On the Diagnosis of Cerebral Death: A Prospective Study on 55 Patients to Define Irreversible Coma." *Clinical Electroencephalography* 2 (1971), 178–99.

Mills, Don Harper. "The Kansas Death Statute—Bold and Innovative." *New England Journal of Medicine* 285 (1971), 968–69.

————. "More on Brain Death." *Journal of the American Medical Association* 234 (1975), 838.

Morison, Robert, and Kass, Leon. "Death—Process or Event?" *Science* 173 (1971), 694–702.

Potter, Ralph B. "The Paradoxical Preservation of a Principle." *Villanova Law Review* 13 (Summer 1968), 784–92.

Ramsey, Paul. *The Patient as Person.* New Haven: Yale University Press, 1970. (See especially chapter 2, "On Updating Procedures for Stating That a Man Has Died.")

Silverman, D., et al. "Irreversible Coma Associated with Electrocerebral Silence." *Neurology* 20 (1970), 525–33.

Taylor, Loren F. "A Statutory Definition of Death in Kansas." *Journal of the American Medical Association* 215 (1971), 296.

Veatch, Robert M. "Brain Death: Welcome Definition or Dangerous Judgment?" *Hastings Center Report* 2 (November 1972), 10–13.

———. "The Whole-Brain-Oriented Concept of Death: An Outmoded Philosophical Formulation." *Journal of Thanatology* 3 (no. 1 for 1975), 13–30.

Wasmuth, Carl E., Jr. "The Concept of Death." *Ohio State Law Journal* 30 (1969), 32–60.

DYING MORALLY: EUTHANASIA AND ALLOWING TO DIE

Bard, B., and Fletcher, J. "The Right to Die." *Atlantic* (April 1968), 59–64.

Baughman, William H., et al. "Euthanasia: Criminal Tort, Constitutional and Legislative Questions." *Notre Dame Lawyer* 48 (1973), 1202–60.

Baylor Law Review 27 (Winter 1975). Symposium Issue on Euthanasia.

Behnke, John A., and Bok, Sissela. *The Dilemmas of Euthanasia.* Garden City, N.Y.: Anchor Press/Doubleday, 1975.

British Medical Association. "The Problem of Euthanasia." London: The British Medical Association, 1971.

Brown, Norman, et al. "The Preservation of Life." *Journal of the American Medical Association* 221 (1970), 76–82.

Byrn, Robert M. "Compulsory Life-Saving Treatment for the Competent Adult." *Fordham Law Review* 44 (1975), 1–36.

Cannon, William P. "The Right to Die." *Houston Law Review* 7 (1970), 654–70.

Cantor, Norman L. "A Patient's Decision to Decline Life-Saving Medical Treatment: Bodily Integrity versus the Preservation of Life." *Rutgers Law Review* 26 (Winter 1972), 228–64.

Catholic Hospital Association. *Christian Affirmation of Life.* St. Louis: Catholic Hospital Association, 1974.

"Compulsory Medical Treatment and the Free Exercise of Religion." *Indiana Law Journal* 42 (1967), 386–404.

"Compulsory Medical Treatment: The State's Interest Re-evaluated." *Minnesota Law Review* 51 (1966), 293–305.

"Constitutional Law—Transfusions Ordered for Dying Woman over Religious Objections." Case Comment. *University of Pennsylvania Law Review* 113 (1964), 290 ff.

Crane, Diana. *The Social Aspects of the Prolongation of Life.* Social Science Frontiers. New York: Russell Sage Foundation, 1969.

Davis, Daniel J. "The Dying Patient: A Qualified Right to Refuse Medical Treatment." *Journal of Family Law* 7 (1968), 644–59.

Dinello, Daniel. "On Killing and Letting Die." *Analysis* 31 (January 1971), 83–86.

Downing, A. B. *Euthanasia and the Right to Die.* New York: Humanities Press, 1970. (Appendix contains Voluntary Euthanasia Bill proposed in British Parliament.)

Fletcher, George. "Prolonging Life." *Washington Law Review* 42 (1967), 999–1016.

Fletcher, Joseph. *Morals and Medicine.* Boston: Beacon Press, 1954. (See chapter VI, "Euthanasia—Our Right to Die.")

Ford, John C. "Refusal of Blood Transfusions by Jehovah's Witnesses." *Catholic Law* 10 (1964), 212–26.

Gazza, Beverly A. "Compulsory Medical Treatment and Constitutional Guarantees: A Conflict?" *University of Pittsburgh Law Review* 33 (1972), 628–37.

Geddes, Leonard. "On the Intrinsic Wrongness of Killing Innocent People." *Analysis* 33 (January 1973), 93–97.

Gruman, Gerald J. "An Historical Introduction to Ideas about Voluntary Euthanasia: With a Bibliographic Survey and Guides for Interdisciplinary Studies." *Omega* 4 (Summer 1973), 87–138.

Gurney, Edward J. "Is There a Right to Die? A Study of the Law of Euthanasia." *Cumberland Samford Law Review* 3 (Summer 1972), 235–61.

Hegland, Kenney F. "Unauthorized Rendition of Life-saving Medical Treatment." *University of California Law Review* 53 (1965), 860–77.

Hoover, James F. "An Adult's Right to Resist Blood Transfusions: A View Through *John F. Kennedy Memorial Hospital v. Heston.*" *Notre Dame Lawyer* 47 (1972), 571–87.

In the Matter of Karen Quinlan: The Complete Legal Briefs, Court Proceedings, and Decision in the Superior Court of New Jersey. Arlington, Va.: University Publications of America, 1975.

Kay, Edward M. "The Right to Die." *University of Florida Law Review* 18 (1966), 591–605.

Kelly, Gerald. "The Duty of Using Artificial Means of Preserving Life." *Theological Studies* 11 (June 1950), 203–20.

————. "The Duty to Preserve Life." *Theological Studies* 12 (December 1951), 550–56.

Kohl, Marvin, ed. *Beneficent Euthanasia.* Buffalo, N.Y.: Prometheus Books, 1975.

————. *The Morality of Killing.* New York: Humanities Press, 1974.

Maguire, Daniel C. *Death by Choice.* Garden City, N.Y.: Doubleday, 1974.

Mansson, Helge H. "Justifying the Final Solution." *Omega* 3 (May 1972), 79–87.

McKegney, F. P., and Lange, P. "The Decision to No Longer Live on Chronic Hemodialysis." *American Journal of Psychiatry* 128 (September 1971), 267–74.

Milhollin, Gary L. "The Refused Blood Transfusion: An Ultimate Challenge for Law and Morals." *Natural Law Forum* 10 (1965), 202–14.

Montange, Charles H. "Informed Consent and the Dying Patient." *Yale Law Journal* 83 (July 1974), 1632–64.

Morgan, Lucy Griscom. "On Drinking the Hemlock," *Hastings Center Report* 1 (December 1971), 4–5.

Pius XII. "The Pope Speaks: Prolongation of Life." *Osservatore Romano* 4 (1957), 393–98.

Rachels, James. "Active and Passive Euthanasia." *New England Journal of Medicine* 292 (1975), 78–80.

Ramsey, Paul. *The Patient as Person.* New Haven: Yale University Press, 1970. (See especially chapter 3, "On (Only) Caring for the Dying.")

"The Right of a Patient to Refuse Blood Transfusions: A Dilemma of Conscience and Law for Patient, Physician and Hospital." *University of San Fernando Valley Law Review* 3 (1974), 91–104.

Sharpe, David J., and Hargest, Robert F., III. "Life-saving Treatment for Unwilling Patients." *Fordham Law Review* 36 (1968), 695–706.

Silving, Helen. "Euthanasia: A Study in Comparative Criminal Law." *University of Pennsylvania Law Review* 103 (1954), 350–89.

Sullivan, Michael T. "The Dying Person—His Plight and His Right." *New England Law Review* 8 (1973), 197–216.

Vaughan, Nancy Lee. "The Right to Die." *California Western Law Review* 10 (Spring 1974), 613–27.

Veatch, Robert M. "Choosing Not to Prolong Dying." *Medical Dimensions* (December 1972), 8–10 ff.

Vodiga, Bruce. "Euthanasia and the Right to Die—Moral, Ethical and Legal Perspectives." *Illinois Institute of Technology/Chicago-Kent Law Review* 51 (Summer 1974), 1–40.

Williams, Robert H. "Our Role in the Generation, Modification and Termination of Life." *Journal of the American Medical Association* 209 (1969), 914–17.

———. *To Live and to Die.* New York: Springer-Verlag, 1974.

Yondorf, Barbara. "The Declining and Wretched." *Public Policy* 23 (Fall 1975), 465–82.

SPECIAL PROBLEMS IN EUTHANASIA:
INFANTS, CHILDREN, AND INCOMPETENT PATIENTS

Baker, James A. "Court-Ordered Non-Emergency Medical Care for Infants." *Cleveland/Marshall Law Review* 18 (1968), 297–98.

Duff, Raymond S., and Campbell, A. G. M. "Moral and Ethical Dilemmas in the Special-Care Nursery." *New England Journal of Medicine* 289 (1973), 890–94.

Eckstein, Herbert B. "Severely Malformed Children: The Problem of Selection." *British Medical Journal* (May 5, 1973), 284.

Fletcher, John. "Abortion, Euthanasia, and Care of Defective Newborns." *New England Journal of Medicine* 292 (1975), 75–78.

———. "Attitudes Towards Defective Newborns." *Hastings Center Studies* 2 (January 1974), 21–32.

Freeman, John M. "The Shortsighted Treatment of Myelomeningocele: A Long-Term Case Report." *Pediatrics* 53 (March 1974), 311–13.

Gustafson, James M. "Mongolism, Parental Desires, and the Right to Life." *Perspectives in Biology and Medicine* 16 (Summer 1973), 529–57.

Heymann, Philip B., and Holtz, Sara. "The Severely Defective Newborn: The Dilemma and the Decision Process." *Public Policy* 23 (Fall 1975), 381–418.

Jonsen, A. R.; Phibbs, R. H.; Tooley, W. H.; and Garland, M. J. "Critical Issues in Newborn Intensive Care: A Conference Report and Policy Proposal." *Pediatrics* 55 (June 1975), 756–68.

Langer, William L. "Infanticide: A Historical Survey." *History of Childhood Quarterly* 1 (Winter 1974), 353–65.

Lorber, John. "Selective Treatment of Myclomeningocele: To Treat or Not to Treat." *Pediatrics* 53 (March 1974), 307–08.

McCormick, Richard A. "To Save or Let Die: The Dilemma of Modern Medicine." *Journal of the American Medical Association* 229 (1974), 172–76.

Robertson, John A. "Involuntary Euthanasia of Defective Newborns: A Legal Analysis." *Stanford Law Review* 27 (January 1975), 213–67.

Shaw, Anthony. "Dilemmas of 'Informed Consent' in Children." *New England Journal of Medicine* 289 (1973), 885–90.

Smith, David H. "On Letting Some Babies Die." *Hastings Center Studies* 2 (no. 2, May 1974), 37–46.

Smith, G. Keys, and Smith, E. Durham. "Selection for Treatment in Spina Bifida Cystica." *British Medical Journal* 4 (October 27, 1973), 189–97.

Stein, Sherman C.; Schut, Luis; and Ames, Mary D. "Selection for Early Treatment in Myelomeningocele: A Retrospective Analysis of Various Selection Procedures." *Pediatrics* 54 (November 1974), 556.

Working Party of the Newcastle Regional Hospital Board. "Ethics of Selective Treatment of Spina Bifida." *Lancet* 1 for 1975 (January 11, 1975), 85–88.

Young, Stephen Grant. "Parent and Child—Compulsory Medical Care Over Objections of Parents." *West Virginia Law Review* 65 (1963), 184–87.

Zachary, R. B. "Ethical and Social Aspects of Treatment of Spina Bifida." *Lancet* 2 (1968), 274.

WHAT TO TELL THE DYING PATIENT

Drillen, C. M., and Wilkinson, E. M. "Mongolism: When Should Parents Be Told?" *British Medical Journal* 2 (November 21, 1964), 1306.

Fitts, Williams T., Jr., and Ravdin, I. S. "What Philadelphia Physicians Tell Patients with Cancer." *Journal of the American Medical Association* 153 (1953), 903.

Fletcher, Joseph. "Medical Diagnosis: Our Right to Know the Truth." *Morals and Medicine*. Boston: Beacon Press, 1964.

Kant, Immanuel. "On the Supposed Right to Lie from Altruistic Motives." *Critique of Practical Reason*. Translated and edited by Lewis White Beck. Chicago: University of Chicago Press, 1949.

Kelly, W. D., and Friesen, S. R. "Do Cancer Patients Want to be Told?" *Surgery* 27 (June 1950), 822–26.

Litin, E. M. "Should the Cancer Patient be Told?" *Postgraduate Medicine* 28 (November 1960), 470–75.

Lund, Charles C. "The Doctor, the Patient and the Truth." *Annals of Internal Medicine* 24 (June 1946), 955.

Oken, Donald. "What to Tell Cancer Patients." *Journal of the American Medical Association* 175 (1961), 1120–28.

Pemberton, L. B. "Diagnosis: Ca/Should We Tell the Truth?" *Bulletin of the American College of Surgeons* (May 1971), 7–13.

Samp, Robert J., and Curreri, Anthony R. "A Questionnaire Survey on Public Cancer Education Obtained from Cancer Patients and their Families." *Cancer* 10 (March–April, 1957), 382–84.

Vernick, J., and Karon, M. "Who's Afraid of Death on a Leukemia Ward?" *American Journal of Diseases of Children* 109 (1965), 393.

THE NEWLY DEAD

Ad Hoc Task Force on Cardiac Replacement. *Cardiac Replacement: Medical, Ethical, Psychological, and Economic Considerations.* National Heart Institute, 1969.

American College of Surgeons/National Institutes of Health Organ Transplant Registry, Advisory Committee to the Registry. "Third Scientific Report." *Journal of the American Medical Association* 226 (1973), 1211–16.

American Medical Association House of Delegates. "Statement on Heart Transplantation." *Journal of the American Medical Association* 207 (1969), 1704–05.

Beard, B. H. "Fear of Death and Fear of Life: The Dilemma in Chronic Renal Failures, Hemodialysis, and Kidney Transplantation." *Archives of General Psychiatry* 21 (1969), 373–80.

British Medical Association. "Report of the Special Committee on Organ Transplantation." *British Medical Journal* (March 21, 1970), 750–51.

"Compulsory Removal of Cadaver Organs." *Columbia Law Review* 69 (April 1969), 693–705.

Daube, David. "Limitations of Self-Sacrifice in Jewish Law and Tradition." *Theology* 72 (July 1969), 291–304.

Dukeminier, J., Jr. "Supplying Organs for Transplantation." *Michigan Law Review* 68 (1970), 811–66.

———, and Sanders, D. "Organ Transplantation: A Proposal for Routine Salvaging of Cadaver Organs." *New England Journal of Medicine* 279 (1968), 413–19.

Fletcher, Joseph. "Our Shameful Waste of Human Tissue." In *Updating Life and Death.* Edited by Donald Cutler. Boston: Beacon Press, 1969, chapter 1.

Fox, Renée C., and Swazey, Judith P. *The Courage to Fail: A Social View of Organ Transplants and Dialysis.* Chicago: University of Chicago Press, 1974.

Gaylin, Willard. "Harvesting the Dead." *Harper's Magazine* (September 1974), 23–30.

Jinks, Robert W. "California's Response to the Problems of Procuring Human Remains for Transplantation." *California Law Review* 57 (May 1969), 671–93.

Miller, George W. *Moral and Ethical Implications of Human Organ Transplants.* Springfield, Ill.: Charles C. Thomas, 1971.

Ramsey, Paul. *The Patient as Person.* New Haven: Yale University

Press, 1970. (See especially chapters 4, 5, and 6: "The Self-Giving of Vital Organs," "Giving or Taking Cadaver Organs for Transplant," and "A Caveat on Heart Transplants.")

Renal Transplant Registry, Advisory Committee. "The 12th Report of the Human Renal Transplant Registry." *Journal of the American Medical Association* 233 (1975), 787–96.

Sadler, Alfred M., Jr., and Sadler, Blair L. *Organ Transplantation: Current Medical and Medical-Legal Status: The Problems of an Opportunity.* Washington, D.C.: U.S. Government Printing Office, 1970.

————. "Transplantation and the Law: The Need for Organized Sensitivity." *Georgetown Law Journal* 57 (October 1968), 9–13.

————. "Transplantation and the Law: Progress Toward Uniformity." *New England Journal of Medicine* 282 (1970), 717–23.

————. "Recent Developments in the Legal Aspects of Transplantation in the United States." *Transplantation Proceedings* 3 (March 1971), 293–97.

————, and Stason, E. B. "The Uniform Anatomical Gift Act: A Model for Reform." *Journal of the American Medical Association* 206 (1968), 2501–06.

Sadler, Blair L., and Sadler, Alfred M., Jr. "Providing Cadaver Organs for Transplantation." *Hastings Center Studies* 1 (no. 1, 1973), 14–26.

"The Sale of Human Body Parts," *Michigan Law Review* 72 (May, 1974), 1182–1264.

Wolstenholme, G. E. W., and O'Connor, Maeve. *Ethics in Medical Progress: With Special Reference to Transplantation.* Boston: Little, Brown and Co., 1966.

NATURAL DEATH AND PUBLIC POLICY

Baltes, Paul B. "Prototypical Paradigms and Questions in Life-Span Research on Development and Aging." *Gerontologist* (Winter 1973), 458–66.

Butler, Robert N. *Why Survive? Being Old in America.* New York: Harper and Row, 1975.

Callahan, Sidney, and Christiansen, Drew. "Ideal Old Age." *Soundings* 57 (Spring 1974), 1–16.

Comfort, A. "Biological Theories of Aging." *Human Development* 13 (1970), 127–39.

Cullman, Oscar. "Immortality of the Soul or Resurrection of the Dead." In *Immortality and Resurrection.* edited by Krister Stendahl. New York: Macmillan, 1965.

Eisele, Frederick R., special editor. "Political Consequences of

Aging." *Annals of the American Academy of Political and Social Science* 415 (September, 1974).

Engelhardt, H. Tristram, Jr. "The Counsels of Finitude." *Hastings Center Report* 5 (April 1975), 29–36.

Goldstein, Samuel. "The Biology of Aging." *New England Journal of Medicine* 285 (1971), 1120–29.

Harmon, D. "Free Radical Theory of Aging." *Triangle* 12 (no. 4, 1973), 155.

Hayflick, Leonard. "The Biology of Human Aging." *American Journal of the Medical Sciences* 265 (June 1973), 433–45.

Illich, Ivan. "The Political Uses of Natural Death." *Hastings Center Studies* 2 (January 1974), 3–20.

Lifton, Robert Jay. "On Death and the Continuity of Life: A Psycho-historical Perspective." *Omega* 6 (no. 2, 1975), 143–59.

Marx, Jean L. "Aging Research (I): Cellular Theories of Senescence." *Science* 186 (1974), 1105–07.

———. "Aging Research (II): Pacemakers for Aging?" *Science* 186 (1974), 1196–97.

May, William. "Attitudes Toward the Newly Dead." *Hastings Center Studies* 1 (no. 1, 1973), 3–13.

———. "The Sacral Power of Death in Contemporary Experience." *Social Research* 39 (Autumn 1972), 463–88.

"The Myths of Old Age Are the Myths of the Young: A Symposium." *Journal of Communication* 24 (Autumn 1974), 74–112.

Nagel, Thomas. "Death." *Nous* 6 (1973), 73–80.

Neugarten, Bernice L. "Social Implications of a Prolonged Life Span." *Gerontologist* (Winter 1972), 323 ff.

Steinfels, Peter, and Veatch, Robert M., eds. *Death Inside Out.* New York: Harper & Row, 1975.

Stendahl, Krister. *Immortality and Resurrection.* New York: Macmillan, 1965.

Williams, Bernard. "The Makropulos Case: Reflections on the Tedium of Immortality." In *Problems of the Self.* Cambridge: Cambridge University Press, 1973, pp. 82–100.

BIBLIOGRAPHIES

Clouser, K. Danner, and Zucker, Arthur. *Abortion and Euthanasia: An Annotated Bibliography.* Philadelphia: Society for Health and Human Values, 1974.

Kalish, Richard A. "Death and Dying: A Briefly Annotated Bibliography." In *The Dying Patient.* Edited by Orville G. Brim, Jr., et al. New York: Russell Sage Foundation, 1970, pp. 323–80.

Kübler-Ross, Elisabeth. *On Death and Dying.* New York: Macmillan, 1969, pp. 249–60.

Kutscher, A. *Bibliography of Books on Death, Bereavement, Loss and Grief: 1955–68.* New York: Health Sciences Publishing Corp., 1969.

McCormick, Richard A. "Notes on Moral Theology." *Theological Studies* 34 (March 1973), 53–103.

National Library of Medicine. Literature Search #71-4: "Attitudes Toward Death."

U.S. Department of Health, Education, and Welfare, Public Health Service, National Institutes of Health, National Institute of Neurological Diseases and Stroke, Applied Neurologic Research Branch. Brain Death: A Bibliography with Key-Word and Author Indexes. Edited by Andrew J. K. Smith and J. Kiffin Penry. DHEW Publication No. (NIH) 73-347, June, 1972.

U.S. Department of Health, Education, and Welfare, Public Health Service, National Institutes of Health. *Selected Bibliography on Death and Dying,* by Joel J. Vernick.

Index